WALKING IN SICILY

About the Author

Gillian Price was born in England but moved to Australia when young. After taking a degree in anthropology and working in adult education, she set off to travel through Asia and trek the Himalayas. The culmination of her journey was Venice where, her enthusiasm fired for mountains, the next logical step was towards the Dolomites, only hours away. Starting there Gillian is steadily exploring the mountain ranges of Italy and bringing them to life for visitors in a series of outstanding guides for Cicerone. When not out walking with her Venetian husband, she works as a freelance journalist and translator. An adamant promoter of the use of public transport to minimise impact in alpine areas, Gillian is an active member of the Italian Alpine Club and Mountain Wilderness. www.gillianprice.eu

Other Cicerone guides by the author

Across the Eastern Alps: E5
Alpine Flowers
Gran Paradiso
Italy's Sibillini National Park
Shorter Walks in the Dolomites
Through the Italian Alps –
   The Grande Traversata delle Alpi
Tour of the Bernina
Trekking in the Alps (contributor)
Trekking in the Apennines – The
   Grande Escursione Appenninica

Trekking in the Dolomites
Walking in Corsica
Walking in the Central Italian Alps
Walking in the Dolomites
Walking in Tuscany
Walking in Umbria
Walking on the Amalfi Coast
Walking the Italian Lakes
Walks and Treks in the Maritime Alps

WALKING IN SICILY

by
Gillian Price

2 POLICE SQUARE, MILNTHORPE, CUMBRIA LA7 7PY
www.cicerone.co.uk

© Gillian Price 2015
Third edition 2015
ISBN: 978 1 85284 785 2
Reprinted 2017 (with updates)

First edition 2000
Second edition 2006

A catalogue record for this book is available from the British Library.
Maps: Nicola Regine
Photos: Gillian Price and Nicola Regine

Printed by KHL Printing, Singapore

Dedication

To my wonderful parents,
as well as little Kieran, and Sicilian nieces Susanna and Sabrina

Updates to this Guide

While every effort is made by our authors to ensure the accuracy of guidebooks as they go to print, changes can occur during the lifetime of an edition. Any updates that we know of for this guide will be on the Cicerone website (www. cicerone.co.uk/785/updates), so please check before planning your trip. We also advise that you check information about such things as transport, accommodation and shops locally. Even rights of way can be altered over time.

We are always grateful for information about any discrepancies between a guidebook and the facts on the ground, sent by email to updates@cicerone.co.uk or by post to Cicerone, 2 Police Square, Milnthorpe LA7 7PY, United Kingdom.

Register your book: To sign up to receive free updates, special offers and GPX files where available, register your book at www.cicerone.co.uk.

Front cover: Great views from Vulcano's crater (Walks 41)

CONTENTS

Acknowledgements

On early trips I dragged along Anna Z., then Marty, whose unrivalled chauffeur services were immensely appreciated; Libby, who miraculously survived Stromboli – inclusive of unpredictable wind changes; and Anna M. and Damiano, who actually enjoy picnicking in the fog.

A special thank you to Girolamo Lombardo of the Palermo Tourist Board, indefatigable pioneer in local cartography; Giovanni Mineo and Luigia Di Gennaro of the Cooperativa Artemisia in Palermo; Gaetano Perricone and vulcanologist Salvatore Caffo of the Etna Park; Carmelo Magaraci and Sara La Rosa at the Alcantara Park; Giovanni Vacante at the Madonie Park. Forestry Department staff photocopied maps and pointed us the right way, Luciano Buccheri and his hospitable crew at Pantalica top of the list. Italian Alpine Club branches at Cefalù and Palermo were very helpful, as was Mario Vaccarella of Petralia Sottana. Melanie Kneip and Andrea Mazzaglia had good suggestions on Etna, as did the Magma Trek staff for Stromboli. Professor Schicchi of Palermo University kindly sent the photo of the rare pine tree in Walk 37. Thanks to the readers who let me know of route changes, Pamela Harris and Alan Norton in particular.

Last, but not least, *Grazie di cuore* to Nick, computerised map-drawer and companion.

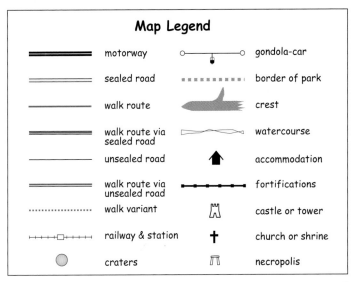

Map Legend

▬▬▬▬	motorway	○——●——○	gondola-car
═══════	sealed road	▪▪▪▪▪▪▪▪▪	border of park
──────	walk route	⬳	crest
▬▬▬▬	walk route via sealed road	⬱⬲	watercourse
──────	unsealed road	⬆	accommodation
▭▭▭▭	walk route via unsealed road	▪━▪━▪━▪	fortifications
··················	walk variant	🏰	castle or tower
+++□+++	railway & station	✝	church or shrine
◯	craters	⛩	necropolis

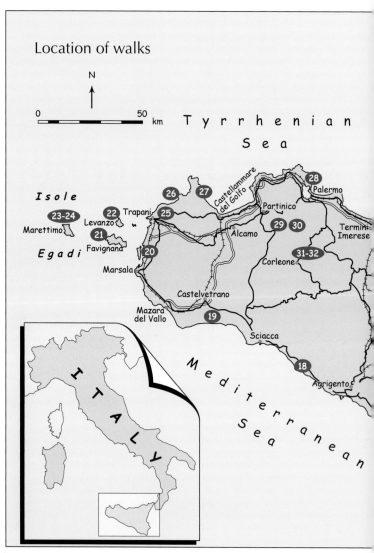

Location of walks

N

0   50 km

Tyrrhenian Sea

Isole

Marettimo

Egadi

Favignana

Levanzo

Trapani

Castellammare del Golfo

Palermo

Partinico

Alcamo

Marsala

Castelvetrano

Mazara del Vallo

Sciacca

Corleone

Termini Imerese

Agrigento

ITALY

Mediterranean Sea

Sorrel brightens the lava fields up to surprising altitudes on Mount Etna

INTRODUCTION

Italy without Sicily forms no image at all in the soul;
only here is the key to everything.
J.W. von Goethe, Italian Journey (1786–1788)

BACKGROUND

The early history of Sicily (Sicilia in Italian) is enveloped in misty legends, with credit for first settling the island going to a motley band of giants. Invincible offspring attributed to Zeus, they enjoyed but a short-lived sojourn as they were punished for challenging the ruling gods. The handful of survivors were bound in chains and banished to underworld forges beneath the island's volcanoes to fashion arms for the gods, such as thunderbolts for Zeus. To this day they struggle and moan, attempting to break free and shake off the weight of the immense mountains. Ancient sources, in fact, refer to the discovery of huge skeletons in caves, though they were assumed to be marine animal remains washed up by the Flood! The mythical one-eyed Cyclops followed, bloodthirsty cannibals who played havoc with passing sailors, including Ulysses on his epic voyage.

Archaeological evidence places prehistoric inhabitants around 13,000 years BC. Sicily's strategic crossroads location in the Mediterranean ensured

Views over the Kalura from the Rocca (Walk 33)

11

Temple at Selinunte (Walk 19)

the arrival of settlers, plunderers, conquerors and visitors from all directions, resulting in a fascinating melting pot of cultures. Major colonisers in the 13th–11th century BC were the immigrant Elymian, Sicel and Sican populations, who lent their name to the island. Subsequently there were Phoenician settlements, prior to a landmark Greek take-over (8th–6th centuries BC) and widespread Hellenisation of language and civilisation, not to mention a name change to Trinacria, for the island's three-pointed shape. Impressive extant temple and city ruins illustrate this period. In the 3rd century BC Sicily became the first province of Rome – the island's fertile land later earning it the denomination 'granary' of the empire.

A brief period of Byzantine rule was followed by the productive Arab epoch, which witnessed the introduction of irrigation techniques, fish preservation and silk farming, as well as some memorable architecture and a wealth of place names: *kalat* for castle is fairly common and has survived in Caltanisetta, *marsa* for port explains Marsala (port of Allah), *gebel* or 'mount' can be seen in Mongibello, another name for Etna. The subsequent Norman period (11th–12th century) added to this precious legacy with religious tolerance, rich art works, feudalism and a Latinising influence. Noteworthy rulers were Roger II, who employed the celebrated Arab geographer al-Idrisi, and William 'the Good'.

Sicily was later joined with Naples to form the 'Kingdom of the Two Sicilies', stretching from the mid-15th to the mid-19th century. It was not until 1860, with the advent of the revolutionary Giuseppe Garibaldi, that the island was freed from Bourbon rule and the Sicilians joined the fledgling united Italy.

More recently, island life was convulsed during World War Two, ending with the Allied landings in 1943 for the move north and the liberation of occupied Italy. In 1946 Sicily was declared an autonomous region, with a special statute and governing body that enjoys a high degree of political independence.

One unique phenomena needs a brief comment in the context of history: the Mafia. It is believed to have originated in the Middle Ages to overthrow foreign invaders, its members taken from the private armies (*mafie*) of landlords. The nefarious organisation known to insiders as Cosa Nostra (our affair) continues to prosper parallel to state authority, rife with age-old payoffs and rivalries. It was dealt a near mortal blow under fascism; however the war years meant recovery, possibly aided by the US use of Mafia cohorts in the Allied invasion. Of late, *mafiosi* turned state witnesses have provided precious evidence about the organisation, though at the terrible price of numerous lives, leading magistrates and lawkeepers in first place. All but invisible to outsiders who are unaffected by events, it is prospering and shows no sign at all of dying out. This is confirmed by recurrent reports in the Sicilian and national daily press and TV of Mafia-related crime and inquiries. Such news should remove any doubts harboured by visitors that it is only the stuff of

films nowadays. Background reading is warmly recommended and several suggestions are listed in the Further Reading section.

Some facts and figures help give a fuller picture of Sicily. The largest of the Mediterranean islands, its territory embraces 37 minor islands, some volcanic. A total of 25,708 sq km are occupied by a population of over 5 million, which averages out at 194 inhabitants per square kilometre, or half a hectare per head. The island is 270km in length and 180km in breadth, though described by Arab traveller Ibn Hawqal in the 11th century as 'seven days long [by walking], four days broad'. It lies a mere 143km north of Tunisia in north Africa, while on the other hand it is divided from the main Italian land mass by the Strait of Messina, 3km across at its narrowest and 20km at its broadest.

An ambitious State project is in the pipeline to bridge the passage. However opposition is widespread as many say the funds could be better used upgrading the island's rail and road networks, in desperate need of maintenance. Others emphasise the unsuitability of the site, citing the disastrous 1908 earthquake and tidal wave that struck Messina leaving over 60,000 dead and 91% of the city flattened. Moreover this natural channel is run through by treacherous swirling currents and whirlpools, the dread of ancient mariners who feared being shipwrecked and devoured by the ghastly lurking she-monsters Scylla and Charybdis, who put paid to many of Ulysses' men.

Modern-day victims of shipping disasters of an entirely different kind are the thousands of hopefuls, asylum seekers, who put themselves at the mercy of unscrupulous criminals for the 'short' boat trip from the north African coast across to the islands of Lampedusa and Pantelleria, as well as Sicily's southern coast. When the sea is calm, thousands at a time disembark, whereas on rough days the navy fishes their corpses from the waves, unless they wash up on the beach first.

Generally speaking Sicily's landscapes are predominantly mountainous. First and foremost is a completely separate elevation, Mount Etna, unrivalled in dominance. Europe's highest active volcano at 3300m above sea level, this unique attraction has an unmistakable dark cone shape and is recognisable from afar by its trademark plume of smoke, a belching chimney when an eruption is in progress. The main ranges, on the other hand, the Peloritani, Nebrodi and Madonie, which rise to maximum heights just short of the 2000m mark, are generally considered a natural continuation of the Apennine chain that reaches down to the coast in neighbouring Calabria on the toe of Italy. Rugged reliefs cloaked with dense woods, these mountains tend to be sparsely populated and are cut through by picturesque valleys and highlands which double as golden fields of wheat in spring then dust bowls in summer.

In striking contrast the coastal belts feature the dark, glossy greens of citrus orchards and vineyards, alternating with chaotic settlements often characterised by an air of abandon. Ancient ruins punctuate rolling hills bright with spring flowers and aromatic herbs. Finally the

The broad rim of extinct volcano Monte Mojo (Walk 3)

offshore islands are worlds unto themselves, surrounded by inviting crystal-clear waters, windswept and often cut off from the mainland in winter.

WALKING AND MAPS

Walking for pleasure is still not widely practised in Sicily and guarded curiosity will often greet ramblers, as getting around on foot has long been equated with hardship. Signposting and way-marking are rare luxuries on pathways. As a consequence, commercially produced walking maps are few and far between, with the exception of those covering the popular Aeolian islands in addition to the Etna and Madonie Parks. Details of any useful exemplars or local material are listed in the individual walk headings, while useful terminology can be found in the Glossary (Appendix A). Each route comes complete with a comprehensive sketch map, for which the legend can be found before the Introduction. The main landmarks shown on each map are also indicated in **bold** in the walk description.

Individual headings include an overall difficulty rating for the route.

- **Grade 1** means an easy stroll, suitable for all.
- **Grade 2** is a little strenuous, with reasonable distances and/or climbs and drops involved. A basic level of fitness is required.
- **Grade 3** is akin to an alpine trek. It may involve occasional problems with orientation, as well as exposed or particularly arduous stretches. Some experience and extra care is recommended, along with suitable equipment.

Distances are given in both kilometres and miles, together with overall height loss and/or gain (ie how much you descend and/or ascend), but only when this exceeds 200m. Measurements in brackets given during the actual descriptions refer to altitude (metres above sea level).

Total timing for the walk is also given in the heading and does NOT include any stops, so always allow more time when planning your day. Timing given en route is cumulative unless otherwise specified.

Note: when 'path' is used it means just that; 'track' is used for a wider path, usually vehicle width; and 'roads' – surfaced or not – are open to traffic.

For visitors who prefer to walk with other people and an experienced guide, the Italian Alpine Club CAI (a volunteer but well-qualified organisation with a branch in virtually every town in Sicily) arranges group walks most weekends throughout the year. Non-members are welcome on many of the excursions. The Palermo office is Tel 091-329407 or http://palermo.clubalpinoitaliano.org. Moreover the Catania branch Tel 095-7153515 or www.caicatania.it periodically takes small groups on an interesting four-day Etna trek.

Mention must be made of the Sentiero Italia project, a mammoth 6000km walker's route traversing the whole of Italy from Sardinia, via Sicily,

Exploring the Silvestri craters (Walk 5)

the Apennines and the Alps, all the way to Trieste. Some work has been carried out on the pathways in Sicily, with way-marking and signposting on the initial 45km in the Palermo area. The question of accommodation is yet to be resolved, but in the meantime sections can be followed on a day basis. Information on this route can be obtained from the Italian Alpine Club.

PARKS, RESERVES AND PROTECTED AREAS

With a plethora of diverse pressing problems to deal with on the island, the environmental movement in Sicily did not get off the ground until the 1980s. A landmark demonstration in 1980 to halt the construction of a coastal road between Scopello and San Vito Lo Capo on the northwesternmost cape led to the

establishment of the Riserva dello Zingaro and heightened awareness of the issues at stake. A string of noteworthy parks and reserves was set up in the wake of the action thanks to appropriate legislation, though it is proving to be a particularly slow and cumbersome process. The Parco dell'Etna, Sicily's first regional park, saw the light of day in 1987; the Parco delle Madonie dates back to 1989; the extensive Parco dei Nebrodi was set up in 1993; while the newest, the Parco Fluviale dell' Alcantara established in 2001, is currently finding its feet while its borders are still being debated. A fifth is rumoured for the Sicani region in the centre-west. More specific information is given in the introductions to each park area. Moreover, www.parks.it is a good source of information.

Furthermore, a host of nature reserves (77 in actual fact) often known as *riserva naturale orientata*, mostly under the auspices of the very capable State Forestry Department of Sicily, the WWF (Global Environment Network) as well as the Italian Alpine Club (CAI), protect some remarkable sites in the provinces of Siracusa, Trapani and Palermo for a start. Generally speaking picking flowers, camping, fishing and dogs are forbidden in protected areas. Marine reserves govern activities such as spear fishing in the Egadi islands. In all some 23% of the whole of Sicily, corresponding to some 6000 sq km, is given over to protected areas.

Groundwork through schools and community-based initiatives is carried out to sensitise local people and prevent them from regarding the protected area solely as an imposition or only in terms of restrictions and prohibitions. Drawing up a workable management plan can take time, and only when it has been implemented can work start on facilities for visitors – funds and staff permitting.

WHEN TO GO

Sicily's climate is typically Mediterranean with hot dry summers and mild rainy winters. It could almost be summed up as having only these two seasons, as the others only appear fleetingly. Fortunately the marvellous range of altitudes and landscapes mean the island can be glorious at any time of year. On the coast temperatures average out at 19°C (13°C inland) and rarely drop below 10°C even in midwinter,

except during the once-in-a-blue-moon snowfall. Generally, March through to June is the best time to go walking in Sicily as the countryside exhibits brilliant carpets of green with extraordinarily dense, and unfortunately short-lived, masses of wild flowers.

In summer, from June onwards, when parched conditions have set in across the lowlands and the island is roasting with temperatures that soar above 30°C under the effect of the blistering *scirocco* wind straight from Africa, the mountain ranges come into their own with deliciously cool conditions, as do the breeze-blessed islands. Late July–August is understandably the busiest time for visitors and high-season prices apply.

Rocky steps at Pantalica (Walk 11)

Strangely, the sea tends to be chilly for swimming until well into the summer but luckily retains its warmth through to the autumn months, when visibility is usually at its prime throughout Sicily. Daylight Saving Time in Italy lasts from the beginning of April to the end of October.

As already mentioned, late autumn–winter is the season when Sicily receives its lion's share of rain, usually desperately needed by the farmers after the near drought conditions of a protracted summer. This is the time of year when sudden downpours cause stony, arid river beds to swell and become *fiumare* (the term for a seasonal watercourse),

Walkers on the old railway track at Pantalica (Walk 12)

and the land starts soaking up moisture in preparation for the imminent explosion of green.

WHAT TO TAKE

In terms of footwear, as the majority of these Sicilian routes follow decent country paths, in most cases nothing more than a good pair of gym shoes is needed. Sandals (with a good grip) are suitable in several cases. However, the exceptions are the volcano routes, notably on Etna and the island of Stromboli, which demand walking boots with thick soles, as anything light will be ripped to shreds by the solidified lava. Ankle support, moreover, is a requisite for the mountainous terrain encountered, for instance, in the Madonie and on the island of Marettimo.

The season and areas visited will dictate specific clothing needs. Loose-fitting cotton garments over a layered base is a good rule, though a pullover or fleece will be appreciated for evenings in the mountain areas. Weatherproof gear is indispensable all year round for the volcano walks as well as the high-altitude routes in the Madonie range. Coastal paths, on the other hand, often call for a windproof jacket outside of summer, while inland routes may require long trousers for the inevitable overgrown thorny stretches. While shorts (for both sexes) are acceptable beachwear in Sicily they are not worn in the countryside, and may cause embarrassment or disapproval in small towns. Discretion is recommended.

EMERGENCIES

The following services may be of help should problems arise. Remember that calls made from a public phone require a coin or prepaid phone card to be inserted, though no charge is made for the short numbers or those starting 800, which are toll free.

- Polizia (police) Tel 113

- For health-related emergencies, including ambulance service (ambulanza) and mountain rescue Tel 118.

- CAI Soccorso Alpino, the mountain and speleological rescue service run by qualified volunteers from the Italian Alpine Club, can be contacted on Tel 095-914141 or 095-643430 for the Catania area, and on cell Tel 339-3533513 for the Palermo region. The service is available to everyone, however those other than members of CAI and affiliated associations covered by insurance will be billed.

- The high risk of fire in the long, dry summer months means that open fires of any nature are totally banned throughout Sicily's park areas, often on a permanent basis. Forest and bush fires should be reported to the Vigili del Fuoco (fire brigade) on Tel 115 or to the Corpo Forestale dello Stato (State Forestry Department) on Tel 1515.

- 'Aiuto!' is 'Help!' in Italian, and 'Pericolo!' means 'Danger!'

It goes without saying that the list of essentials includes a water bottle, sunglasses, a hat (shade is a rare commodity in Sicily) and high-factor protective sun cream, which can double as a remover for the treacherous blobs of tar that occasionally stain the shoreline. Swimming and snorkelling equipment (goggles at least) are optional but warmly recommended, while an altimeter and compass come in handy where waymarking and useful landmarks are lacking. Bird enthusiasts will appreciate a pair of binoculars. A basic first-aid kit with plasters and insect repellent is suggested, as is a torch or headlamp for the cave in Walk 9 and the tunnels in Walk 12.

REACHING SICILY

By plane

Sicily is served by both low-cost and regular airlines from overseas, along with the odd charter flight in summer. Alternatively travellers can fly in to other main Italian destinations such as Rome and reach Sicily by a connecting domestic flight. The island's two useful airports are listed below with their websites, which give the companies that use them.

Palermo's Falcone-Borsellino airport at Punta Raisi (www.gesap.it) takes flights operated by Ryan Air (www.ryanair.com) from the UK. A 40min trip by train will see passengers in the city

Petralia Sottana (Le Madonie area)

centre, otherwise it's 50min by bus. Several long-distance coach lines, such as those going to Trapani and Agrigento, also stop at the airport.

Catania's Fontanarossa airport (www.aeroporto.catania.it) takes British Airways' flights (www.britishairways.com) and Air Malta (www.airmalta.com). Located a mere 6km to the city's south, it has frequent shuttle buses to and from the centre and the main railway station. Coaches to more distant destinations (eg Siracusa) also call in.

By ferry

Sicily is easily reached from mainland Italy by train or car; the journey entails crossing the legendary Strait of Messina on the non-stop ferries from Villa San Giovanni to Messina. Long-distance trains from central and northern Italy use this route, and the carriages are shunted into the ship's hold for the crossing. Drivers, on the other hand, can make

their way to the well-signed port area for the car ferries.

Finally, Palermo is linked by high-speed and normal passenger ferries at various times of year with Naples, Cagliari, Civitavecchia (near Rome), Livorno and Genoa. Milazzo has year-round links to Naples, while Trapani has ferries to Cagliari and Tunisia, and Catania is accessible from both Malta and Ravenna by sea.

TRAVELLING AROUND SICILY

An extensive network of public transport serves even the most remote angles of the island, and visitors are encouraged to make use of it. Though this may limit flexibility and be more time-consuming, it provides ideal opportunities to meet local people and, of great relevance, means one less polluting vehicle on the roads. Details of relevant public transport are provided in the 'Access' paragraph of each itinerary, and contact information for the companies is listed below.

By rail

Enthusiasts with time to spare will have a field day on the train lines, many single track, that snake their tortuous and scenic way through the marvellously varied country landscapes of Sicily. The nationwide phone number for State Railways (Trenitalia) timetable information and reservations is Tel 892021, otherwise the web site is www.trenitalia.com.

In addition, a privately run 'toy' train circles Mount Etna: the Circumetnea starts out from Catania and climbs gradually northwest, reaching almost 1000m above sea level. It skirts the volcano base, terminating at Giarre-Riposto on the Ionian coast once more, from where

it is a short journey by State Rail south back to Catania. Service is suspended on Sundays and holidays. For timetable information Tel 095-541250/1 or www. circumetnea.it.

By bus

Veritable fleets of local buses and long-distance coaches operate across Sicily. Timetables are usually posted at the main stops, while tobacconists and cafés in small towns often act as ticket offices. Try to be at the bus stop early as drivers often depart ahead of schedule!

By ferry

Sicily's island groups, including the Egadi and Aeolians dealt with in this guide, have permanent ferry and hydrofoil links, as outlined in the relevant sections.

Cefalù and its headland (Walk 33)

BUS CONTACT DETAILS

- AMAT www.amat.pa.it Palermo Tel 091-6902690.
- AST www.aziendasicilianatrasporti.it Catania Tel 840-000323, Marsala Tel 840-000323, Palermo Tel 091-6800030, Siracusa Tel 0931-462711 and Trapani Tel 0923-21021.
- Caruso, Noto Tel 0931-894528.
- Citis, Salina Tel 090-9844150.
- Fratelli La Spisa, Cefalù Tel 0921-424301.
- Interbus www.interbus.it Taormina Tel 0942-625301, Messina Tel 090-661714, Siracusa Tel 0931-66710
- ISEA, Misterbianco (Catania) www.iseaviaggi.it Tel 095-464101.
- Lumia, Agrigento Tel 0922-20414.
- Prestia & Comandè www.prestiacomande.it Palermo Tel 091-586351.
- Russo, Castellamare del Golfo Tel 0924-31364.
- SAIS www.saisautolinee.it Catania Tel 095-536168, Palermo Tel 091-6166028.
- Salemi, Marsala www.autoservizisalemi.it Tel 0923-981120.
- Sberna, S. Agata Militello Tel 0941-701029.
- Urso, Lipari www.ursobus.com Tel 090-9811026.
- Zappala & Torrisi www.zappala-torrisi.it Catania Tel 095-7647139.

By car

Car rental firms abound at the major airports and cities and are best booked from abroad, often as fly-drive package deals. One good road map recommended for drivers is the Touring Club Italiano (TCI) 1:200,000 'Sicilia'.

Sicily has a limited and unfinished *autostrada* (motorway) network, free of charge on many stretches. Off the

The following terminology can be of help in understanding timetables:	
Cambio a ... /coincidenza	change at ... / connection
Estivo/invernale	summer/winter
Feriale	working days (ie Monday to Saturday)
Festivo	holidays (ie Sundays and public holidays)
Giornaliero	daily
Lunedì a venerdì/sabato	Monday to Friday/Saturday
Sciopero	strike
Scolastico	during school term

motorways is a reasonable network of state roads, referred to on maps and signposting as *strada statale* (or SS with an identifying number), not to mention the smaller roads, *strada provinciale* (SP plus a number), for which the provinces are responsible. The Italian Automobile Club (ACI) breakdown service is Tel 116.

Avoid driving through major cities such as Catania and Palermo, if possible, as traffic congestion is rife and parking an adventure to say the least. For towns in general it is advisable to park outside the old walled perimeter and venture in on foot.

Local taxis are worth using to reach out-of-the-way archaeological sites or walks. If none are around, a good bet is to ask at the main village café. People tend to be extremely helpful and go out of their way to help visitors.

ACCOMMODATION

All the walk descriptions come complete with listings for accommodation. These range from the modest hotel or *albergo*, to a room in a private home (known variously as *camera privata*, *affittacamera* or bed & breakfast), simple apartment (*apartamento*), and a hostel (*ostello*) or two. Otherwise there are the flourishing *agriturismo* farm establishments, many of which are restored historic properties.

The odd mountain hut (*rifugio* abbreviated to Rif.) has also been included where relevant. Unlike the spartan establishments in the Alps, these

are hybrids – all can be reached by road and are more like country hotels. Sheets are provided as is a private bathroom in many cases, and guests need take only a towel. Charges are generally moderate and home-style meals are available. Those run by the CAI (Club Alpino Italiano) offer discounted rates for members of affiliated organisations. A separate organisation, the CAS (Club Alpino Siciliano), has a couple of well-run manned refuges in addition to unmanned chalets in wonderful positions, though the latter are for the exclusive use of members.

Unless specifically mentioned, all establishments are open all year round. *Mezza pensione* (half board) may be on offer, and this combination of lodging with breakfast plus dinner (usually excluding drinks) can be advantageous.

The main tourist offices in Sicily supply excellent booklets, updated yearly, listing all the accommodation (camping grounds included), with prices and opening periods, for the relevant province. It's advisable to stock up with these handy booklets in the towns as little information is available in the

Rifugio at Piano Battaglia

hinterland. Prices are generally lowered at off-peak times and may be negotiable.

Though advance reservation is only really necessary in high season (essentially Easter and late July–August), it's a good idea to call ahead to small hotels or private rooms to give them advance warning of your arrival. English is not widely spoken outside the main tourist cities or resorts, making a sprinkling of Italian highly desirable.

TELEPHONES

When phoning in Italy remember to use the full area code including the zero, even for local calls. Exceptions are mobiles (*cellulare*), that commence with '3', and toll-free numbers that begin with '800' or '840'. Calls to Italy from overseas must likewise include the zero of the area code.

Mobile phones can be extremely useful when travelling around the island, for booking accommodation for instance, however coverage is by no means comprehensive.

Note: many toll-free numbers for information services cannot be called from a mobile.

Public phones are generally easy to find in small towns and villages, either in the main piazza or the at the bar/coffee shop. Coins are rarely accepted these days it's a good idea to purchase a pre-paid phone card, *carta telefonica*, available from tobacconists, cafés and paper shops. **Note:** the corner with the dotted line needs to be removed before the card can be used.

FOOD AND DRINK

One legacy of Sicily's colourful history is the unique combination of ingredients, spices and herbs that have been grafted onto the simple fare of the peasant people. The Arabs are credited with the majority of imports, from couscous to pasta, and from fish preservation techniques to sorbets and confectionery. The fertile land and hard-working inhabitants mean a vast range of fruit and vegetables is grown on Sicily, with a large measure of success.

All attempts to speak Italian will endear you to the locals. Say '*Pronto*' to start a phone call, then try with these:

Buon giorno (Buona sera). Cerco una camera matrimoniale (singola) con (senza) bagno per una notte (due notti) da oggi (domani).
Good morning (evening). I'm looking for a double (single) room with (without) bathroom for one night (two nights) as from today (tomorrow).
Avete un lettino per un bambino?
Do you have a small bed for a child?
Avete qualcosa di più grande (economico)?
Do you have anything larger (cheaper)?

To familiarise themselves with the raw materials, visitors can do no better than wander around a fresh-produce market. The strictly regional nature of Sicilian food, and its relative lack of sophistication compared to what is usually expected of Italian cuisine, means delicious surprises can be expected by adventurous eaters.

The **snack** front is dominated by the *arancino*, a luscious ball of moist rice around an inner core of meat and tomato sauce (*ragù*), crumbed, fried and eaten warm. Those served on board the ferries that cross the Strait of Messina are legendary! Another snack found prevalently around Palermo is *panelle*, squares of chick pea pastry, battered and fried and served on its own or as a roll filling, preferably accompanied by fried eggplant. *Schiacciata* and *focaccia*, types of pizza-like bread, are good lunch fare and found in all bakeries. A modest restaurant or trattoria may not always have a menu, however by asking '*Che cosa avete oggi*?' (What's on today?) or '*Quale sono le vostre specialità*?' (What are your specialities?) something unfailingly interesting is guaranteed.

Antipasti (**starters**) are usually in a mouth-watering display to be served at room temperature, and could easily constitute a meal on their own. You may find *sarde alla beccaficco*, fresh sardines stuffed with capers and breadcrumbs and lightly fried (the name alludes to the serving manner, as the fish is arranged to resemble a prized game bird, the garden warbler). The eggplant (*melanzana*) is omnipresent, mostly the light mauve bulbous type. Lightly salted and left so the bitter juices drain away, it has a deep, rich taste enhanced by light frying, before serving with a splash of tomato purée and oregano. In combination with celery and capers it also features in the rich *caponata* stew. *Alla parmigiana* sees it layered with tomato and melted parmesan cheese. Mushrooms, sundried tomatoes and an infinity of olives are usually on offer as well.

TOURIST INFORMATION

Masses of helpful information and useful links can be found on the Italian National Tourist Authority web site www.enit.it. The island's main tourist offices are listed here, while other relevant offices can be found under individual walks.
Catania: Via Etnea 63 Tel 095-311768 www.turismo.provincia.catania.it
Cefalù: Corso Ruggiero 77 Tel 0921-421050 www.cefalu-tour.pa.it
Messina: Piazza Cairoli 45 Tel 090-2935292 www.azienturismomessina.it
Palermo: Piazza Castelnuovo 34 Tel 091-583847 or 091-6058351 www.palermotourism.com
Siracusa: Via S. Sebastiano 43 Tel 0931-67710 www.apt-siracusa.it
Trapani: Piazza Saturno Tel 0923-29000 www.apt.trapani.it

The Pizzo Carbonara peak (Walk 35)

Primo piatto or **first course** inevitably means pasta, thought to have been invented in Sicily, if not brought in by the Arabs. In any case, a 12th-century account of the island by the geographer al-Idrisi made mention of busy pasta factories near Palermo where vermicelli and macaroni were produced for exportation to both Muslim provinces and Christian countries. Noteworthy present-day dishes include *pasta alla Norma* (a reference to the opera by Vincenzo Bellini, who hailed from Catania), the sauce a delicious combination of stewed eggplant and tomato. In the Trapani area you'll come across pasta with *pesto trapanese*, a fragrant cold sauce of fresh tomatoes with crushed garlic, almonds, parmesan cheese and basil, or *pasta con le sarde*, topped with fresh sardines combined with tangy wild fennel and pine nuts, not to mention *cuscus*, the dish of north African origin of steamed semolina served with a spicy fish-based sauce. In contrast the Nebrodi mountain villages specialise in fresh *maccheroni*, long

hollow tubes smothered in a rich meat sauce (*sugo*), while the Monti Iblei district offers home-made *ravioli di ricotta* flavoured with a pungent tomato and pork sauce and *cavatelle*, generous fresh pasta coils.

A **main course** (*secondo piatto*) in the hills around Siracusa will include the excellent aromatic braised rabbit, alias *coniglio alla stimpirata*, alongside myriad choice grilled meats flavoured with oregano, garlic and lemon.

Menus with **seafood** (*pesce* or *frutti di mare*) will feature *pesce spada* (swordfish) prepared *al cartoccio*, 'wrapped' to guarantee its moistness while baked, otherwise it is popular grilled on skewers (*spiedini*). Fortunately *tonno* (tuna) is easily found in summer: grilled, baked, sautéed or stewed in onions and vinegar, it is unfailingly luscious. The Sicilians leave the flesh under running cold water until the blood has completely drained away, making for a much lighter meal in both the colour and digestive sense. *Calamari* or similar *totani ripieni* (stuffed)

26

can be a treat, likewise fresh *alici* or *masculini* (anchovies), while any recently caught fish is worth sampling if delicately poached in *acqua di mare*, seawater. Delectable ricci di mare or sea urchins, sliced open to show off their bright orange and crimson flesh, are consumed raw with abundant lemon juice or tossed with pasta and garlic.

Sicily is not a great cheese producer, though fresh *ricotta* is hard to beat. Usually made from sheep's or goat's milk, it comes in a delectable creamy fresh form as well as smoked or dried for grating over pasta dishes. Seasoned, if somewhat bland, cheeses worth trying are *caciocavallo* and *canestrato* – known as tuma when fresh, then *primu sali* when salted.

Notables in the vast vegetable field are *pomodori* (tomatoes), which ripened under the African-like sun can be memorable, as well as *carciofi* (artichokes) and broccoli tossed over pasta. *Contorno* means a vegetable side dish.

Fruit is dominated by citrus, namely *arancie* (oranges), *arancie sanguigne* (blood oranges), *limoni* (lemons) and the monstrous knobbly fruit known as *cedri* (citrons), similar to a lemon and excellent for candying and confectionery.

Last but by no means least are the *dolci*, pastries, ice creams and sweets in general. This class, an art form, encompasses generous mouth-watering cakes made of melt-in-the-mouth *pasta di mandorla*, a lighter version of marzipan, as well as the famous *cannoli*, tubes of fried flaky pastry stuffed with a rich mixture of ricotta cheese and candied fruits,

virtually a meal in itself. In a similar vein is *cassata*, often an ice cream concoction, then there's the superb *torrone*, alias nougat, which comes in mind-boggling variations based on honey, almond and pistachio. *Gelato* (ices) assumes a new meaning and dimension in Sicily. The creamy types can be unforgettable and the lighter fruit flavours are usually *sorbetto*, said to have been invented by the Arabs who used snow from Etna combined with the juice of locally grown citrus fruit.

The *granita* on the other hand is a marvellous thirst-quenching invention for the hot summertime – a finely shaved ice mixture flavoured with sweetened lemon juice (*al limone*), pureed strawberries (*alla fragola*) or whatever takes the maker's fancy, even *al caffè*, coffee, popular breakfast fare. Rumour has it that *al gelso*, or mulberry, is the best and most loved of all. Thick cream is an optional but favourite topping. One special icy treat prepared in Palermo for Saint Rosalia's feast day (September 4th) is *gelo al mellone*, made with watermelon and scented with jasmine flowers. Lastly, try *latte di mandorla*, a sweet almond-based drink.

Climate and history have produced an excellent and currently expanding range of wines. One widely distributed substantial red is Corvo, Duca di Salaparuta, though connoisseurs will appreciate superior full-bodied wines such as Cerasuolo di Vittoria (from the Ragusa province), as well as several recommended reds from the Cefalù hinterland – namely the Passomaggio and

Cabernet Sauvignon from Castelbuono. Top grade Shiraz has also recently emerged. Lighter vintages are the red from the flanks of Etna (with a guaranteed DOC rating, also available in white and rosé) or the house red from San Cipirello in the Palermo hinterland, if not special whites such as those from the Castiglione area.

Notable white wines are the Bianco d'Alcamo (Trapani province), Donnafugata (whose place name means 'spring of health') and Glicine, unfailingly crisp and hard to beat served well chilled in summer.

Dessert and after-dinner wines are many and varied. Marsala hardly needs an introduction, thanks to its 18th-century 'discovery' by English trader John Woodhouse, then there is *zibibbo*, *moscato* (Noto district), and *malvasia* from the Aeolian islands.

Beer, refreshing in the heat, is widely consumed.

FLOWERS AND TREES

Visitors in spring will be overwhelmed by the multi-coloured masses of wild flowers in Sicily. A huge variety of native Mediterranean and introduced plants flourish on terrain that can be both harsh and extraordinarily lush. The range embraces delicate insect orchids, the unusual *Orchis italica* whose straggly pink petals resemble outstretched men, broom shrubs with explosive clusters of golden blooms, bright wild irises, rare white peonies, resplendent sun or rock roses (*Cistus*) and spiky pink-bloomed

caper plants straggling over old masonry, not to mention a generous array of aromatic herbs, the likes of thyme, rosemary, sage, marjoram, oregano ('splendour of the mountain' in Greek) and pungent seaside wild fennel – a dream for any cook. In spring hillside fields are carpeted with carmine velvet crops of *Hedysarum*, like sainfoin, grown for forage.

Memorable surprises also come in the form of minuscule alpine plants that bloom on the blackened lava terrain of Etna up to a record 3050m above sea level, a mere incandescent stone's throw from the very active central craters! The vast slopes of the volcano, in fact, host an astonishing variety of unique flowering plants (*Astragalus* or milk-vetch) and trees (the pale Scandinavian-like birches) endemic to the mountain, along with dense forests of chestnut and majestic Corsican pines.

In all a mere 4% of Sicily's territory is estimated to be occupied by forests. Medium-altitude mountainous zones mean vast woods of downy and evergreen holm oak and their affiliates, together with areas of the silvery-barked Aleppo pine with long, bright green needles – as it is drought resistant, it is often used for reforestation, particularly on rocky terrain close to the coast. A special mention is due the curious manna ash, a flowering tree long cultivated in both Sicily and Calabria for its sugary sap containing mannitol, a white alcohol once used for medicinal purposes (a mild laxative) or in dietetic sweets, now all but substituted by synthetic substances. Long slashes were made in the bark of

Orchis italica *is a rare delight*

Pretty rock roses

tree in August and the manna (not to be confused with the biblical substance, a lichen in all probability) was scraped off then dried as *cannoli* tubes. The Madonie and the Zingaro Reserve are good places to see old trees still marked with the cuts. Abandoned carob trees are also common, the seed pods fed to livestock or cooked up for confectionery. A further example of man's inventiveness can be seen in the exploitation of a mountain variety of the ubiquitous euphorbia, or spurge, whose acrid milky juice, an irritant, was employed to stun river eels.

Back in the lowlands, the unusual dwarf fan palm, the sole native palm in Europe, is widespread in Sicily, and its dried fronds are still woven into robust baskets, as in the past. A stockier, orange-tinted ornamental palm which harks from the Canary Isles can be found in many a public garden. The spiky fleshy leaves of the monstrous agave, or century plant, punctuate the Sicilian landscape nowadays, far from its native Mexico. Its impressive candelabra-like flowers, marking the end of the plant's

life, appear on stems reminiscent of gigantic asparagus, straight out of a science fiction film. The very first agave in Italy was planted in the botanical gardens of Padua in 1561.

Zàgara is the Arabic/Sicilian name for the heady scent of oranges and lemons in blossom, a familiar delight to springtime travellers. The trees were imported from Asia long ago and now form the backbone of the agricultural world in Sicily. Loquat trees laden with their refreshing orange globe fruit, a 19th-century arrival from Japan, are a common sight alongside the citrus orchards. Another staple, the olive, native oleasters were improved by grafting cuttings from related cultivated types which came with early Greek settlers.

Another colourful immigrant, bougainvillea, from Brazil (introduced to Europe in 1829), brightens many a garden wall and terrace, its papery flowers ranging from burgundy-purplish through to orange. One unmistakable landmark plant that spreads like wildfire through abandoned fields, forming impenetrable thorny barriers, is a cactus – the prickly pear, also known under the colourful if misleading name of Barbary fig. Its introduction to Italy from South America is attributed to none other than Christopher Columbus. From spring through to summer it sports pretty, bright yellow, paperish flowers amidst its long, bristling spines, as well as reddish-purple egg-shaped fruit, edible if not particularly tasty once all the insidious prickles have been carefully extracted.

Visitors from the Antipodes will be surprised at the sight of numerous eucalypts, originally introduced to the Mediterranean over past centuries to help drain swampy areas, and which have since themselves become a paradoxical drain on the precious water resources in many cases.

Many of the species referred to above can be grouped under the vast class of Mediterranean maquis, which still accounts for a considerable range

Prickly pear blooms

of altitudes on Sicily. Hardy, low, evergreen tree and impenetrable shrub cover combined with aromatic plants are apparently resistant to the scorching near-drought conditions of a typical Sicilian summer. However they succumb to fire, as oily substances ignite in a flash, but growth can be restored in a matter of months.

Seashore walks are always rich in plant life, with interesting examples such as the stunning yellow horned poppy, lilac sea rocket, purple-tinged sea holly and pungent artemisia. The rather nondescript glasswort, or *Salicornia*, found on salt-ridden marshes and dunes, has jointed, bright green fleshy stalks which supply potash-rich ashes, long used in glass-making throughout the Mediterranean. Underwater plants include an unusual flowering seaweed which forms meadows and comes under the evocative appellation *Posidonia oceanica* ('king of the sea'). Its fronds form floating cushions, though is more commonly seen in dried form, as the old leaves are pulverised then rolled into curious pebble-shaped balls by wave action, to be washed up on the beaches especially along the southern coast. Vast banks of seaweed strands deposited on the sand can even provide a habitat suitable for the endemic marigold.

While spring is undeniably the best time to go walking in terms of the flowers, autumn has its own specialities, such as unusual concentrations of cyclamens in the woods and the striking purple flowers of the poisonous mandrake. Also known as the love apple for

*Cyclamens are common
in upland woods*

its use in potions, not to mention as a painkiller in medieval times, it is similar to the gentian, though is enclosed by spreading dock-like leaves.

WILDLIFE

Crocodiles from the Nile, believed to have been imported by Arab conquerors during the 10th century, once prospered in Sicilian waters. Reports as late as the 16th century described the fearful creatures in lakes and rivers, not to mention Siracusa's famed fountain Fonte del Ciane, where they lurked amongst the giant papyrus. On the other hand, fossil evidence from the Nebrodi mountain range clearly speaks of elephants, rhinoceros and hippopotamus, whereas prehistoric graffiti and cave paintings on the island of Levanzo depict donkeys and bison, along with tunny fish and dolphins. Present-day species are those that managed to live through the ravages of World War Two and extensive deforestation, after centuries of relatively peaceful cohabitation with agricultural man. Survivors range from shy deer and foxes to the wild boar and elusive porcupine (introduced by the ancient Romans for its delectable flesh), and even noisy walkers can count on seeing hordes of wild rabbits and the occasional larger creature such as mouflon. A Mediterranean native, this wild sheep frequents rugged scrub mountain flanks and can be distinguished by its showy curved horns.

A fair range of snakes enjoy this sun-blessed island, and one of the longest and most commonly encountered is a swift and irritable black colubrid, which is harmless. The viper or adder (*vipera* in Italian), a venomous snake with diamond/zigzag markings on its light brown-grey back, is to be taken seriously. Bare feet and flimsy sandals are best avoided, as is sitting on sun-baked rocks without giving prior occupants time to slither away.

The delightful transparent, creamy-coloured Sicilian gecko abounds, distinct from the more usual Mediterranean type. This miniature dragon darts about striking daring poses on walls inside and out in search of insects.

Despite the over-fished state of the Mediterranean, majestic swordfish and silvery tuna of up to 200 kilos are a common sight in the markets, especially towards summertime. The former are pursued predominantly around Messina from curious boats (*feluca*) whose masts are fitted with slender lookout towers some 22m high. A similar extension of the prow serves the harpooner. Tuna, on the other hand, are subjected to a complex group hunt and meet their end according to age-old traditions that see them first captured in a labyrinth of nets and chambers, as per the *mattanza* still practised in the Egadi islands.

The picture on the bird front is a little more cheerful. Pink flamingos have returned to coastal bird sanctuaries along with an impressive number of waterfowl such as herons, egrets and the elegant black-winged stilt (the *cavaliere d'Italia*), easily recognised by its long, spindly and unsteady crimson legs, almost comical as it fishes in shallow water. Dominant birds in the countryside tend to be flashy magpies and squawking jackdaws, though there are also melodious skylarks and nightingales, and some impressive birds of prey. In spite of the annual slaughter many are subjected to on their return south across the Strait of Messina, the list includes buzzards and

kestrels, the peregrine falcon, Bonelli's eagle and elegant Eleonora's falcons, most of which are to be considered endangered. The latter are renowned for their evening group hunting forays when they prey on smaller, weary species. The unusual Egyptian white vulture, or pharaoh's chicken, reportedly survives in the mountains, as do rare pairs of golden eagles.

A frequenter of stony ground and clearings, the Sicilian rock partridge is not an unusual sight scurrying along a track trailing its young, while memorable is the eye-catching hoopoe running and bobbing its way along pathways. This unusual and showy bird is identifiable by its trademark crest of black-tipped, chestnut-brown feathers and black and white striped wings. A summer migrant in northern Europe, it often winters over in Sicily in preference to Africa.

Sunset over the Sciara del Fuoco (Walk 46)

THE NORTHEAST COAST

WALK 1

*Taormina and
the Castello Saraceno*

Time	2hr
Distance	3.5km/2.2 miles
Ascent/descent	400m/400m
Grade	1
Map	Town map from Tourist Office
Start/finish	Taormina railway station
Access	Taormina's railway station (Taormina-Giardini) is served by all Messina–Catania trains. Buses (Interbus) also stop here before proceeding uphill to the town, where it is feasible to slot directly into the upper part of the itinerary if desired. A novel way to access the town is by cable-car (*funivia*): from Mazzarò on the coast it ascends the mountainous eastern flank, to terminate a short distance from Porta Messina.
	Drivers on the A18 autostrada will need the Taormina Sud exit, then the SS 114 coast road, and are advised to seek parking on the outskirts of town.

This popular scenic route makes use of old winding trails on the picturesque hillsides around the erstwhile Graeco-Roman settlement of Tauromenium, now a charming tourist attraction. The site was originally occupied by the native Sicel population and is set in a dominating position high over the sea in a series of spacious recesses and terraces on the flanks of lofty Monte Tauro. The actual town was founded in the 5th century BC by refugees fleeing from the destruction of nearby Naxos, the pioneer Greek colony in Sicily; in fact, Taormina's landmark, an unusual and beautiful theatre ensconced in the mountainside, dates back to that period. The thriving settlement was eventually seized by the Arabs in the 10th century, only to fall to the Normans some time afterwards, as happened all over the island.

Path closure: due to minor landslips the path from the railway station up to the town is currently closed after Madonna delle Grazie – and awaiting repairs.

Piazza IX Aprile,
Taormina

Taormina enjoys a marvellous Mediterranean climate with mild winters, long ensuring its fame as a haven for foreigners of a literary penchant, such as Goethe, D.H. Lawrence and Lawrence Durrell. A must for all visitors to Sicily, the town offers attractive, stately buildings set amid lush vegetation – the likes of the ornamental palm from the Canary Isles shade many a garden. Bougainvillea adds splashes of colour, while omnipresent orange trees thrive in this sun-blessed climate, their divine perfume wafting down back-streets and alleys.

The walk itself follows well-graded mule tracks and, once the town has been traversed, continues uphill to a photogenic sanctuary and Saracen castle. Magnificent views range over the sparkling Ionian Sea and coastline and take in the majestic spread of Etna. An easy route for anyone who can deal with gradual climbs from sea level to 400m in altitude. It is however unsuitable in the central part of the day in summer as shade is scarce, but highly recommended at other times of the year, preferably late afternoon to catch the sunset from the castle. Naturally Taormina has no lack of opportunities for refreshment or accommodation.

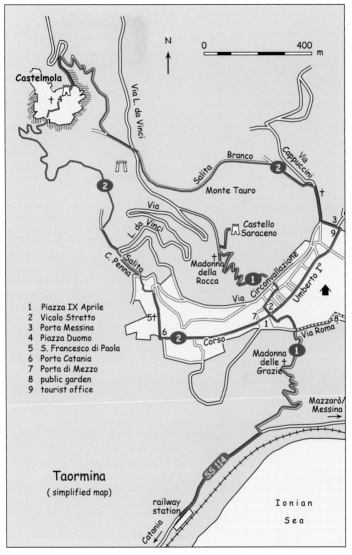

N

0 — 400 m

Castelmola † 4

Via L. da Vinci

Branco

Via Cappuccini

Salita ② †

Monte Tauro

Via L. da Vinci

Castello Saraceno

② C. Penna Salita

† Madonna della Rocca ①

Via Circonvallazione

3
9

Umberto I°

7 ②

1 8

Via Roma

1 Piazza IX Aprile
2 Vicolo Stretto
3 Porta Messina
4 Piazza Duomo
5 S. Francesco di Paola
6 Porta Catania
7 Porta di Mezzo
8 public garden
9 tourist office

5 †

6 ② Corso

Madonna delle Grazie † ①

Mazzarò/ Messina →

Taormina
(simplified map)

SS 114

railway station

Catania

Ionian Sea

The Walk

The route starts from the beautifully restored Art Deco-style **railway station**, enveloped in heady orange blossoms that are nothing short of overwhelming in spring. Take the road northeast in the direction of Taormina and after some 300m, where it squeezes through a row of houses, turn off left, following the signpost for the *'centro'*. Right past a grotto-cum-shrine, a ramp leads to a pathway for the winding ascent through scrubby vegetation. Views over the sea are impressive from the word go. After the modest church of **Madonna delle Grazie** is a stiff but short climb to the verge of a sprawling hotel complex – go left up the stairs to Via Roma. ◄

Here it's well worth detouring briefly right (east) to the delightful shady public gardens Parco Duchi di Cesarò for brilliant views of Etna.

Resume the uphill stretch on a broader flight of steps alongside Hotel Villa Schuler, then it's left at the subsequent fork and up in a matter of minutes to the town's main street, Corso Umberto 1°, close to **Piazza IX Aprile** (45min from the railway station). In terms of height, you're halfway now, as Taormina stands 200m above sea level.

Directly across the road, squeezed between an antique shop and a *gelateria*, is the narrow arched alleyway Vicolo

Cloud-capped Monte Etna, visible from Taormina's gardens

Stretto, all of 60cm wide. It emerges at a lane in the residential area, where you go right for a brief stretch, then take the next flight of steps uphill. Busy Via Circonvallazione is crossed, and close by (left) is the start of the old mule track for the Castello Saraceno and Via Crucis.

Climbing gradually above town, a series of steps and ramps passes through a lovely profusion of wild flowers, majestic agave spikes and wild fennel, not to mention the prickly pear outlined on the rocky mountainside. Needless to say there are good views down onto the town's famous Greek theatre.

Twenty minutes from the square will see you at the well-placed scenic sanctuary of **Madonna della Rocca**, a 16th-century church partially built into the limestone bastion, as its curious uneven rocky ceiling reveals. Outside, a vast expanse of the Ionian coast stretches into the distance, with a curve of Calabria on mainland Italy to the northeast. Below, set in the gentle sweep of the bay at modern day Capo Schisò, are the scanty remains of the first Greek colony in Sicily, namely Naxos.

Just around the corner from the church is drinking water, a modest souvenir stand and the start of the final but brief leg to the castle. At the commanding height of 398m on the very top of Monte Tauro, the 12th-century **Castello Saraceno** (1hr 15min) occupies the site of the acropolis built in classical times. Several extant lengths of defensive walling, a tower and remains of a cistern can be seen, but the best thing is the panorama: the solemn spread of Monte Etna lays southwest, while the bird's-eye views over the coast, Taormina and environs are breathtaking. If the castle is closed, enquire at the souvenir stand, as the custodian may be on hand to let you in.

Return the same way to Taormina's centre and the Corso to join the locals on their traditional evening promenade, and from there continue to the **railway station** (grand total 2hr).

Tourist Office
Taormina
Tel 0942-23243

Accommodation
Affittacamere Il
Leone
Tel 0942-23878
Casa Grazia
Tel 0942-24776

WALK 2
Castelmola

Time	2hr
Distance	4.15km/2.6 miles
Ascent/descent	300m/300m
Grade	1
Map	Taormina map from tourist office. For sketch map of route please see Walk 1.
Start/finish	Porta Messina
Access	To reach Taormina see Walk 1. The occasional Interbus run climbs to Castelmola itself.

This rewarding walk departs from picturesque Taormina to gain the dizzy perch of Castelmola, erstwhile fortress constructed to defend the prominent settlement through the ages. Paved lanes climb to a height of 531m above sea level to reach the peaceful village overlooking the Ionian Sea, Monte Etna and a tract of northeastern Sicily. The return, on the other hand, is on a path that drops through old orchards and wilder hillside colonised by masses of prickly pear, whereas the final stretch is a delightful stroll along Taormina's main pedestrian-only street. Several steep parts make it unsuitable for the middle of a hot day.

The Walk
At the northernmost entrance to Taormina (200m), a short distance uphill from the bus terminal and cable-car is Porta Messina, where the walk starts. Take Via Costantino Patricio in gradual ascent, and turn right at the fountain under the arch onto Via Cappuccini. Curving left the road passes extant arches of a Roman aqueduct, and you bear left again at the next junction onto Via Dietro Cappuccini. A little after a hotel and masses of brilliant bougainvillea take the way signed Salita Branco. The old stepped track, now mostly concrete-ridden, climbs a dry side valley cutting the northern flank of Monte Tauro below the Castello Saraceno, while offering sweeping views back to the

Calabrian coast. After the tarmac road for Castelmola is crossed (Via Leonardo da Vinci), a steeper surfaced ramp opposite leads quickly upwards – keep right at the arrow. The original track, for foot traffic only these days seeing as a wider vehicle road has been constructed on a lower level, has been pleasantly paved. It passes beneath buildings constructed in somewhat precarious positions on the cliff edge. A final stretch along the bridge-cum-road, quite a feat of engineering, terminates in the charming shady main *piazza* of Castelmola (531m) ▶ .

Subsequently it is recommended you follow the side alley on the uphill side of the square. Marked 'Salita Castello' it leads through restaurant premises to an even higher lookout point with stunning all-round views (1hr total). The gently sloping flanks of Monte Etna provide a particularly interesting landscape even at this distance: the succession of lava flows can easily be made out, some of the most ancient clearly reaching right down to the coast around Catania.

Once back down at the *piazza* for the return walk, direct your steps downhill towards Piazza Duomo and the immaculately restored church. Take the lane under an arch, then follow signs down steps for the Pizzeria Le Mimose. After crossing two minor roads you quickly reach the lower edge of Castelmola, and close on hand left is a wide flight of steps high over the motorway. The way quickly becomes a lovely panoramic path winding through abandoned gardens thick with all manner of aromatic herbs, and olive and fruit

A rest at one of the inviting outdoor cafés to drink in the breathtaking panorama along with an apt refreshment is a suitable reward after the effort of the climb.

View to Castello Saraceno from Castelmola

orchards, now the domain of towering prickly pear, ablaze with pretty yellow blooms in early summer. A curve left leads through an old arch in view of a hillside pitted with the ancient tombs of the Sicel necropolis dating back to the Iron Age (10th–7th centuries BC), and now at risk from encroaching construction above.

The path passes well below, in a blaze of pink olean-ders and shaded by fig trees, before joining a surfaced road lined with broom close to a spread of modern apartments. Minutes later you touch on Via Leonardo Da Vinci once more, and essentially follow your nose for the final stretch back to town – namely take the steps down right, cross straight over the intersection for Salita Celestino Penna, and notice the lovely angle onto the Castello Saraceno and sanc-tuary. The subsequent leg is called Via della Chiusa, part of the route dating back to prehistoric times between Taormina and Castelmola.

These steps between houses bring you out on Via Diodoro Siculo–Via Apollo Arcageta, just uphill from the town's original cathedral, now the church of **S. Francesco di Paola**. Next is the square and car park preceding **Porta Catania** (keep left), leading back into the heart of Taormina along Corso Umberto I°, reserved for pedestrians. This broad avenue faithfully retraces the axis of the Graeco-Roman set-tlement, while the Via Valeria, the 3rd-century BC Roman road that linked Messina with Siracusa, also passed this way. Nowadays it is lined with ceramic workshops, *pasticcerie* crammed with mouth-watering almond pastries, and cafés where thirst-quenching *granite* can be had. This western medieval section of town includes a stately duomo and mon-umental fountain, before the **Porta di Mezzo** (clock tower) leads to the charming Piazza IX Aprile, featuring a terraced belvedere and several pastel stuccoed churches.

Proceeding along the Corso don't miss the brief detour right on Via Numachia for the massive Roman 122m-long brick wall, former support for a cistern or gymnasium. The Corso soon takes you past the magnificent 15th-century Palazzo Corvaja (and **tourist office**) which once hosted the Sicilian parliament, its striking two-tone facade the result of alternating limestone and lava blocks. After Piazza Vittorio Emanuele, erstwhile agora and forum, is **Porta Messina** and the conclusion (1hr for the return).

Tourist office and
Accommodation
– see Walk 1.

THE ALCANTARA RIVER VALLEY

The Alcantara River rises at 1200m above sea level in the Nebrodi mountains in the northeastern triangle of Sicily, and flows eastwards for 48km to the Ionian Sea. En route it passes between the rugged Peloritani range and the imposing volcanic flanks of Etna. Heading towards the coast it runs through several striking gorges, patiently channelled out over geological time by the impetuous watercourse, which swells with spring snowmelt from the volcano and seasonal rain.

Eons ago a minor volcano discharged a massive flow of lava that followed the same course, spreading a good 20km. The rock is basalt, solidified from a long-gone volcanic cone. This translates into flashing black walls of infinite angles that reflect the sparkling waters.

Tree trunks carried by the current once served as makeshift links between one bank and the other, though ruins of numerous bridges still dot the banks – presumably the reason for the Arabic origin for Alcantara, from al Qàntarah for 'bridge'. Fertile imaginations however attribute the origin to a legendary construction thrown across by the devil in a single night. In any case historical records of navigating the waterway date back to ancient times, many involving the proximity of the first Greek colony in Sicily, at Naxos below Taormina.

The most spectacular stretch of the river – and one of Sicily's top tourist attractions – is the Gole di Larderia, usually referred to as the Gole dell'Alcantara, 15km inland and well signposted. A narrow gauge railway ran along the valley 1958–1978 and encouraging talks are currently underway to re-open the line for tourists. In the meantime the area is accessible by either car or Interbus on the SS 185. Steps lead down to the valley floor (there's a free-of-charge 'Comunale' entrance).

Teeth-chilling cold water flows through the narrow cliff passage, and many visitors opt for waders to explore. Be warned that it is usually closed after heavy rain due to debris which obstructs

Wading up the Alcantara gorge

the river and poses dangers for visitors, while on good days it can get very crowded.

In quieter spots, animal life can be expected in the shape of frogs and toads, the rare Hermann's tortoise and other more common types, a number of harmless snakes, and a host of water birds such as grey herons.

In addition to the gorge, the surrounds offer worthwhile walks in the realms of a newly established park which extends along the course of the river, encompassing over 31,000 hectares. The Parco Fluviale dell'Alcantara (Alcantara River Park) has its headquarters at Francavilla di Sicilia Tel 0942-9899 or www.parcoalcantara.it.

Bathing at the Alcantara River gorge

WALK 3
Monte Mojo

Time	2hr 15min (1hr 15min with a car)
Distance	4km/2.4 miles
Ascent/descent	200m/200m
Grade	1–2
Start/finish	Mojo Alcantara
Access	Mojo Alcantara lies some 28km inland from Taormina and 10km from Francavilla, to which it is linked by bus on weekdays, courtesy of the Interbus line. Those arriving by car need the SS 185 which turns east away from the Ionian coast, a short distance south of Taormina. Drivers coming from Randazzo can take the SS 129 as far as Passo Pisciaro then turn north for Mojo.
Variant	If you are arriving by car you can cut 1hr off timing by driving as far the path start. Refreshments are available at Mojo.

Mojo (also spelt Moio) is a sleepy backwater in the Alcantara hinterland. In addition to the sweet juicy peaches it produces, the main reason to pay a visit is the curious 703m-high mound at the rear of the village. The long-extinct volcano is recognisable from afar standing out in a blaze of unbelievably bright yellow broom in springtime. It was long believed to have pre-dated Etna itself, and fed on the same underground lava pool. Back in the mists of time the modest *vulcanetto* exploded and spewed ash and volcanic bombs over the surrounding countryside. Moreover Monte Mojo was long held responsible for spilling the thick river of lava that flooded the Alcantara valley, partially blocking the course of the river and leading to the formation of its spectacular gorges. However, more recent credible theories attribute this to Monte Dolce on the Etna massif.

The local people tell a different tale to explain the mount's presence. Once upon a time two farmers who were brothers made their home here. One was unfortunately blind and the other, named Mojo, decidedly evil-intentioned, and

43

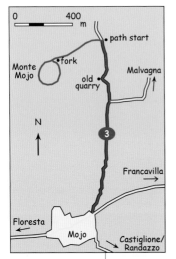

hid the harvest. This was brought to the attention of the Almighty who took appropriate action: a massive bolt of lightning struck the wrongdoer, turning him into a huge black volcano, rooted to the spot; it consequently exploded as Mojo spewed out his anger!

While unpretentious, the remaining cone is well worth visiting both for its panoramas and the wonderful display of wild orchids it puts on in the late spring.

THE WALK

Leave the sleepy village of **Mojo** (525m) and head north past the petrol station at the start of Via Vanella Mojo. Not far after the cemetery as the road curves right for Malvagna, leave it for a minor road straight ahead (closed to heavy traffic). Climbing a little, it passes a fascinating **old quarry**, where contrasting deep red and black layers of pyroclastic material underlie the bright green and yellow of broom and ferulas. A little way uphill at a stone hut is the **path start**, announced by a signpost (30min). At a sharp left a broad, well-constructed path of lava blocks heads west between olive groves and oaks. Check the low walls for pieces of volcanic bombs. An easy steady climb ensues to the grassed rim of the extinct volcano and a **fork**. Below, survivors of a long-gone orchard straggly grape vines and chestnut trees nestle inside the crater. Turn left for the narrowing path which ascends more steeply on rougher terrain. This slope is thick with insect orchids. On top of **Monte Mojo** (703m), the wonderful views are dominated by majestic Etna, with the Nebrodi range to the northwest and Peloritani northeast, including Monte Castelluzzo close-by.

Accommodation
see Walk 4 for
Francavilla or
Walk 41 for
Randazzo

It's worth completing the entire circle of the rim, taking care on the steep descent to the **fork**, Return to the **path start** and **Mojo** the same way you came.

WALK 4
Francavilla and the River

Time	2hr
Distance	3km/1.8 miles
Grade	1–2
Start/finish	Municipio at Francavilla
Access	Francavilla lies on the SS 185, 18km inland from the Ionian coast. The daily Interbus service from Taormina stops outside the Municipio (town council), as does the weekdays-only direct run to and from Catania.

When the pioneer Greek colony of Naxos on the Ionian coast was devastated in 403BC by the tyrant of Siracusa, exiles made their way inland to found less vulnerable settlements such as that on the hilly location of present-day Francavilla in the Alcantara valley. It expanded and flourished over the centuries under noble dynasties, and was defended by a castle in Norman times. Its position is strategic *par excellence*, occupying a slender triangular ridge surveying the inland and mountain ranges including Etna, while looking down to the Ionian coast at the same time. The Alcantara river below was said to have run red with blood during a fierce battle in 1719 between the Spanish and Austrians for the control of Sicily (won by Spain, the start of a lengthy period of domination). Though the late medieval fortress itself now stands in tattered ruins, the marvellous views are intact.

The name of the town – officially known as Francavilla di Sicilia (to distinguish it from the other seven eponymous settlements in Italy) – is explained in several ways: according to the authorised version it comes from the French, 'Franc Ville', as the town was exempt from feudal taxes until 1538. However, the locals seem to prefer the fanciful story that tells of Louis, a Dauphin of France, falling in love with and kidnapping Angelina, a lass from the town. In vain had she encouraged her governess to keep watch, encouraging her with 'Franca, vigghia!' the dialect for 'Franca, keep watch!'

Francavilla's ruined castle and views to the coast

The walk entails a straightforward if steep climb to the castle lookout, followed by a pleasant stretch through citrus orchards along the renowned river. Most of the route corresponds to the Alcantara Park nature trail '*le Gurne*' with info boards.

THE WALK

From the Municipio at **Francavilla** (320m) turn southeast along an old basalt-paved road through the old part of town. Many houses still sport elaborately decorated stone balconies and hefty carved portals. Past the Chiesa del Carmine keep straight on Via Ruffo, in ascent. At lovely Villa Luisa Maria, its garden shaded by swaying Canary palm trees, fork left to reach the squat belltower and church in **Piazza Matrice**.

The lane above the fountain leads past a sign for the 16th-century castle (*ruderi castello mediovale*), and to a concrete ramp uphill. A path takes over, climbing steadily south past derelict sheds. Overgrown at times, it leads onto open hillsides thick with stunning spring orchids. A ridge is soon gained, where inspiring views range from the Peloritani mountains west, with the highest peak Montagna Grande, and all the way down the Alcantara River valley past the precarious village of Motta Camastra to the Ionian Sea. Moreover close at hand are the **castle** ruins (50min, 450m), beyond which stands the photogenic town of Castiglione di Sicilia backed by the almost ghostly presence of Etna. ▸

Return the same way to **Piazza Matrice** (20min). Turn left down the narrow street lined with tiny stone dwellings to **Piazza San Francesco**, site of a museum. Continue in the same direction on Via S. Francesco. This passes an archaeological site under plastic roofing where evidence of a 4th-century BC settlement of exiles from Naxos has been discovered. Take the next lane left for the descent towards the river. Through

It is possible to clamber up a narrow path amongst the crumbling walls on the narrow ridge, but take special care as it is a little exposed and can be slippery.

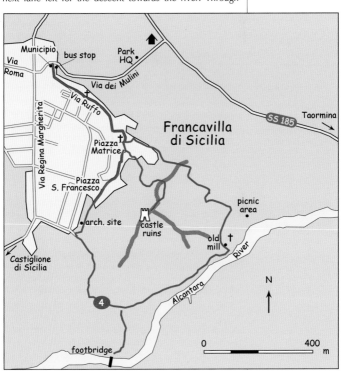

47

The Alcantara River below Francavilla

Accommodation
Hotel L'Orange
Tel 0942-981374
B&B Quattareddu
Tel 0942-982693
or 333-2972877

scented orange groves you curve beneath the castle. Soon after a prominent oak tree, turn right on a path lined by a high stone wall. Not far along are stone steps that drop to the peaceful banks of the Alcantara River at an iron **footbridge** (30min, 300m), property of the Electricity Commission ENEL. This is a good spot for a picnic with the shade of oleander trees, and allows you to admire the smooth black rock flanks, and even a kingfisher or harmless black snake. Note the curious system of irrigation channels that branch off at the nearby cascades; they date back hundreds of years to the Arabic period and, still referred to in local dialect as *saja*, the original term, they convey precious water to the thirsty citrus orchards. Long stretches are hewn into the volcanic rock face.

Return to the upper lane and turn right (east). A major irrigation channel is soon crossed, followed by a drop beneath a curious overhang of smooth lava overlaying jagged strata. Remnants of an ancient bridge are visible on the opposite riverbank, while close at hand an **old mill** stands well below the castle. Here fork left as per the nature trail, in gentle ascent along the flanks of the hill, thick with orchids in springtime. A picnic area is a good spot to enjoy the lovely views, before you enter the town again and shortly reach **Piazza Matrice**. Walk back along Via Ruffo to the Municipio of **Francavilla**.

MONTE ETNA

'When I look at her, low, white, witch-like under heaven, slowly rolling her
orange smoke and giving sometimes a breath of rose-red flame, then I must
look away from earth, into the ether, into the low empyrean. And there, in
that remote region, Etna is alone.'
D.H. Lawrence, *Sea and Sardinia*

The fire-breathing giant and its devastating eruptions have left deep inspirational impressions on Mediterranean cultures all through the ages. Early conjecture by the Greeks explained its activity as banished giants working underworld forges, along with the grisly monster Typhon, imprisoned there by Zeus, who made the earth tremble with his twisting and turning. The fitting name of 'Etna' derives from a Greek word meaning 'to burn', though the Arabs preferred to refer to it as Jebel Utlamat, 'mountain par excellence', whence derives its modern-day Latinised alias, Mongibello.

However for the Sicilians it is simply *a' muntagna* ('the mountain'), and strictly feminine.

Sicily's massive landmark volcano began life thanks to submarine activity in a long-gone gulf in eastern Sicily over half a million years ago, and appears to rise directly from the Ionian Sea. It needed Scottish geologist Charles Lyell in 1858 to demonstrate that it was the outcome of small-scale recurrent eruptions instead of a single cataclysm, the prevalent theory of the time.

With its 3300m in altitude, Monte Etna is Europe's highest active volcano,

Shepherds' hut backed by Etna's central craters (Walk 6)

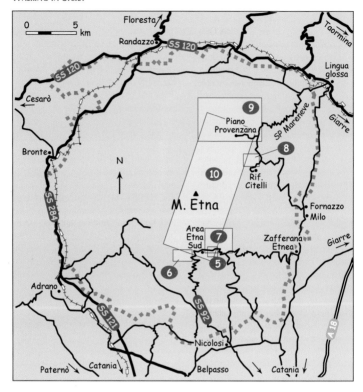

dominating the whole of Sicily. The volcano covers an area of 1600 sq km, has a diameter of 44km and a base circumference of some 160. The height of the upper crater is currently around 3340m, though this varies considerably with lava build-up. Views from the summit can range as far as 240km.

At present four craters are active on the summit: the North East, the Bocca Nuova (new mouth), the South East and the Voragine (chasm); while around 320

secondary or adventive cones dot the slopes, witnesses to recurrent decentralised activity.

The first recorded eruption, and possibly the most violent, occurred in 475BC, though a subsequent episode in 396BC was evidently of mammoth proportions as it obstructed the progress of the Carthaginian army. Over 250 more have since followed, often catastrophic events such as in 1669 when 15 villages were obliterated and Catania was inundated by lava, which reached the sea and resulted in a 2km extension of the coastline. Over the last 30 years there has been an eruption every three years on average, for a duration between a few hours to a matter of years. The explosive activity has become Strombolian in nature, namely small explosive eruptions and often accompanied by spectacular lava fountaining. Noteworthy recent flows include that of 1985, which cut across the road from Nicolosi, and the 1991 streams which threatened Zafferana Etnea. Moreover the 1991–93 period meant over 250 cubic metres of lava over 473 days. In late 1999 a voluminous river of lava from the Bocca Nuova made its way down the western flanks in the direction of the township of Bronte. On the other hand the extended 2000–2003 eruptions made headlines all over the world. Columns of thick smoke and ash of biblical dimensions towered into the sky, showing up on satellite pictures – and incidentally closing Catania's airport. A new mouth opened up, discharging mammoth amounts of lava in a sluggish but destructive red-black river north-northeast that slowly submerged the northern resort of Piano Provenzana. Fortunately there have been few victims; life-threatening explosions are rare and the creeping lava flows are slow enough to give people time to evacuate their homes.

As an alternative to mechanical diversion of lava or dynamiting, forbidden practices nowadays, the protection of Catania's patron Saint Agata is often evoked to halt the fiery rivers. In the wake of her martyrdom in the third century, her veil miraculously saved the city from being engulfed by magma and continues to be revered and borne in procession on her feast day, 5 February.

Another remarkable story, of obscure origin, stars none other than Queen Elizabeth I of England. During her early imprisonment she evidently drew up a pact with Beelzebub, prince of the devils, exchanging for her soul the throne of England and victory over her enemies, the Catholic Church included. On her death at the ripe age of 70, she requested a final favour of him: that her body not be interred in the cold, damp earth of England, but on an immense mountain on an island she had dreamt of in the middle of the Mediterranean. Her wish was fulfilled, and the devil bore her body dressed in full royal regalia into the fiery magmatic depths of none other than Sicily's Etna!

Some notes on the natural inhabitants of the mountain are in order. Lava, 'the black milk of Etna's breast', in the words of Carlo Levi, means a dearth of nitrogen, an essential element for plant life. Notwithstanding, it is colonised by a succession of fascinating plant types and can even be dated by the vegetation it supports. First off the mark are lichens and algae, which obtain nitrogen from the air and attach themselves to the rock surfaces, paving the way for the pioneer species such as milk vetch and the ubiquitous Etna broom shrubs, whose strong roots help break up the solidified lava. Then come prickly pear, fruit-bearing trees and olives, with grape vines last of all.

Vegetation on the mountain fits into three clear altitude bands: the lowest, from sea level to around 1000m, densely cultivated, is characterised by

Endemic mouse-ear on lava

grapes, pistachios, almonds, walnuts, hazelnuts, figs and fruit orchards that thrive on the fertile volcanic soil; this is followed by steeper terrain which is cloaked with broom and woods of chestnut, oak and beech (which holds the European record for altitude here, growing as high as 2250m), as well as a relic from the ice ages, the endemic birch, which resembles the Scandinavian variety. These precede the over 2000m band, or 'desert', of ashes and sand. This apparently barren lavic terrain is suited to a surprising array of flowering species, such as two special daisies, Etna camomile and ragwort, which make it up to an incredible 3050m, closely followed by a sort of crimson sorrel. A little beneath them, the fine sand is anchored by striking tussocks of milk-vetch,

Astragalus siculus or *Spino santo*, 'holy thorn', which provides hospitality for other plants such as Etna mouse-ear. Further endemics, the Etna violet and soapwort, which comes in pink cushions, also belong here.

A bright range of butterflies is to be seen, while feathered wildlife is abundant across the volcanic slopes, notably birds of prey such as golden eagles and red kites, while a host of hardy, tiny ground nesters (such as black and white tailed wheatears, stonechat, blue rock thrush and black redstart) can be seen darting across the high-altitude lava fields. The woods on the other hand are home to jays and woodpeckers. The animal front is dominated by wild cats, foxes and rabbits, whose populations have reputedly reached plague proportions since hunting has been banned in the Park. A curious phenomenon can be observed in early summer with the arrival of incredible 'clouds' of scarlet ladybirds that are airlifted helplessly en masse and easily spotted against the dark terrain.

The extraordinary world of Etna – an island within an island – lends itself to an enthralling series of visits punctuated by phenomena such as *fumarole* (hissing gas vents), immense lunar expanses thick in soft ash and lapilli, adventive cones, volcanic bombs akin to huge cannon balls of viscous lava which are spun out of craters, and unique underground tubes or lava tunnels. If conditions are favourable, the actual summit craters can be reached, lying on the level of the trademark 'cloud' – smoke in actual fact. However it is the striking contrast between life and death that leaves lasting impressions. Flourishing vineyards are half-buried by dark lava, roofs of erstwhile houses emerge from under a sombre solid avalanche, newly reconstructed stretches of road and rail make their tentative way across blackened wastes. Despite the persistent onslaughts, life goes on around the volcano, its lower slopes densely populated.

In 1987 an area of 59,000 hectares came under the auspices of the Parco dell'Etna. The headquarters at Nicolosi (Tel 095-821111) occupy an atmospheric Benedictine monastery, recently restored with great care. Several *sentieri natura*, marked nature trails, run through zones of special interest. In general walking is on forestry tracks, though waymarking is all but absent on many routes. Orientation can be tricky in the thick woods as well as on the open lavic terrain which is all but devoid of useful landmarks; it is especially difficult and dangerous if low cloud and mist roll in – not uncommon. Moreover, the high iron content of the rock can play havoc with compass readings. **Remember that stormy conditions, snowfalls and strong winds high up are common even in summer, and it is extremely inadvisable to set out on any of the walks in adverse weather.**

As the seasons go, remember that the upper half of Etna is usually snowbound for approximately four months of the year (December through to March), an attractive proposition for experienced ski tourers and marvellous for photography. Unless snowshoeing appeals (the Park runs a programme with guides) walkers are better off waiting. May–June is recommended for the high-altitude flora, July–August can be scorchingly hot on the lower reaches, while the autumn months bring crisp clear skies and russet woods.

There is a long-distance trail known as the GTE (Grande Traversata Etnea) around the mountain's midriff; however, patchy waymarking, ongoing lava flows and dearth of support structures mean it is only really feasible with a guided group: contact the Catania branch of the CAI (Tel 095-7153515 or www.caicatania.it).

Thanks to the panoramic road SP 92 via Nicolosi, the majority of visitors flock to the most accessible zone of the mountain, Area Etna Sud, 1900m above sea level. Day-in, day-out, coach-loads are disgorged at the sprawl of restaurants and kiosks peddling an unbelievable range of souvenirs and postcards.

Volcanic bomb

Its landmark is the Italian Alpine Club's mythical Rifugio Sapienza, which has miraculously survived countless onslaughts of incandescent lava, and has recently been transformed into a hotel. Close by, a brand new gondola car whisks visitors up to the 2500m mark, where 4WD minibuses continue towards the 3000m threshold. Quite frankly a trek to the volcano's breathtaking summit craters is an unforgettable experience. For safety reasons, at the present time visitors are only allowed to venture to the highest rims in the company of the qualified alpine guides, who are also experts in vulcanology. Metereological conditions permitting, from May through to October the excursions leave the Area Etna Sud (adjacent Rifugio Sapienza) on a daily basis, and are well-worth considering (Tel 095-7914755 or www.etnaguide.com.) Another agency is www.etnaest.com, tel 327 7972212.

The northeastern realms of Etna are much quieter and accessible thanks to the SP Mareneve and Rifugio Citelli and Rifugio Bruneck at Piano Provenzana – the friendly staff can help with local transport and will pick guests up at bus stops. They also organise local walks with a guide. Unaccompanied walkers can venture on the walk itineraries described in the following pages.

For more detailed and constantly updated information in English, together with links to weather forecasts and stunning images of the upper reaches of Mount Etna where the action is, not to mention a thrilling read, log on to 'Italy's Volcanoes: the Cradle of Volcanology' at www.italysvolcanoes.com, as well as the guides' site above. The Parco dell'Etna website www.parcoetna.it has all manner of information, including itineraries, while readers of Italian will appreciate highly informative www.cataniaperte.com/etna.

Maps

- 'Mt Etna' 1:25,000 by Selca, Florence, is the most useable map for walkers, and is available at Area Etna Sud and bookshops in large towns.
- There is a clear 1:50,000 map 'Parco dell'Etna' put out by the TCI (Touring Club Italiano) in conjunction with the Catania Provincial Tourist Board.
- The Park Authority itself publishes a simplified diagram-cum-map in leaflet form (in English – 'Etna Regional Park') showing the location of highlights around the mountain and providing plenty of background information. However, it is not much help for walking.

Note Remember that Etna is an active volcano and the situation can change dramatically at a moment's notice. Intending walkers should check locally for route information to avoid dangerous situations. In any conditions it's good practice to let someone know which route you intend to follow on a given day to facilitate rescue operations if needs be.

WALK 5
The Craters of Monte Silvestri

Time	1hr 20min
Distance	2.2km/1.4 miles
Grade	1–2
Map	'Mt Etna' 1:25,000, Selca
Start/finish	Restaurant, Monte Silvestri
Access	Area Etna Sud (also referred to as Rifugio Sapienza) is located 21km from Nicolosi. It is served by daily AST runs from Catania via Nicolosi. Drivers will need the parking area near the restaurant shown on the map, a short distance east from the gondola-car lift and Rif. Sapienza, along the road for Zafferana Etnea. On foot, it's a 5min stroll from the bus stop.

This route offers two easy but spectacular circuits around a number of colourful craters, long inactive. Ranging between altitudes of 1846–1908m above sea level, a good distance below the smoking summit of Etna, is the cluster of six craters belonging to Monte Silvestri. Strictly speaking they belong to the group of 300 or so adventive (or parasitic) lateral cones that have over time opened up on the flanks of the great giant – in this case along a radial fault during a six-month eruption in 1892. This batch is especially attractive for its rainbow of coloured soils – green, red, white, yellow – in addition to the wide-ranging panorama on offer.

Hotel-style accommodation is available at nearby Rif. Sapienza, as well as Nicolosi, which has a good choice of restaurants.

THE WALK
From the **restaurant** (1880m), where visitors are exhorted *'Visitate i crateri Silvestri'*, take the clear path south flanking the first small exemplar of the **Monte Silvestri Inferiore** craters with its vivid chromatic tones. The broad rim of the main hole, some 50m in diameter, is circled next on prevalently reddish terrain. From the opposite side take the steep

Monte
Silvestri
Super.

Rif. Sapienza

• bus stop

Zafferana Etnea

5

Nicolosi

restaurant

**Monti
Silvestri**

N

Monte
Silvestri
Infer.

Monte
Nero

0   200
              m

path which drops quickly on loose soil towards a further crater, unmistakable **Monte Nero** (black mount). Take care following its rim.

Return to the main crater the same way – or via any of the numerous side paths which invite further exploration. The entire area is quite breathtaking. There are vast stark extensions of lava flows, their dark masses interrupted by islands of greenery that escaped the carnage. Further groups of adventive cones punctuate the landscape right down to the broad valleys that circle Etna, preceding the Ionian coast. The circuit is completed left around the main lower crater and back to the roadside **restaurant** (40min).

Those with energy to spare should cross the road and embark on the steep path for the upper crater. A tiring red-black sand ramp bears north, at first skirting the recent lava flows which appeared to everyone's surprise on the lower slope of La Montagnola in 2001. Swinging east then south, the path gradually gains the wonderfully scenic rim of **Monte Silvestri Superiore** (1998m). The views range over neighbouring Monti Calcarazzi and the elongated Schiena dell'Asino crest, not to mention much further afield. A clear path continues west around the rim, before descending to join the ascent path, whence left back to the **restaurant** (40min).

Accommodation
Rif. Sapienza
Tel 095-915321 CAI
Nicolosi:
B&B La Giara
Tel 095-7919022

Dwarfed to the size of ants, people explore the lower Silvestri rim

WALK 6
Monte Nero degli Zappini Loop

Time	1hr 40min
Distance	5km/3.1 miles
Grade	1
Map	'Mt Etna' 1:25,000, Selca
Start/finish	Piano Vetore
Access	As per Walk 5, but leave the main road 2.5km west of the Area Etna Sud. There is ample roadside car parking. Those travelling by the daily Catania–Etna bus should ask to be let off at the *'Sentiero Natura'* turn-off, then it's a matter of minutes to walk in.
Note	After a lava invasion in 2003, the central section was modified. This may not be shown on older maps.

This rewarding *Sentiero Natura*, the very first nature trail to be marked by the Etna Park authorities, leads through an interesting range of volcanic landscapes. It is within easy reach of the main Etna Sud zone, but is thankfully quiet and little visited. Moreover, the routes gives great angles onto Etna's main summits and the columns of smoke issuing from the craters. Pockets of endemic plant life up the interest level. The sole note of 'warning' concerns the dearth of shade on all but the central stretch, making sun protection essential. Good trainers instead of boots are OK on this route.

THE WALK
From the **Sentiero Natura signpost** (1741m) on Piano Vetore, turn right (northwest) onto the broad trail with M. Vetore behind you. You strike out over black sand and past a flag pole, accompanied by a spread of endemic broom bushes. Ahead is the huge spread of Etna, its desolate southern flanks marked by dark stripes of recent lava flows and punctuated by the split secondary cone M. Nero degli Zappini, NNW, among others. (Zappini refers to the landmark conifer that grows on it). Keep left at an old road, then immediately right as per observation point 1 (*punto di osservazione*, PO1) and

proceed between the hardy cushions of milk-vetch and Etna violets, more often than not adorned with rabbit droppings. The foot of a 'fresh' lava lobe is soon traversed, in a zone that is home to a surprising number of songbirds. At PO3 detour left to inspect a curious crumbling cone, witness to an ancient eruption.

After a stretch west, in the proximity of the next marker, turn off left towards a hut. Only minutes away is the fascinating fenced-in **Grotta Santa Barbara** (1778m), one of the few caves of its type left on the mountain. Accumulated compressed snow from the winter was once transported in wicker backpacks, insulated with ferns, down to coastal locations. The hut used to be the abode of the 'snowkeeper'.

Retrace your steps to where you turned off and go left to resume the *sentiero natura* with views ranging southwest to the Nebrodi range. ◄

Close by in the shade of a conifer at PO4 is an unusual hollow tree trunk that had been enveloped in lava; the wood crumbled away leaving only the solidified mould.

Keep on the right fork in slight ascent through a carpet of juniper and masses of broom, to a copse of beech. Soon the original route undergoes a change due to the 'invasion' of lava in 2003. By all means proceed further as a faint path has been trodden a short way across. However you will then need to backtrack and follow the front of the lobe, making your way downhill towards a building and small dam where a good track is joined. The black-stone **shepherds' hut** Casa Carpentieri (1hr, 1735m) long served herders, and still sports

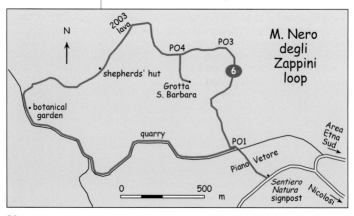

58

a stone-enclosed sheep pens and a curious outside drying rack for cheeses.

On the Zappini route

A short distance downhill metal piping is crossed, and a lane joined (southwest) through a reforestation zone, now conifer wood. A left at the ensuing T-junction means tarmac, all but buried in pine needles, leading to the Nuova Gussonia **botanical garden** belonging to the University of Catania (and rarely open to visitors). Some 10min along, the *sentiero natura* branches left past a road barrier and across old lava, with superb views of upper Etna. An abandoned quarry is traversed (PO11) and the road returns to the start point and **Sentiero Natura signpost**.

Accommodation
See Walk 5

WALK 7
Schiena dell'Asino

Time	3hr
Distance	7.4km/4.6 miles
Ascent/descent	420m/420m
Grade	2–3
Map	'Mt Etna' 1:25,000, Selca
Start/finish	Area Etna Sud
Access	See Walk 5

This marvellous walk ascends the massive ridge known as the Schiena dell'Asino, or 'donkey's back', located on the southeast flank of Etna, at the foot of La Montagnola, the mountain's most impressive adventive cone that opened up at 2500m in the summer of 1763. It overlooks another notable phenomenon, the gaping Valle del Bove, an immense open canyon that measures 7km x 6km and has walls that tower as high as 1000m. It receives the majority of lava discharged from the central craters and is streaked with an unbelievable series of greys. (Its curious name supposedly refers to 'oxen', as this was apparently the limit for cart transport drawn by the creatures.)

Despite its proximity to the main visitors' zone, usually packed with coaches and crowds, this walking route is a solitary and memorable venture. While the initial stretch follows a clear, marked track, the central stretch is over rougher unmarked terrain, before the conclusion – a traverse of sandy slope, preferably executed running. In any case no-one should venture onto the ridge in uncertain weather as low cloud spells disorientation, and what's more wind gusts whirling around the precipitous edge can be dangerous. Sun protection and drinking water are essential, as are boots and a wind jacket. Gaiters are handy for keeping sand out of your boots during the descent. An altimeter is a great help for calculating the level where the descent can begin.

As concerns the difficulty, the route rates Grade 2 as far as the Malerba plaque on the spectacular edge of the Schiena dell'Asino, then becomes Grade 3 as the path as such disappears and special care and experience are essential. Even as a shorter (2hr 30min) return trip, it is highly recommended.

THE WALK

From **Area Etna Sud** (1880m) follow the road past the restaurant at the Monte Silvestri craters heading east in slight descent. Crowds and souvenir stands are quickly forgotten, while the triangular point of La Montagnola appears above, due north. At 1832m a clear walkers-only track breaks off left, signed 'Sentiero Schiena dell'Asino'. Initially east-northeast, it climbs steadily with a good gradient over fine volcanic sand alternating with rock. Pine trees are encountered, many bearing traps for the ravenous processionary caterpillars. Endemic broom, violets and astragalus cushions take over on the barer slopes. The path winds eastwards marked by the occasional pole marker amidst abundant rabbit droppings. ▶ A section due north concludes at the 2000m mark on the breathtaking

Vistas are immense, over the sombre wasteland of volcanic origin and down to the sparkling Ionian coast beyond Catania in stark contrast.

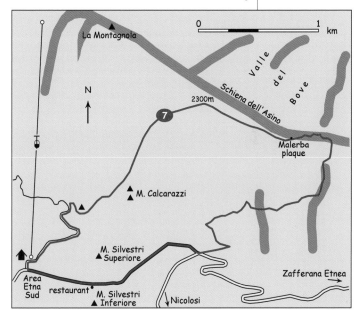

61

Looking over the depths, eastwards, a monumental cliff drop is just discernible – the Salto della Giumenta (the 'mare's leap'), a dark, frozen-in-movement waterfall.

edge of the **Schiena dell'Asino** (1hr 15min). At your feet is the horribly black-grey-red expanse of the Valle del Bove with streaky waves of superimposed lava streams. ◀

Now proceed left (west) uphill along the knobbly ridge, taking great care to keep well in from the edge. Agile birds such as the wheatear are surprisingly numerous in these apparently barren wastes. Only 5min up is the **Malerba plaque** (2043m), placed in memory of a rescuer who lost his life on a mission here in 1987.

Now make your way up the steepening ridge, though almost immediately an impassable rock outcrop forces you to detour left via a lower crest. Then continue making your way across the soft sand, anchored by plant mounds, and upwards (northwest) in the direction of La Montagnola (though momentarily out of sight). About 1hr of steady climbing, with dips in between, will see you at the **2300m level** below La Montagnola. In view well below are the colourful Monte Silvestri cones and Area Etna Sud. Faint paths become obvious west-southwest as you head across the soft sand, suitable for a running descent, though take care not to go off course. Head for the minor craters (from the year 1766) of **Monti Calcarazzi** (2064m) where several broad paths appear, as does a hint of sulphur. Chances are that you'll subsequently end up on the rough service track that drops to the station for the gondola-car lift. But however you descend, you'll inevitably end up on the road in the vicinity of **Area Etna Sud** (1880m).

Accommodation
See Walk 5

Gaiters are handy for a volcanic-sand-running descent

WALK 8
The Monti Sartorio Circuit

Time	1hr 30min
Distance	3.5km/2.2 miles
Grade	1
Map	'Mt Etna' 1:25,000, Selca
Start/finish	*Sentiero Natura*, on the Rif. Citelli road
Access	From the wonderfully panoramic road SP Mareneve (sea-snow) that runs across the eastern flanks of Etna, take the signed turn-off for Rifugio Citelli, some 12.5km from Fornazzo and 5.5km from Piano Provenzana. The start of the walk is signposted 1km along. Unfortunately there is no public transport to this zone.

This fascinating and easy loop skirts the Monti Sartorio, a group of seven modest mounts (adventive volcanic cones) which came into being on January 30th, 1865. Located at 1800m altitude on the eastern flank of Etna, they succeeded in exuding a total of 96 million cubic metres of incandescent lava over a total of 150 days, and were named after 19th-century scholar Sartorius von Waltershausen, one of the first to chart the volcano's eruptions.

Amidst the stands of Corsican pines, elegant endemic birch, and a multitude of grasses and flowers that have succeeded in finding a hold on the lava and ash terrain in the 140 years since the eruption, is a fine range of volcanic oddities. Included are over-sized cannon balls for which the appellation 'bombs' has been coined; they are formed when viscous lava is flung out of a volcano and spins through the air, cooling in the process.

The walk is feasible any time of year except for the mid-winter months, when snow cover can be expected. Though an old shepherd's route is followed on the first leg, a broad lava flow is subsequently crossed and is rough on the feet, making thick-soled boots essential. What's more, there are long stretches with no shade – so have a sun hat handy in spring–summer. A mere 100m height gain is entailed, and as the route is a *sentiero natura* it is waymarked courtesy of the Parco dell'Etna. The welcoming Rifugio Citelli is only 1.5km up the road from the walk, and can provide all manner of refreshment as well as accommodation in addition to further suggestions for local walks, thanks to the expert staff.

THE WALK
Park at the curve in the road where signposting announces the start of the **sentiero natura** (1660m). Short yellow poles lead the way (northwest) along a broad track through clumps of the delicately pale birch trees that are endemic to Etna and grow predominantly in this zone. Out of the trees, the hot sandy landscape takes on a desert-like appearance, reminiscent of central Australia. However, closer inspection reveals hardy grasses and even flowers; the likes of tansy and the endemic Etna milk-vetch.

Past a junction (for the return path, 5min) you bear left (west) drawing closer to the highest of the bare Sartorio mounts bordering the path, north. The slopes sport the odd slender pioneer Corsican pine not far from birch, windblown and precarious on the volcanic sand and debris base. Some

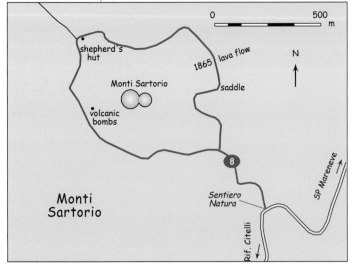

Volcanic bombs on the Monti Sartorio circuit

20min from the start keep your eyes peeled for a low marker for an interesting group of **volcanic bombs** just off the path. Quite a number in different shapes and sizes lie scattered among the pines. In the other direction (southwest) is the impressive sight of Monte Frumento delle Concazze, one of Etna's largest adventive cones, carpeted to a fair height with a sequence of grasses.

Back on the main path you proceed north, the way fringed by stunning white-green cushions hosting lightly scented Etna mouse-ear. A short distance on is an old **shepherd's hut** (at 1715m) where the *sentiero natura* turns right off the main track. You soon find yourself winding through a peaceful birch wood, heading east around the mount to emerge at an astonishing contrast – the massive **lava flow** dating back to 1865 (20min from the hut). In all the solid river extends for eight sq km, with an average thickness of 12m. The hardened surface is surprisingly jagged and crossing requires a deal of clambering, which can be rough on the hands.

Some way up you leave the lava for a **saddle** between two of the major cones, before dropping gradually across a plain bright with flowers. The main path is not far away now, then it's left for the short distance back to the road.

Tourist Office
Linguaglossa
Tel 095-643094
Milo
Tel 095-955437

Accommodation
Rif. Citelli
Tel 095-930000 or
333-8706144 CAI
**www.rifugiocitelli.
com**

WALK 9

*Monte Nero Circuit
and Grotta dei Lamponi*

Time	3hr 15min
Distance	10km/6.2 miles
Ascent/descent	400m/400m
Grade	2
Map	'Mt. Etna' 1:25,000 Selca
Start/finish	Piano Provenzana
Access	Piano Provenzana is located on a branch of the SP Mareneve road that runs along the eastern side of Etna between Linguaglossa and Fornazzo. Unfortunately there is no public transport beyond Linguaglossa (on the Circumetnea railway line).
Note	Enquire locally for access conditions to the *sentiero natura* for the Monte Nero circuit before setting out. Otherwise be prepared to skip that section and start out directly from Rifugio Brunek: follow the *pista* (unsurfaced track) that strikes out northwest, climbing easily for the 7km as far as Grotta dei Lamponi, allowing 3hr return time.

These high-altitude reaches of the scenic northeastern flank of Etna feature a vast array of volcanically formed marvels, guaranteeing fascinating – not to mention educational – walking. After a circuit of 2049m Monte Nero, the undeniable highlight of this itinerary is a curious lava cave, the Grotta dei Lamponi. The 'cave of the raspberries' (they grow in the vicinity) is an incredible spacious, tubular cavity that was formed when lava streamed down from the volcano's summit in the 17th century. A crust formed on the upper surface as the lava solidified on cooling, though the flow continued undisturbed beneath it. The lava also released gases that supported the roof, though further heating actually caused occasional cave-ins. As the flow terminated towards the end of the eruption, the tunnel emptied out, leaving the long, hollow cylindrical structure. A number of such lava caves underlie the mass of Etna, but this is probably the finest and easiest to visit.

As far as the walk goes, don't forget that as well as the actual distance, it entails a fair amount of ups and downs – 400m in descent and the same in ascent. Furthermore, much of the route traverses dark lava terrain where the going can be hot in summer, so don't forget your sun hat. May–October is best to minimise the chances of snow, though low-lying cloud can lead to fog-bound conditions at any time. All food and drink must be carried, and a torch will enhance the visit to the cave.

The start point of the walk, Piano Provenzana, is a low-key winter ski-resort at 1774m above sea level. However, the scatter of buildings was submerged by lava during the 2003 eruption of Etna when a new mouth opened up at a relatively low altitude on the mountain's southeastern flank; the stunning forest of majestic Corsican pines surrounding the area was also badly burnt and damaged. Plans are already underfoot to reconstruct facilities and clear tracks, and in the meantime accommodation is available at good refuges down the road at the 1400m mark.

Another cave, the fascinating 150m-long Grotta del Gelo, is a somewhat gruelling climb uphill from the Grotta dei Lamponi. For three centuries, snow funnelled in during winter

Ropey lava formation en route to Grotta dei Lamponi

M. Nero/Grotta dei Lamponi

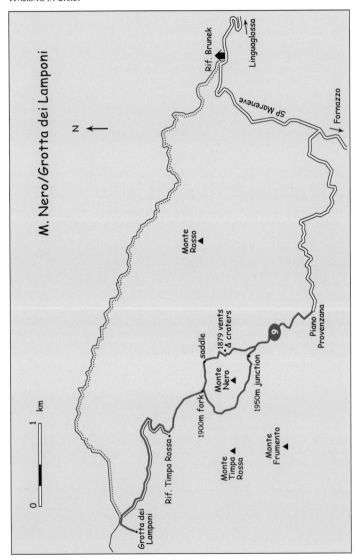

has been compressed into a 'fossil glacier', needless to say it holds the record for the southernmost ice field on the whole of the European continent! Curious ice stalactites also survive year-round. Intending visitors are advised to contact the Park headquarters beforehand to check whether or not the cave is visitable, and arrange for a guide.

THE WALK

At **Piano Provenzana** (1774m), a *sentiero natura* sets out northwest for Monte Nero. After 10min the 4WD track (for the summit craters) is crossed and you continue in the same direction past a **1950m junction** (for the return route). The wood is left behind and the dark bare outline of Monte Nero faces you against the broad background of the distant Peloritani mountain range; in the opposite direction on Etna the domed volcanic observatory stands out clearly. Crunchy lavic terrain dating back to the 19th century is soon underfoot, a perfect petrified glacier in black, with parallel ridges of dense flow forever frozen in their tracks. On the opposite edge, you follow (right, north) an unusual crest consisting of a series of minor **vents and craters** formed in 1879. At a **saddle** the path turns left (west) and dips before climbing to 1935m, with even wider-reaching views that also take in the Nebrodi range northwest and the broad underlying valley formed by the Alcantara River. On a northern corner of Monte Nero, in stark surrounds relieved only by the odd conifer, is a **1900m fork** (40min) for the path downhill for the cave extension. (The *sentiero natura* proceeds on a level around left, west, circling Monte Nero.)

You head in the direction of a copse sheltering several huts. It is a steady descent on a good, if narrow, path across dark sand mixed with volcanic ash and detritus. Hardy flowering plants such as Sicilian soapwort, Etna mouse-ear and sorrel continue to surprise with their bright colours, while playing an essential soil-anchoring role and paving the way for larger species in the centuries to come. Down at the trees, a couple of minutes through the pretty beech wood stands the chalet **Rif. Timpa Rossa** (1850m). A well-kept Forestry Department hut, it is always open and equipped with a stove, fire-wood and water in the cistern outside. There are no beds but it could be used for emergency shelter.

From here you need the forestry track down right at first through the pine plantation, then curving around westwards in gradual descent. There are woods of conifer and beech alternating with meadows and clearings that sport Etna

Grotta dei Lamponi

violets, camomile and a multitude of hares and wild rabbits, before you emerge onto the vast lava spread dating back to 1947, its starkness relieved by *dagala*, striking islands of greenery which have escaped the devastating black tentacles. Turn left to join the *pista*, dirt road from Rif. Brunek (1706m, 1hr 30min). There are some superb examples of ropy lava formations on the edge of the track, this being the easternmost edge of the Passo dei Dammusi, the result of Etna's greatest ever recorded eruption (lasting 10 years, from 1614 to 1624), famous for its spectacular Hawaiian-style lava formations. (*Dammuso* itself comes from the Arabic word for 'ceiling, covering' after the superimposed lava flows which form layers that resound when walked over.)

At the signpost for the Grotta del Gelo, take the faint rocky path for the short climb towards a huge cairn for the yawning entrance-cum-collapsed roof of the **Grotta dei Lamponi** (1762m, total 1hr 45min). An easy clamber and you enter the refreshing recesses of this extraordinary tunnel, some 2m high and 4m wide. A torch is helpful for anything but a brief perusal, however a little experience and a strong flashlight mean you can actually proceed uphill in the tunnel to a higher exit, as suggested by the draught as the cooler air is entrapped and channelled downhill. The cave/tunnel is 900m in length in total, and runs south–north.

Return to the dirt road and backtrack via **Rif. Timpa Rossa** to the junction where you left the *sentiero natura* (50min from the cave).

Right, the level path heads for a saddle with a curious fractured slab wall of lava. Yellow poles point the way up a series of pillow-like steps towards wooded Monte Timpa Rossa. Following a brief area wooded with beech trees and low juniper shrubs, you enter a bizarre broad corridor around 2000m in altitude – the landscape unworldly, pure volcanic. A dark sea of huge, rough waves frozen in choppy movement, through which the path proceeds, like Moses' passage through the Red Sea! Weird and wonderful 'sculptures' are everywhere, and the zone is also pitted with old craters. Red painted arrows lead south across a gaping fracture, then a vast smooth curved lane takes you back past more frozen glaciers of lava, massive cushions of flowers, then eastwards to the **1950m junction** encountered in the first stage. It's not far back to **Piano Provenzana**.

Tourist Office
Linguaglossa
Tel 095-643094

Accommodation
Rif. Brunek
Tel 095-643015
www.rifugio-brunek.it
Rif. Clan dei Ragazzi
Tel 095-643611 with camping ground
Rif. Ragabo
Tel 095-647841

WALK 10

Monte Etna:
The North–South Traverse

Time	7hr 30min (can be reduced)
Distance	22.5km/14 miles
Ascent/descent	1450m/1450m (can be reduced)
Grade	3
Map	'Mt. Etna' 1:25,000 Selca
Start point	Piano Provenzana
Access	See Walk 9 for the start point. The conclusion is at Area Etna Sud, accessed via the excellent road (SP 92) from Nicolosi, while a minor road climbs via Zafferana Etnea. Daily AST buses leave the area in descent via Nicolosi to Catania, an enthralling trip in its own right.

The traverse on foot from north to south of this massive active volcano is a very exciting prospect. You can approach the central crater zone under your own steam – a once in a lifetime experience. Solitude is not lacking, and furthermore you are guaranteed experience of earthquake rumblings, minor eruptive explosions accompanied by detonations and even recent lava flows close up. Conditions permitting (see the Warning Note below), you may be lucky to reach the uppermost rims of the volcano to see mouths spitting red hot molten lava amidst banks of dark smoke, though at present the zone is strictly out-of-bounds to unaccompanied walkers for safety reasons. Four craters are currently active – the North East, the Bocca Nuova, the South East and the Voragine.

   The sombre lunar-like landscape en route is a constant reminder that the giant only slumbers for brief spells, and evidence of the ongoing activity is manifest and plentiful in the shape of vast lava fields, ash and lapilli, and a host of adventive cones on lower slopes.

   At the high altitudes reached the track is inevitably panoramic, affording stunning views of both the Ionian and Tyrrhenian seas on opposite coasts of Sicily. Moreover, given the harsh inhospitable terrain, the varied array of flow-ering plants that presents itself comes as quite a surprise. Lava-pioneer types include the unusual cushions of the Sicilian milk-vetch, which actually host other flower such as the mouse-ear, and the list of endemics is long.

The walk in itself is not difficult, as the straightforward (if monotonous) tracks used by 4WD vehicles are followed most of the way. It's hard to lose your way unless there is particularly bad weather with thick, low-lying cloud pre-senting as banks of fog, in which case it is inadvisable to set out in the first place. Remember that the traverse is long and tiring and signifies a total height gain of 1450m, no mean feat. You climb from an altitude of 1774m to 3250m (or 3100m if the summit craters are not accessible) and subsequently re-descend to 1880m, though this can be eased by means of the gondola-car lift from 2500m for the final drop. Plenty of food and drink must be carried as there is absolutely nothing en route. Moreover a compass, pro-tection from the sun (hat, glasses and sunscreen) and the cold (woollens and wind-proof jacket) are essential all year round. Even if it's hot enough to start out in shorts and a T-shirt, remember that 1500m higher up a jumper and long trousers are minimum requirements. Begin walking as early as you can, as the ascent can be pretty hot in midsummer once the day is under way. As early as April–May is feasi-ble, though in all likelihood this will entail encounters with snow and possibly ice, so be equipped accordingly. June and

WARNING NOTE

Intending walkers on this route must check on the conditions of the track and the volcano itself, before embarking on the traverse as all four central craters have been unusually active in sporadic bursts since 1995. Of course, conditions vary dramatically, but at the time of writing (2012) reports warned visitors that it was 'extremely dangerous' and often 'absolutely impossible' to climb as far as the summit craters. The uppermost stretch of path was considered at risk and sub-sequently out of bounds as material such as lapilli, ash and dangerous so-called volcanic bombs were being ejected at unpredictable intervals and heights. The authorities post multilingual signs at the relevant access points and these must be adhered to. Rash behaviour can put lives at risk; furthermore, insurance poli-cies do not cover salvage operations. At 'worst', you can take a guided tour from the southern side – see the Monte Etna introduction.

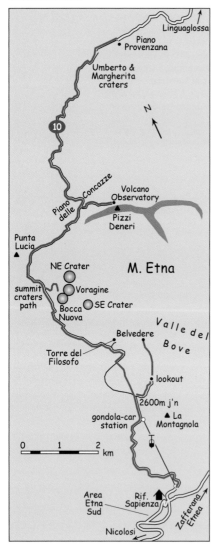

thereafter is fine. Autumn can be splendid for visibility. The risk of abrupt changes in the weather, dramatic drops in temperature and electric or snowstorms can never be excluded.

The traverse has been described starting from the northern Piano Provenzana side, instead of the more popular south, for several reasons. On the whole it is a much quieter and more pleasant place to start than the Area Etna Sud, and offers good views of the summit craters, which usually put on firework displays on clear nights. **Note** Piano Provenzana was invaded by lava in 2003, so until reconstruction happens, accommodation is down the SP Mareneve road at 1400m (see Walk 9).

THE WALK

Leave **Piano Provenzana** (1774m) on the 4WD track southwest. Enjoy the beech and pine wood while it lasts, as there's not much in the way of shady trees very soon. Once you reach 2000m in fact, it's the domain of hardy shrubs and the cushion flowers which typify Etna's high-altitude flora. A short-cut soon presents itself to avoid a wide curve in the track, however the sand can make the going tiring. At 2300m (1hr 15min) the top of a ski lift is passed, while close at hand are the impressive gaping adventive from 1879, the **Crateri Umberto e Margherita**, named after king and queen of Italy at the time. Several lobes of the 2003 lava may have caused slight modifications in the track on this stretch. Otherwise it makes for problem-free, if somewhat monotonous, walking, leaving you free to concentrate on the ever-broadening views of Etna itself, its lazily smoking rim still a long slog away, not to mention what amounts to the entire northeastern point of Sicily – with the Peloritani and Nebrodi ranges, the Tyrrhenian coast and even the Aeolian islands. At closer range, in contrast, is the surprisingly flourishing flora such as the Etna camomile and ragwort, as well as the sorrel, whose delicate hues of purplered often blend right in with the lavic terrain.

Rough lava from 1966–7 is traversed, then a lighter coloured stretch at the broad saddle known as **Piano delle Concazze** and a junction (2789m, 2hr 15min).

Detour to the Volcano Observatory (30min return time)

The branch left leads to the observatory for volcanologists, set at 2847m on the Pizzi Deneri ridge. While the building itself, property of the Italian National Research Council (CNR), is not visitable, the site provides a marvellous outlook to the Ionian coast and, of course, over the gigantic gash of the Valle del Bove. Believed to owe its form to the collapse of parts of the ancient volcano structure due to explosions, this dramatic basin-like valley now measures some 7km by 6km, and has walls that tower as high as 1000m.

Back at the **Piano delle Concazze** junction, proceed with the slog along the main track, which continues relentlessly upwards (southwest), cutting the western flank of Etna, in the shadow of the towering North East crater (the highest, dating back to 1911). A number of visibly active *fumarole*, or volcanic gas vents, punctuate the bare slopes above. The belching cloud emitted by the central craters is soon much closer, vastly unlike the innocent slivers or plumes of pale cloud as seen from the coastal level. At around 2900m (3hr 15min) a track turns off down right for Punta Lucia, which saw considerable action in 1983, as attested by its sulphurridden surrounds.

Further along the main track is the **fork** (3100m, 3hr 45min) where, eruptions and authorities permitting, you can proceed towards the actual summit craters (see below). Otherwise stick to the wide track which proceeds south.

Path to the summit craters (1hr return)

Only if conditions are favourable and you feel up to a further 150m climb should you proceed on this path. Steeper and narrower, it can be subject to dangerous gases if a strong wind is blowing the wrong way! You climb among volcanic bombs, ash and lapilli to the breathtaking rim which affords amazing views of the inner and very active crater mouths, busy shooting out clots of lava or fountains along with clouds of smoke and ash.

Return the same way to the main track.

Back at the **fork**, resume the main track southwards skirting the base of the Bocca Nuova ('new mouth', formed in 1968) and the adjacent Voragine 'opening'. In the opposite direction, the landscape spread out below is a fascinating sea of rolling green contrasting with the petrified rivers of dark lava. In October 1999 flows headed toward the township of Bronte, west-northwest from here, while Randazzo to the north had an especially narrow escape in the 1980s. A little further around a vastly different landscape awaits. These lower sloping reaches of the South East crater are a lunar desert – the ground a thick covering, several metres deep in places, of large-grained ash embedded with knobbly lapilli (hardened shapes of magma). To add to the

Etna viewed from the northeast

atmosphere the chances are good of the unmistakable stink of sulphur. Experts say the crater itself is more appropriately called the South East cone, as the build-up of debris means the inner section now towers 100m over the outer rim. Furthermore molten rivers as recent as 2001 have spread this flank with a carpet of black.

At the forthcoming fork, keep to the lower track; with it come views of the gondola-car lift station in the shade of La Montagnola. This eventually brings you to the junction (2800m, 5hr 15min) for a fork left leading to the so-called **Torre del Filosofo** (philosopher's tower), a dilapidated building used by guides and forms the upper limit of the vehicle-bound tour groups at the time of writing; it was named for Empedocles, the 5th-century BC Greek philosopher from Siracusa who was believed to have spent time there while studying the volcano. As legend would have it, he flung himself into the crater of Etna as proof of his divinity. It is thought an original tower was constructed around AD117 by Emperor Hadrian, who made several trips to the summit to study the goings-on of Etna and enjoy the view. A cable-car once ran this far up, long since swept away by the fury of the magma.

Continuing downhill, you are obliged to keep company with the dust-raising tourist vehicles for 10min before a short-cut off to the left. This side track drops to a **2600m junction** (5hr 40min), where the direct route for the gondola-car lift is on the right; however, time permitting, it's worthwhile taking the left branch for the Valle del Bove lookout and Belvedere (see below).

Back at the **2600m junction**, head straight down now towards the gondola-car station. Towering above the track

Detour to the Valle del Bove lookout and Belvedere (50min return)

The track passes a number of gaping former craters and, climbing briefly, reaches the guard rail marking the marvellous lookout (2615m) over the Valle del Bove. A breathtaking spot, frequented by darting swallows and scavenging crows, it provides views of the full extension of the valley flooded with layers of lava, then right down to Catania and the coast. The curving ridge on the right, the Schiena dell'Asino, terminates with Monte Zoccolaro, southeast. From the minibus parking area a path continues north along the narrowing crest to a further **belvedere** at 2761m, reputedly the best place for viewing the effusive vents of the early 1999 activity below the South East cone.

is La Montagnola, the largest adventive cone on Etna, which came into being after the 1763 eruption. En route is a black river from recent eruptions but a clear track drops to the **gondola-car station** (2500m, 6hr 45min total).

Now the great decision: to enjoy the (extortionately priced) convenience of the gondola-car lift or slog down the monotonous track for the final 600m descent. Either way there are continuing vast views. One hour should suffice on foot for this last leg to the **Area Etna Sud**, the bus, or board and lodgings in the form of Rif. Sapienza (1880m, grand total 7hr 45min, detours included).

As so vividly illustrated by the postcards on sale here, the *rifugio* has miraculously 'survived' being enveloped in incandescent lava during countless eruptions. Drawn-out restructuring has been necessary before it could open its doors to visitors once more – now as a hotel. It continues to play an essential role for walkers on this side of Etna and is a good place to meet people. The helpful custodian is a mine of information about the mountain. Alternatively the closest town, Nicolosi, has B&Bs, a hostel as well as shops and a camping ground in the shade of the Monti Rossi, an interesting series of adventive cones dating back to 1669 and extolled by Goethe.

Tourist Office
Linguaglossa
Tel 095-643094
Nicolosi
Tel 095-914488

Accommodation
Area Etna Sud:
Rif. Sapienza
CAI (hotel-style
accommodation)
Tel 095-915321
Nicolosi:
Ostello (youth
hostel)
Tel 095-7914686
B&B La Giara
Tel 095-7919022

Rifugio Sapienza, at the conclusion of the trek

MONTI IBLEI AND THE SOUTHEAST CORNER

WALK 11

Wondrous Pantalica and its Necropolises

Time	Part A – 45min; Part B – 2hr
Distance	Part A – 1.7km/1.1 miles; Part B – 4.8km/3.3 miles
Ascent/descent	Part B – 300m/300m
Grade	2
Map	'Pantalica' 1:20,000 at park entrances
Start/finish	Part A – eastern end of tarmac road; Part B – Palazzo del Principe car park
Access	A car is preferable. Follow the SS 124 from Siracusa, then 14km after Solarino take the winding road for Ferla, whence the narrow 9km road along the ridge of upper Pantalica to the walk start.
	The AST bus company operates Mon–Sat runs from Siracusa to Buccheri, Ferla and Palazzolo Acreide. However, ongoing transfers then mean taxi, shank's pony or hitch-hiking, and traffic is light.

Five thousand simply hewn tombs honeycomb the limestone cliffs, the final resting places of the ancient inhabitants of Pantalica, set on magnificent high plateaux with plunging gorges. Proposed for World Heritage Site rating, it encompasses a perfect combination of nature and archaeology, not to mention some of the best walks in this guide. Located in the Monti Iblei (or Hyblaei Hills) a mere 25km inland from Siracusa and civilisation, the wondrous heights of Pantalica, together with the Anapo and Calcinara river valleys that cut through the limestone tableland isolating the main isthmus-shaped site, are now run as a 2600-hectare nature park under the auspices of the Forestry Department.

Of the open-air necropolis, said to be the most extensive of its type in Europe, the earliest rock tombs date back to the 13th century BC, when indigenous people fleeing from the coast took refuge in the safety afforded by these

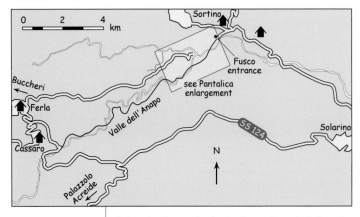

sheltered valleys and uplands. Successive arrivals from the
Italian mainland helped consolidate and develop the settlement, which grew into a kingdom. It was known originally
as Hybla (from the Sicel goddess), whereas Pantalica, the
name used today, is believed to derive from the Greek for
'caves' or 'cavities'.

The sole surviving building from what must have been
a huge township is the so-called Palazzo del Principe (or
Anaktoron) and there are remnants of trench-style fortifications. Hybla's power ranged over a modest territory, and
it is known that in 728BC the last king, Hyblon, granted
Greeks an area on the coast to found Megara Hyblaea.
Around the same time an aqueduct was constructed from
the Calcinara watercourse to supply Siracusa (Hybla's
port); the monumental fountain over the famous Greek
theatre still spouts water channelled from the Pantalica valley. The town itself was probably destroyed following the
expansion of Siracusa. (A modest collection of finds from
the archaeological digs is on display at Siracusa's Museo
Archeologico Regionale).

Several centuries of decline were remedied during the
Byzantine period, as scattered churches testify. However
the original inhabitants had in the meantime moved over to
found Sortino. In the wake of the Arab invasions Pantalica
was all but abandoned, with the exception of transitory
shepherds, brigands and partisans.

In the early 1900s work started on the narrow-gauge Siracusa–Ragusa–Vizzini railway line. Unfortunately service on this scenic run along the river valley floor ceased in 1956, though the track (minus rails) now serves walkers and the Forestry Department, along with the occasional horse-drawn carriage.

Pantalica's wild setting and vegetation make for an unforgettable visit. Spring (March–May) is highly recommended for the extraordinary riot of wild flowers, which keep the bees fed for the area's renowned honey-making. In mid-summer the depths of the valleys are shady, but it can be hot going climbing to the plateau. Later, despite the biting winds, even winter has its own special fascination, with the landscape particularly stark.

This walk has two sections: the first a straightforward return path to the Calcinara valley floor, with a mere 180m descent. The second is a marvellously rewarding circuit touching on the Anapo river, and involves greater height gain and loss. Food and drink must be carried, as nothing is available in the park. Sun protection is essential, together with swimmers for a dip in the river. A modest entrance fee may be charged for entrance to the *riserva*.

Palazzo del Principe at Pantalica

81

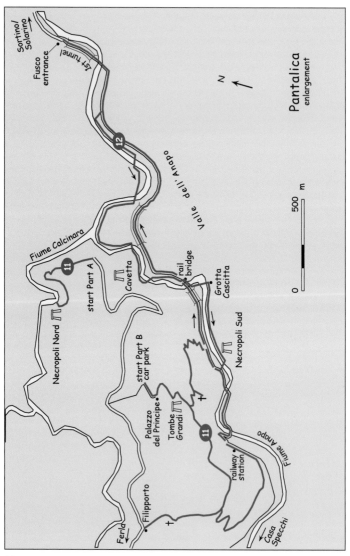

Pantalica
enlargement

There is excellent accommodation on the valley floor near the Fusco entrance (see Walk 12) as well as in nearby towns. The region deserves a visit for its precious Baroque palaces and churches, laid-back community life, and dense calendar of popular religious processions and feast days.

THE WALK
Part A: Valle del Calcinara (45min)
Having travelled eastwards along the narrowing ridge of Pantalica, park your vehicle at the very **end of the road** (330m). A wide track marked 'Necropoli Nord' leads around northwest in gradual descent and enters the beautiful valley excavated over time by the modest river. The bird song can be deafening, and masses of flowering red valerian, golden marigolds, a riot of mauve vetch, handsome acanthus and veritable domes of tree spurge line the path. Yawning caves appear in the limestone flanks opposite, while the path passes numerous scattered sites of ancient tombs with low rectangular entrances hollowed out in the hillside. The old roadway itself is partially excavated into the stone, the final stretch to the stream particularly evocative (20min). At the water's edge, on the **Calcinara** (180m), the vegetation becomes denser and lusher with every step you take. There are oleanders and figs overhanging verdant azure pools complete with cascades – and an invitation to explore further.

Retrace your steps to the road.

Part B: Valle dell'Anapo (2hr)
Some 2km back from the end of the road and Part A, a lane turns south to a modest car park. Then it's 5min on foot to the **Palazzo del Principe** aka Anaktoron or *castello* (450m). All but smothered in sweet broom, wild gladioli and stately giant fennel plants, massive regular stone blocks mark the site of what is believed to have been a princely palace or castle. It is the sole above-ground construction ever found here, and has been compared to Mycaenean architecture. The position affords long-ranging views over the rolling Monti Iblei, and cruising birds of prey are not an uncommon sight.

You now need the stone-bordered path curving southwards down the sunbaked hillside coloured with purple stonecrop and alive with bird song. The **Tombe Grandi a**

Camere (large tombs with chambers) grouping is quickly reached, while clusters of dark square holes, namely wall tombs belonging to the spread-out Necropoli Sud come into sight over the valley.

Turn left (east) at the ensuing fork for the 'Chiesetta Rupestre' (straight ahead connects with Filipporto). A little steeper and narrower, the path is partially worn into the rock and occasionally marked with red paint splashes. Only minutes along is a 5min detour right to a **lookout** and railing for plunging views of the Anapo valley, next to the tiny Byzantine **rock church** dedicated to S. Nicolicchio.

Back on the main path you soon need to branch off left on a fainter path, dropping beneath a notable cavity surrounded by countless rock tombs. The vegetation is profuse to say the least, and the steep way often overgrown – keep an eye out for the occasional red paint splash marker as you continue valleywards. About 25min from the car park you reach a junction marked by an noteworthy old olive tree: bear right now to zigzag the final leg to the deep, shady floor of the **Valle dell'Anapo**, beneath the Necropoli Sud which occupies cliffs on opposite flanks.

The old railway station at Pantalica

In the cool domain of the valley, accompanied by the refreshing sound of running water, follow the broad dirt track alias one-time railway line, right (southwest), in common with Walk 12. The river is crossed briefly and cool citrus groves precede Pantalica's former **railway station** building (228m, 40min), set at the foot of towering pale cliffs. Now it houses a modest museum of old farming implements, while outside adjacent are toilet blocks.

A couple of minutes further along the track lined with monstrous agave plants, is a fork right. The delightful rock-based path climbs through the sweet scents of a veritable herb garden: marjoram, yellow Jerusalem sage and grey artemisia, not to mention the colourful masses of miniature purple iris and love-in-a-mist. A fork is ignored (left) and the way starts zigzagging, helped by iron railing on brief stretches. Past yet more rock faces riddled with tombs, the path affords countless superb lookout points, and before you know it you're back up on the higher rock terrace level, to be joined by the path from the Palazzo del Principe (30min from the railway station).

Keep left (north) through pretty stretches of marigolds and huge purple thistles to rock dwellings dating back to Byzantine times. The miniature rock cave-church San Micidiario is situated on the branch path left from the dwellings. A further 5min will take you via ancient rock trenches built for defence purposes to the road at **Filipporto** ('outside the door', 380m, 15min). According to local lore in ancient times prisoners were cast to their deaths from the elevated saddle.

From here it's 2km right (east) along the quiet road back to the turnoff for the **Palazzo del Principe** car park (2hr). (Otherwise retrace your steps to the junction and take the marvellous scenic high path that returns via the Tombe Grandi a Camere and Palazzo del Principe to the car park – allow an extra 30min).

Accommodation
Floridia–Fusco road:
Pantalica Ranch
Tel 0931-942069,
338-680181 or
333-3258612
Le Sacre Pietre
Tel 0931-954798
or 336-8365110
Cassaro: B&B
L'Aquila
Tel 0931-877020
Ferla: B&B Pantalica
Tel 0931-870147

WALK 12
The Pantalica River Walk

Time	2hr 15min
Distance	6.4km/4 miles
Grade	2
Map	'Pantalica' 1:20,000 at park entrances. See Walk 11 for sketch map for this walk.
Start/finish	Fusco entrance
Access	By car follow the SS 124 from Siracusa, and turn off at Floridia or Solarino for the minor road that drops northwest into the Anapo river valley. Some 10km along, a short distance after the turnoff for Pantalica Ranch, ignore the road that climbs (right) to Sortino, and continue straight ahead. Take the middle lane of the three soon encountered, for the Fusco entrance to the reserve.
	The AST bus company has Mon–Sat runs from Siracusa to Sortino, however you'll then need to walk 7km downhill to Fusco.

See Walk 11 for information on Pantalica and its *riserva*. This delightful walk follows the winding course of the Anapo river, in the depths of the valley below Pantalica, criss-crossing from one bank to the other. The river must have been impressive in Phoenician times as the water level was believed to reach most of the way up the cliffs, and boats could actually sail up from the coast.

Numerous side paths linking with the old railway track enable walkers to leave or enter at will. At present the route is feasible as far as the former railway station of Pantalica, but plans are underway to extend it to the photogenic masonry premises of Casa Specchi, a further 3.5km along the track. Waymarking may also be on the cards, to supplement the few wooden arrows in place. It is most suitable May–September as outside that period the handful of wooden bridges will be dismantled in view of the risk of winter flooding. Picnic supplies and swimming gear are warmly recommended, as is a torch for the tunnels on the return route. Sandals with decent grip are fine as footwear if you prefer fording streams instead of balancing on stepping stones. A modest fee may be charged for entrance. The *agriturismo* on the valley floor are perfect bases for the walk.

THE WALK

From the reserve entrance at **Fusco** (220m), walk along the train track through the first tunnel. Out the other side 5min on at a break in the fencing, take the path right, parallel to both the Anapo River and the old railway track. Cliffs loom on your left. As the path reaches the water it's either stepping stones or a bridge, depending on when you come. Over on the right bank, steps lead through old terracing with a citrus orchard. Back down at the waterside are bleached pebbles and thick reeds beneath steep cliffs. Another water traverse then you continue around a beautiful loop in the river, involving some clambering over rocks. An atmospheric stretch hewn out of the cliff passes high above the confluence of the Calcinara and Anapo rivers, and tomb cavities

Wooden bridge across the Anapo River

87

Shady picnic area along the river

belonging to the Necropoli Cavetta appear opposite. Bearing south amidst red valerian and euphorbia, past an abandoned sheep pen and wild fig trees, then steps drop back to the water level near a massive fallen boulder. The next crossing takes you over to the shady right bank and a bridge. A path resumes parallel to the railway amidst oleanders and ivy, below cliffs riddled with natural cavities. Picnic tables are close-by as is a ford under a **rail bridge**, though you immediately return to the left bank. The gaping recess of **Grotta Cascitta** appears, turquoise water filling its mouth.

The path hugs the river now so you end up clambering over stones, past sets of picnic tables, well below the extensive Necropoli Sud. A quick succession of crossings will see you over on the right bank and joining the old rail track. Then it's a swing back to the opposite bank and a picnic area where the path resumes at the rear of a citrus grove. Underground chambers soon passed once served as monks' cells, and small niches for water collection are also obvious.

Back on the main track (in common with Walk 11) it's a short stroll through an orange orchard and across the river uphill to Pantalica's former **railway station**, complete with a toilet block. (1hr 30min).

Accommodation
see Walk 11

The return means a relaxing 3km stroll along the old railway track and back to **Fusco** (45min).

WALK 13
Cava Grande del Cassibile

Time	2hr
Distance	6.5km/4 miles
Ascent/descent	300m/300m
Grade	2
Start/finish	Cava Grande car park
Access	By car from Avola (20km south of Siracusa on the coastal road SS 115), the main entrance to the Cava Grande is 12km inland northwest. Signposting is clear and the remains of Avola Antica are passed en route.
	Public buses from Siracusa (Interbus) and trains are only useful as far as Avola on the coast.

The Cava Grande del Cassibile is a marvellous canyon cut deep through the limestone plateau of the Monti Iblei, which comprise the southwestern hinterland of Siracusa. The rock was formed during the Miocene, 15 million years ago. Though not far off the main tour routes, the valley is well hidden from view, and the stiff descent to the Cassibile River (known under the Greeks as the Kacyparis) is a guarantee against crowds and an assurance of peace and quiet. The delicious emerald green waters in deep 'kettle' pools at the base of sheer cliffs are inviting to say the least, and a swim on a glaring hot day is heaven.

Path closure: the paths described are currently closed and awaiting maintenance after forest fires. Check **www.cavagrande delcassibile.it** for news and alternative paths.

The upper reaches of the Cava Grande consist of rolling meadows and vast sparkling extensions of gorgeous wild flowers in spring – March is said to be the best month, though the oleanders down at the waterside tend to flower a little later (May–July). The valley flanks are cloaked in typical Mediterranean shrubs the likes of broom and lentisc, which afford but minimum shade, while the bottom of this marvellous gorge is of interest to botanists as it hosts Italy's healthiest colony of oriental plane trees – in contrast to the hybrids that shade many town squares. All in all, a wonderful spot.

A 10km stretch of the river and environs has been declared a nature reserve (Riserva Naturale Orientata

*Inviting pools at
Cava Grande*

After heavy rain
the reserve may be
closed to the public
for safety reasons.

Cavagrande del Cassibile) under the watchful eye of the
Forestry Service. Included is an 11th–9th century BC cave
necropolis encompassing over 80,000 tomb sites, located in
the seaward reaches of the protected area. In addition to this
itinerary, new walking routes are being planned: enquire at
the Forestry Department hut at the start point. You may be
required to register there before embarking on this route. ◀

Backpacks for the day's trip should be loaded with food
and drink, swimming and protective sun gear. There is a
recommended bar-cum-trattoria at the car park, should any
supplies be needed.

THE WALK

The **Belvedere** at the car park (505m) certainly lives up to
its name and offers spectacular plunging views into the
Cassibile valley, a broad gash in the undulating Iblei plateau.
It is backed by the unmistakable volcanic pyramid of Etna far
to the north, without forgetting the spread of Siracusa on the
coast. The **Scala Croce** or Cruci (named after a shrine en
route) rock steps zigzag downwards amidst masses of brilliant rock roses, broom and reedy grasses. The descent is
often knee-jarring; the steps were presumably fashioned for
giant legs. The opposite side of the valley is scarred by a gaping natural cave, the Grotta dei Briganti, one of the numerous sites inhabited in prehistoric times.

At a **junction** marked by a wild pear tree (330m,
20min), take the lower left fork. (The path encountered, the

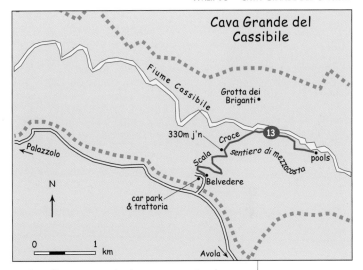

sentiero di mezzacosta, leads east–west cutting the steep flanks parallel to the river; it follows the cleverly concealed underground water conduit originally laid by the Electricity Commission in the early 1900s terminating at a small-scale hydroelectric plant.)

The path continues dropping then narrows, curving right into thickets of ferns, oleanders, wild fig trees and graceful poplars, not to mention the important – though somewhat nondescript – oriental plane trees. The going can be slippery in places. The Fiume Cassibile and a first rank of terracing is close-by, the banks of limestone worn bare by the action of the flowing water and later exposed when the water level was lowered by the offtakes used to generate hydroelectricity. Clamber along the terraces right (east), watching your step on the tricky moss-ridden stretches. You proceed gradually along the overgrown riverbank to a stunning series of vast green **pools** (210m, 45min). Known locally as *uruvi*, 15m deep at the most, they are linked by vast slabs of pale rock and lovely cascades, and dominated by towering cliffs. ▸

Return to the **Belvedere** the same way (1hr 15min should do), unless you opt for a detour to explore the path intersected at the pear tree junction.

Accommodation
Avola: Hotel L'Ancora Tel 0931-822875 B&B La Terrazza sul Mare Tel 0931-823973

A refreshing swim is definitely in order, with the dainty swallows skimming the surface for insects and submarine inhabitants in the shape of tiny freshwater crabs.

WALK 14
Noto Antica

Time	1hr 45min
Distance	5.3km/3.3 miles
Grade	1
Start/finish	Noto Antica car park
Access	Noto itself is on the SS 115 south of Siracusa, whereas Noto Antica lies 10km northwest out of town. You'll need the SS 287 (for Palazzolo), and later on the turn-off signed for the picturesque convent and church of S. Maria della Scala, after which it's narrow and winding for 3km via an old bridge before the car park at Noto Antica.
	There is no public transport to Noto Antica, though Noto itself is well served by Interbus from Siracusa, as well as the train.

This walk provides a fascinating wander amongst the evocative ruins of a long-standing town laid to waste by the ruinous earthquake that flattened Sicily's southernmost provinces in 1693. The original town of Noto (or Neas for the ancient Sicel founders) was spread over the broad V-shaped expanse of 420m high Monte Alveria, a site carefully chosen in the 5th century BC for its naturally fortified plateau edged with plunging cliffs, reinforced with defensive walling against Greek invaders. It became a renowned centre of culture and knowledge, ruled in succession by the Greeks themselves, the Romans, Arabs, Normans and Spanish.

Despite the damage and relative dearth of visitable remains (much was recycled for the new town), the sprawling overgrown site warrants a wander both for the archaeological highlights in the form of the impressive ramparts of the medieval castle and modest necropolises dating back to the prehistoric era, as well as for the wealth of spontaneous vegetation that ranges from the wild asparagus to a variety of flowers as well as olive and pomegranate trees. For the most part a broad motorable dirt road is followed, and there are neither difficulties nor climbs involved. The description of the route helps give an idea of the vast expanse of the area formerly occupied. No water or sustenance is available at Noto Antica, so go prepared.

In the wake of the destruction wrought in 1693, the new town of Noto was rebuilt 10km away on a lower hillside site closer to the coast. Over time, with the collaboration of a vast army of architects, nearly all the churches were reconstructed in the elegant Baroque style in vogue in the 1700s, with the addition of monasteries, fine public buildings and palaces through the next century, when it acted as provincial capital and Episcopal see. The town of Noto is considered a masterpiece of Sicilian Baroque architecture and urban planning, and a visit is simply compulsory. A local type of limestone was employed for the constructions, a material that assumes rich gold and pastel hues with age, making for an unforgettable spectacle at sunset when the entire town appears to be illuminated. Restoration is ongoing, as the forests of scaffolding and reinforcing braces attest, though a word must be spared the magnificent cathedral – the interior of which collapsed inexplicably in the wake of restructuring in 1996.

This delightful town is an excellent base with its plentiful B&Bs and excellent range of modestly priced *trattorie* with memorable country-style game dishes or home-made pasta with ricotta cheese or eggplant. As wines go, those containing locally grown nero d'Avola grapes (red) include the superb Cerasuolo di Vittoria and a vintage from Eloro near Vendicari. Dessert is mandatory; either a gelato or one of the luscious almond pastries crafted by the town's master pastrycooks accompanied by a glass of the local moscato wine.

THE WALK

From the **car park** beneath the castle walls at **Noto Antica** (400m), go back down the road past olive groves carpeted with marigolds, high above the 9th-century BC Sicel necropolis. Prior to the bridge is a lane left to a curious stretch of ancient sunken roadway – worth exploring despite the all but impenetrable undergrowth. Back on the modern road, you need the sign for the Grotta delle Cento Bocche ('cave of the hundred mouths') and stone steps climbing to a modest group of joined manmade cavities in the rock face, said to be a

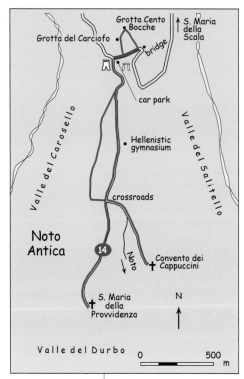

Byzantine oratory. Wild flowers abound, including orchids in spring and the everlasting with its felted yellow tufts. From here, facing downhill, make your way diagonally right to a sizeable rock tomb entrance surmounted by a weathered engraving of a candelabra (or artichoke). It is referred to as the **Grotta del Carciofo** ('cave of the artichoke'); it is believed to be an ancient Jewish burial site.

Return to the road and **car park** (15min so far) for the impressive entrance to the city proper by way of the castle gate, the Porta della Montagna. A path takes you up to the sturdy battlements and lookout points. Back down on the dusty track, continue south past the massive

This peaceful area is punctuated by eucalypts and more collapsed caves, probably artisans' workshops, while the mills and tanneries were at the river below.

surviving 15th-century round tower, then as the main route veers left, go straight ahead on the stone-based path to a lookout over wild, beautiful **Valle del Carosello**. A narrow path leads due south from here along the top of the cliffs, passing a number of evocative cave dwellings before exiting the city via a stone portal. The way, none too clear at times, deteriorates a little and drops slightly, following a line of barbed wire for the most part. ◄

At a stone wall a wider track leads up left to join the main route at the **crossroads** (45min).

A monument here commemorates the destruction wrought by the earthquake. The track along right leads through olive groves and the now derelict monastery and church of **S. Maria della Provvidenza**, founded in the 18th century in memory of the victims of the catastrophe, and inhabited up until the 1940s. From the rear of the buildings, set on a promontory overlooking the Valle del Durbo (the local name for plane tree), are marvellous views over the wild countryside, neighbouring valleys and right out to the coast. Wild fig trees and artemisia are at home here, while the church walls have been colonised by caper plants.

Go back to the crossroads with the monument and take the right branch for 10 minutes straight along the track (ignore the fork right for the winding descent to Noto) and through the gate at the end, where a pleasant path takes you through the scenic position of the long-abandoned **Convento dei Cappuccini**, built on the base of a 14th-century fortress at the erstwhile southern gateway.

Return to the **crossroads** once more and head north along the dirt road back to the **car park**, passing the ruins of several religious complexes and what is held to be the foundations of a 3rd-century BC **Hellenistic gymnasium**, after a total of 1hr 45min.

Tourist Office
Noto
Tel 0931-573779
www.comune.
noto.sr.it

Accommodation
B&B Arca
Tel 0931-838656
or 333-1404324
B&B Trinacria
Tel 0931-573786
or 335-7322516

15th-century tower at Noto Antica

95

WALK 15
Riserva Naturale di Vendicari

Time	Cittadella – 2hr; Eloro – 3hr 20min
Distance	Cittadella – 7.7km/4.8 miles; Eloro – 11.8km/7.5 miles
Grade	1–2
Map	Brochure at reserve entrance
Start/finish	Main entrance
Access	10.5km south of Noto on the road to Pachino is the signed turn-off towards the coast for the Riserva Naturale di Vendicari. Once over the disused railway line, it's a further 2km to the main entrance. There is roadside parking.

Access by public transport is feasible by the daily Interbus Siracusa–Noto–Pachino run. Ask to be let off at the Vendicari turn-off at Roveto for the short walk in to the entrance (allow 20min).

There is also a handy weekday bus by Caruso from Noto to Eloro Marina, a short distance from the northernmost perimeter of the reserve and a summer entrance. **Note** This may entail a minor river crossing unless the weather has been particularly dry.

Flamingos, exquisite insect orchids and pristine stretches of endless white sand characterise this simply stunning wetland reserve. It also offers a string of ample lagoons, which double as bird nurseries, fronted by the beaches and scattered with photogenic buildings in the shape of medieval watchtowers, an old tuna cannery and fishery with structures dating back to Greek times. There's also the odd traditional farm house, without neglecting the minor archaeological site at Eloro on the northernmost edge. This marvellous area provides great interest for lovers of birds and perfect beaches, and has a good measure of manmade and natural history thrown in.

Over 200 species of birds – both permanent and transitory – have been observed at Vendicari; the list headed by spectacular flamingos, which nest there, along with the elegant black-winged stilt, followed by spoonbills, cranes, herons, black stork, pelicans, ducks galore, coots and memorable flocks of sea gulls. Other land-based curiosities are the pond turtle and harmless snakes. A variety of habitats is encompassed, and visitors cross from the salt marsh settings, featuring the curious glasswort plant, to the low sand dunes colonised by hardy grasses and reeds, through to the arid red rocky headlands punctuated with dwarf palms and century plants, as well as zones of typical dense Mediterranean maquis. The salt-water lagoons or *pantani*, on the other hand, were used as either salt pans or profitable fish farms (eels included) until recently, whereas a port is believed to have operated here in long-gone Phoenician times.

The Riserva Naturale Orientata di Vendicari (www. riserva-vendicari.it), capably managed by the Forestry Department, came into being in 1989. Any time of the year is good for a visit except perhaps midsummer, when the heat is usually too oppressive to encourage exercise and the lagoons have often dried up. Spring, of course, brings more colour in the way of flowers; autumn means decent swims in the still-warm sea; while winter, despite chilly winds, is more rewarding for the masses of birds that stop over during their long-distance migrational flights: especially October–November on their way south, or February–March in the reverse direction. Nesting turtles are another attraction.

The two linear walk routes (one to Cittadella and the other to Eloro) follow flat ground and are both easy and well marked, if lengthy; they can be linked. Visitors should bring food and drink as nothing is available locally, as well as the usual sun protection gear and swimming costumes; don't forget binoculars. No camping or fishing is allowed, and visitors must keep to marked routes. Before starting out, ask at the entrance booth for clues on the whereabouts of the flamingos (*fenicotteri* in Italian).

THE WALK
Cittadella (2hr)
From the **main entrance** booth a shady eucalypt-lined lane leads seawards (southeast). A path soon branches off right for Capanno Roveto via a wooden walkway through a swampy zone where visitors are dwarfed by reeds

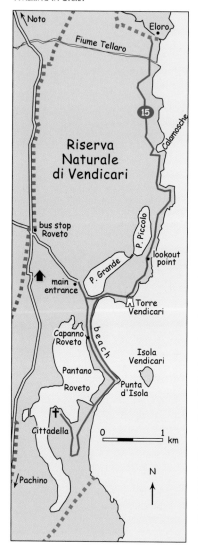

and lentiscs. An expanse of sandy meadow is traversed to the cane-screened birdwatchers hut, **Capanno Roveto**, set amongst wattle trees and facing the vast reed-bordered lagoon of Pantano Roveto (10min).

A track continues south on the narrow sandy strip between lagoon and sea, and keen eyes will be rewarded by the tiny wild insect orchids that flourish here. The divine white sand beach is only a matter of metres away through low bushes of broom, and you soon round **Punta d'Isola** opposite Isola Vendicari. Then it's southwest along the beach, backed by low dunes colonised by colourful sea holly, to a silted-up lagoon outlet, where the path heads inland once more. You pass a turn-off for a birdwatching hut then a ruined house surrounded by magnificent century plants, and along to a junction where you need the right branch. A gradual climb in a north-westerly direction leads onto a minor headland over the lagoons and to the remains of the curious Trigona church, **Cittadella** (1hr). The site once hosted a Byzantine-era (4th–5th century) settlement, with a skeletal necropolis in the proximity.

Return to the beach the same way. To proceed with the northern Eloro route keep north along the sand past a signboard, towards the overgrown buildings on the next point, to pick up the route described below. Otherwise retrace your steps via **Capanno Roveto** back to the **main entrance**.

Eloro (3hr 20min)

Starting out from the reserve's **main entrance**, take the lane heading southeast towards the sea, past a birdwatching hut and eastwards towards the chimneys of the old **tonnara** (15min). Extraordinarily dense banks of golden chrysanthemums have invaded the ruins of the erstwhile fish cannery, which was active right up until World War Two. However, the operation was launched well back in the 4th century BC, the Hellenistic period, with a processing plant for mackerel and tuna. Surplus catches would be preserved in salt, while a significant by-product was garum, a piquant condiment made from fermented leftovers. Things evidently flourished on a vast scale under the Arabs.

Adjoining the fish cannery on the water's edge is the picturesque medieval **Torre Vendicari** (also known as Torre Sveva), shaded by conifers, just one of the numerous defensive towers that sprang up along this southerly coastline in response to repeated Barbary incursions from north Africa. This particularly elegant tower was constructed by the Duke of Noto in the 1500s, and later restructured and equipped with heavy-duty artillery.

The track continues around the now rocky coastline, with low dwarf palm domes here and there amongst humps of limestone outcrops alternating with oversized clumps of thyme, giant fennel, prickly pear and contrasting pink-purple blooms of the borage family's oyster plant. A dry-stone wall precedes an old house, and you shortly reach a hut and **lookout point** over Pantano Piccolo, its surface often alive with jumping fish. The town of Noto can be seen north-northwest, set on the edge of the gently sloping Monti Iblei.

Take the lane heading (right) for the coast over rolling open terrain. Down at sea level once more you reach a junction (1hr) over the stunning aquamarine waters of the cove of **Calamosche**, perfect for a dip. Ignore the paths off left and stick to the coastal route north for Eloro. It runs essentially parallel to the sea through scrubby vegetation and eventually reaches the modest estuary of the **Fiume Tellaro**, which may need fording outside of summer. A final stretch of sand leads to a canal where bashful pond turtles breed, and the nearby **Eloro** archaeological site, accessible from the reserve in summer (total 1hr 40min).

Return to the main entrance the same way.

Accommodation
Roveto: *Agriturismo Il Roveto*
Tel 0931-66024
or 339-4123148
Noto: see Walk 14

WALK 16
Isola delle Correnti

Time	45min
Distance	2.8km/1.8 miles
Grade	1
Start/finish	Car park 6km SE of Portopalo
Access	A visit is inadvisable without a private vehicle as the route starts 6km (via monotonous tarmac) southeast of Portopalo and the dearth of traffic off-season is not propitious to hitchhiking. That said, Portopalo di Capo Passero is served by the daily Interbus coach from Noto via Pachino to substitute for the rusting railway still shown on maps.
	Drivers can reach Pachino from the main SS 115 (Siracusa to Ragusa) from various points such as Noto (24km) to its north or Ispica to the west-northwest (19km). Portopalo di Capo Passero is then a further 6.5km southeast. The walk itself starts a 6km southwest out of town: follow the signs for Isola delle Correnti and park where the road comes to an end in sight of the beach.
Warning	Crossing to the island is not advisable if there is a high tide and a rough sea as the sunken causeway may be swept by unpredictable and strong currents.

The diminutive low-lying island known aptly as Isola delle Correnti is actually the southernmost point of Sicily, and furthermore is located at a slightly lower latitude than Tunis in north Africa. On the other hand Malta is the closest land mass, only a matter of 100km south-southwest. This is a lovely corner of the world, apparently living a life of its own. Turtles even used to visit the beaches here at three-year intervals to deposit their leathery eggs. Isola delle Correnti is not strictly an island as it is still joined to land by what is now a submerged neck from the eroding isthmus, so that reaching it means embarking on a half-walk half-wade. Understandably a swimming costume is useful, and plastic sandals make the going more pleasant as the grassy cover on the island conceals spiky specimens insidious for bare feet.

In spring the walk is delightful: though the water is still chilly and a dip bracing, to say the least; the beaches are colonised by marvellously coloured flowering plants, not to mention the 'king of the sea' seaweed *Posidonia oceanica*, whose curious dried, fibrous balls like airy pebbles drift along the sand amidst thick spongy banks of ribbon-like algae. A visit in autumn can be divine, as the water is still perfect for swimming and visitors are few and far between. Summer at these latitudes, on the other hand, means decidedly African temperatures and a popular beach resort in full swing.

The hinterland of this southerly angle of Sicily is an unbroken 'sea' of greenhouses and market gardens specialising in delicious tomatoes and strawberries and protected by plastic sheeting in the cooler months.

The nearest township, Portopalo di Capo Passero, is a drab backwater fishing centre reminiscent of a settlement from the wild west. However, it served as a key landing point and bridgehead during the Allied Forces' Operation Husky on 10 July 1943 at the start of the move northwards

Braving the water crossing to Isola delle Correnti

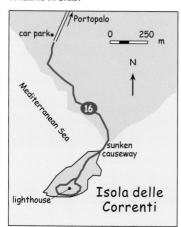

Tourist Office
Portopalo di Capo
Passero
Tel 0931-848035

Accommodation
Hotel Vittorio
Tel 0931-842181
Affittacamere Scala
Corrado
Tel 0931-842701
Agriturismo Il Ranch
Tel 0931-842754,
a short way out
of town on the
Pachino road

to liberate Nazi-fascist occupied Italy. Portopalo also boasts a picturesque old *tonnara* fish processing plant silhouetted on its waterfront. Freshly-caught fish and seafood are served in the town's excellent restaurants in simple but singularly effective ways. One traditional dish is *ghiotta alla marinara*, a fish similar to mackerel which is flavoured with a stew of tomato, capers, celery and olives.

THE WALK

From the **car park** a lane leads through rustling shoulder-height canes to the beachfront and the stunning deep blue Mediterranean. Ahead is the inviting island, its buildings akin to a fortress. The sand on this wind-blown corner is anchored down in great patches by an astonishing array of hardy vegetation that includes glasswort, sea holly, blue-mauve sea lavender, and silver-green velvety sea wormwood – insignificant in appearance but aromatic to the touch. The narrowing isthmus to your left around the waterfront extends into the water as a **sunken causeway** to the island, usually nothing more than a waist-deep immersion. **Isola delle Correnti** has rigorous plant cover and exuberant wild rabbits and makes for a delightful visit especially out of season, when it is all but deserted with the exception of solitary fishermen. It is easily explored with the help of a faint path that circles the **lighthouse** and outbuildings. Visible further up the coast northwest is the Punta delle Formiche (point of the ants), namely the diminutive rocky islets scattered off the headland.

Return to the **car park** the same way.

WALK 17
Cava d'Ispica

Time	Part A – 45min; Part B – 2hr 30min
Distance	Part A – 4km/2.5 miles; Part B – 9.4km/5.9 miles
Grade	1–2
Start/finish	Part A – archaeological zone entrance; Part B – upper Ispica
Access	A car is essential for Part A. Approximately halfway between Modica and Ispica along the SS 115 is the turn-off for the Cava d'Ispica archaeological zone.
	For Part B, the township of Ispica lies on the Siracusa–Ragusa train line, and is also served by daily AST buses. Drivers will easily find Ispica on the southernmost curve of the SS 115 between Noto and Modica.

Cava d'Ispica is an ancient, tortuous 13km-long canyon cutting through the southernmost reaches of the Monti Iblei limestone plateau. An open-air museum to all effects and purposes, its sites of habitation reveal life and death from prehistoric times as early as the Bronze Age (14th–15th centuries BC) through Byzantine times to the late 17th century, when a catastrophic earthquake wrought widespread devastation and the sites were abandoned. These days the odd vegetable patch or orchard spread along the Cava are the sole signs of 'civilisation', otherwise it has long since reverted to its natural state, conjuring up images of a Garden of Eden. Sheer pastel-coloured rock flanks cleft dramatically by the cataclysm and extensively weathered reveal layers of interconnected manmade cavities of vast proportions. A grand total of 5000 have been documented as rock tombs, cave dwellings and churches, many decorated with rupestrian art, though all but inaccessible to visitors.

While part of the northernmost extremity of Cava d'Ispica has been fenced off and protected as an archaeological site, with the inclusion of intriguing early Christian catacombs, the southernmost part near the township of Ispica is more accessible and attractive in natural terms, as it is deeper cut, wilder and crammed with a surprising array of plant and

*Cava d'Ispica
archaeological zone*

bird life. Ideally a complete itinerary would run the entire 13km length of the valley; however, at the time of writing the unkempt overgrown state of the central part made exploration prohibitive beyond the paths described here.

Overall this walk rates average on archaeological and natural interest, however it is of minor interest compared to Pantalica. It is unsuitable after May as the valley can become airless and the oppressive heat does not abate until October. As usual, drinking water should be carried. Neither difficulty nor significant height gain or loss are entailed, though boots are a good idea for Part B, as the going can get a little rough and ankle support is desirable.

On a prominent outcrop overlooking the southern end of the Cava stands the present town of Ispica, very traditional and conservative in nature. It dates back to the 18th century, and is said to be virtually an identical reconstruction – churches included – of the original valley settlement reduced to rubble by the massive 1693 earthquake.

The two routes described are located in separate parts of the Cava d'Ispica – the archaeological zone area (Part A) and the Parco della Forza (Part B).

THE WALK
Part A (45min)
To visit the enclosed **archaeological zone** in the northernmost part of Cava d'Ispica, 20min is usually enough. Inside, just

past the ticket booth (400m), turn down right for the intriguing **Catacomba Larderia**, the early Christian (4th–5th centuries) catacombs with a curious honeycomb appearance. The nearby former mill has been transformed into a museum. The main path leads to a series of former cave dwellings (**Grotte Cadute**) and ancient necropolises, which mean several storeys' worth of yawning cavities in the rock flank.

Leave the **archaeological zone** and cross the road for the concrete ramp and the lane curving left below the road bridge. Not far along you'll need the faint path up right (next to a shed) for the brief climb to a sizeable outcrop and erstwhile Byzantine church and tomb site. A gaping cave in the

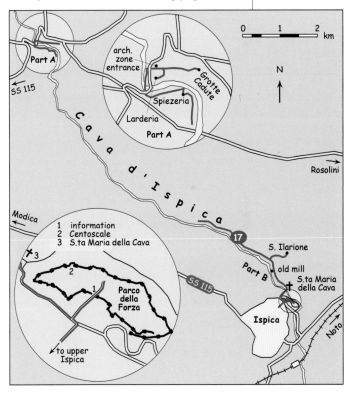

crumbly chalky stone is known as the **Spiezeria** as it was believed to house a medieval pharmacy run by monks, as attested by rock-hewn shelving.

Back on the lower valley track, it is worthwhile proceeding southwards a little further via the dry stream bed to admire the extension of the cliff settlements, where partial collapse has revealed more labyrinthian premises. The modest cliffs are silhouetted with bizarre prickly pear outlines while the valley floor, in contrast, is a flourishing, fertile oasis of towering reeds and unusually thick concentrations of yellow chrysanthemum-type flowers edging orange and lemon orchards. However, passage is soon hindered by barbed wire and untamed brambles.

Return the same way.

Part B (2hr 30min)

The most straightforward entry to Parco della Forza is from the upper part of **Ispica** (170m). 'Tourist information' signs point over to the northeastern flank, where vehicles can be left near a school (10min on foot from the main square). A flight of steps then a winding concrete-based ramp drop through citrus groves ensconced amidst medieval-era necropolises to a quiet road. Opposite is the access track for **Parco della Forza** (the name derives from 'fort') on the former stronghold, a natural outcrop. A series of drawbridges is believed to have once afforded entrance to this 3.5 hectare strategic rock island at the southernmost mouth of the lengthy Cava d'Ispica. Allow 30min for a thorough visit of Ispica's former nerve centre.

◄ Beyond the children's playground is an amazing underground staircase known as Centoscale ('one hundred steps' – even though it actually has 240), probably excavated in the Norman period to guarantee a water supply for the besieged fort. A diagonal tunnel leads to a spring at stream level, with a recess and water storage basin every 100 steps as buckets were evidently passed up. Other features of the site are ruins of medieval palaces and churches, not to mention fortifications, cisterns, numerous caves, rock stairways and stables and stalls for livestock, featuring ingenious channelling to drain off rainwater and keep the premises dry. A small *antiquarium* (museum) completes the picture.

Leave Parco della Forza and turn right for the '*chiesa rupestre*'. A steep track winds down to the enchanting valley

Ask at the timber information booth for the helpful multilingual leaflet.

floor where the light-coloured cliffs are pockmarked with natural caves and man-made caverns. The old church of **Santa Maria della Cava**, shaded by generous European nettle trees, half in half out of the rock face, is believed to date back to the 6th–7th centuries; it is generally locked to protect its frescoes. The track (left) into the deep canyon threads its delightful way northwards past a huge boulder topped by a cross; high up left the cliffs are said to host a sculpted face of Christ, which is venerated by the inhabitants. Continuing below crumbling cave dwellings, you pass the ruins of an **old mill** (110m), then where the track enters fenced-off private property a clear path keeps right, following old stone fortifications. At a substantial gap in the walling marked by a huge gnarled **carob tree**, branch off right for old stone steps hewn out of the cliff for the ascent to a natural platform, **Sant'Ilarione**, below orangey rock, affording lovely views of Ispica. The limestone here has been colonised with the bright pink and lilac blooms of stonecrop, straggly wild figs, heather, domes of tree spurge and aromatic patches of wild sage. ▶

A worthwhile option is to continue into the shallow inner valley; the old path alternates clear stretches with jungle, and there are dwarf palms, thyme, butcher's broom and wild asparagus. It climbs up left to the topmost level of the cliffs before petering out at a scenic area.

Return to the **carob tree** and junction on the valley floor the same way.

A little further along a cave-cum-animal stall is passed, then you join the dry stony torrent bed near the recognisable ruins of another mill building. The path runs along smooth slabs of rock or pebbles. The cultivated gardens have been left behind now and the area is wilder and the vegetation more luxurious. The valley floor is thick with pomegranate and medlar trees loaded with fruit, oleanders, giant spiky century plants, acanthus and lentisc. Keep your eyes skinned for the myriad wild orchids. The further you venture into the Cava d'Ispica, the more interesting the bird life becomes: there are darting swallows, cooing pigeons and an array of birds of prey including the buzzard. Soon an interesting and extensive complex of rock caves can be seen high above right in the sheer cliff face (marked by a modest electricity pylon above). Perfect cross-sections of a series of interconnected rooms have been exposed by a rockfall (1hr 15min).

Further exploration along the valley and its side valleys depends on the conditions of the undergrowth and heat. Return to **Ispica** the same way (2hr 30min grand total).

Accommodation
B&B Casa Timponelli
Tel 0932-951079
2.5km out of Ispica

ANTIQUITIES IN THE WEST

WALK 18

The White Cliffs of Eraclea Minoa

Time	2hr + 40min extension
Distance	6km/3.8 miles
Grade	1–2
Start/finish	Sabbia d'Oro restaurant
Access	From the main coastal road (SS 115) 38km northwest of Agrigento and 30km southeast from Sciacca, you'll need the turn-off towards the sea (southwest, close to the Fiume Platani) for the final 3.5km to the coast and Eraclea Minoa.
	The closest public transport is the Agrigento–Sciacca bus line (Lumia) which takes the main road; ask to be let off at the above mentioned turn-off. A summer-only line from Cattolica Eraclea covers the remaining distance.

A dazzling white headland extends out over a long run of a pristine beach of golden sand backed by a shady scented pine wood. Capobianco, the aptly-named promontory, hosts the surviving fraction of the 6th-century BC colony of Eraclea Minoa. A vast slice of the crumbly chalky land has long disappeared into the Mediterranean Sea, carrying with it a good part of the erstwhile settlement, but remnants of dwellings, a modest theatre, streets and a curious shaft for loading ships at the port guarantee an interesting visit. This low-key site is quiet as it receives far fewer visitors than the famed Selinunte (see Walk 19), yet the surroundings are beautiful and the site is a riot of wild flowers in springtime.

Over time the settlement of Eraclea Minoa has been run by varied groups, starting with the Minoans of Crete: hence the appellation. History is confounded with legend in accounts of King Minos hot on the heels of Daedalus in flight, literally, on his wings of wax. In Sicily, however, Daedalus was sheltered by King Cocalus, whose daughters wasted no time in disposing of mighty Minos by pouring boiling water over him at bath-time.

Other occupants of the site were possibly the Phoenicians, colonisers from Selinunte, then settlers from Sparta, conquerors from Agrigento and Siracusa, and the Romans in the final period, before it was abandoned once and for all in the 1st century BC. As well as the finds on display at the site's modest *antiquarium* (museum), other items are held at the Museo Regionale Archeologico at Agrigento.

Along with the archaeological site, this walk takes in a stunning stretch of coast as well as the edge of a nature reserve (Riserva Naturale Orientata Foce del Fiume Platani) that encompasses the mouth of the River Platani and an adjacent pine wood. An optional extension is also given. In this area, en route to and from Africa, winged migrants such as kestrels and the buff-coloured squacco heron stop off for a rest and meal of river eels. Another wayfarer, the handsome hoopoe bird, is often seen on the pathways of the archaeological site. A final faunal note: the locals warn of a copious viper population, so wear shoes in preference to sandals and don't sit on sunny rock surfaces without checking first.

The walk itself, after an initial approach via a quiet surfaced road, covers ancient Eraclea Minoa and the old port before returning to the starting point via the beach. However, by parking at the entrance to the archaeological site and following the itinerary as far as the old port/beach then backtracking to the car park, it can be shortened by some 40min and the road thus avoided.

No difficulty is involved, though the passage via the beach on the return stretch could see you wading around the point at high tide. A swimming costume and a picnic are handy, as well as binoculars for bird watchers. There is a summer-only grocery shop close to the beach, though the Sabbia d'Oro bar-restaurant may do snacks as well. Accommodation in bungalows is on offer at the camping grounds in summer, otherwise ask at the restaurant for rooms.

The Walk

From the **Sabbia d'Oro** bar-restaurant on the seafront, walk back up the access road. After the initial climb to the cliff-top level, take the first turning left – a narrow surfaced road lined with scattered remnants of the ancient settlement's defensive walls and fortifications. There are sweeping views of the white cliffs at Capobianco and long curve of

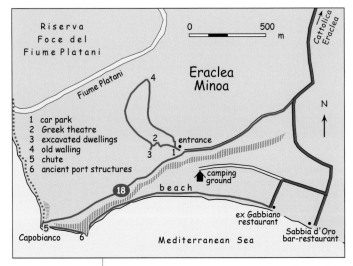

1 car park
2 Greek theatre
3 excavated dwellings
4 old walling
5 chute
6 ancient port structures

coastline. Curious pinkish salsify flowers are here in abundance, along with multicoloured thistles and, of course, the omnipresent majestic agave. Half an hour from the beach are the car park, ticket office and entrance for the archaeological site of **Eraclea Minoa**.

A quick visit is in order to the *antiquarium*, then take the wide track west for the modest **Greek theatre**. Down left, a series of excavated dwellings (*abitazioni*) and cleared streets can be found. Highlights range from the ancient shop incorporated into a house, latrines, household altar and a cistern.

Back near the theatre, follow the main lane left (north). It is shaded by perfumed mimosa trees and scant conifers, and looks over the shallow valley thick with vineyards and irrigated by the Fiume Platani, its banks smothered in tall rushes. Downhill, where a locked gate bars the way, take the path off right to the remains of Eraclea's northernmost **outer walling**, equipped with lookout posts. You then proceed back uphill (south) to a prominent knoll occupied by an incongruous World War Two bunker. Keep left along the ridge for the steps that return via gardens of geranium to the ticket office (40min for the visit, total 1hr 10min).

From the **car park**, take the wide lane right (southwest). After a gate it follows the edge of the cliffs in the direction of the point, heading for masses of gigantic prickly pear and spear-like agave plants. It soon crosses a decent stretch of the original paved north–south road that extends down from the site amidst thickets of acacia with impressively long thorns. At a fork in the track keep straight on, following the cliff edge through vineyards and fields. After a stile the track becomes a little rougher and passes a modest house. A narrowing path leads a little further round to **Capobianco** and masses of showy yellow crown daisies. Briefly right is fencing marking the southernmost limit of the Riserva Foce del Fiume Platani: a breathtaking spot overlooking turquoise sea and endless white beach. Now make your way with care down over the pebbly conglomerate underlaid with smooth chalky rock to the lower point with a huge circular hole. Obstructed nowadays by debris, this manmade **chute** was used in ancient times for loading ships moored in the cave directly below. To reach it is a simple matter of a clamber (diagonally right) down an easy ledge via a pole marker. Pass the grove of eucalyptus and turn in left for the roomy cave, now the exclusive domain of bats (20min from the car park).

The white cliffs at Eraclea Minoa

Riserva Foce del Fiume Platani extension (40min return)

From the chute it is feasible to extend the walk along right (north) to the modest reserve – a sandbank often forms at the river's mouth and is easily crossed at low tide. On the opposite bank, back from the unspoilt beach, several camouflaged huts for bird watching have been constructed in the mixed pine, acacia and eucalyptus wood carpeted with the brilliant blooms of the Hottentot fig. The best time for observing the migratory species is late autumn through to spring, though even in summer the odd heron or egret will be fishing, competing with terns and seagulls.

The reserve can also be reached by road and is well signposted.

Accommodation
Campeggio
Eraclea Minoa
(also does B&B)
Tel 0922-846023
or 0922-29101
www.eraclea
minoavillage.it

To return to the start point, if the tide is not excessively high, head left (east) along the beach below the crumbling pale stratified cliffs. Remains of ancient port structures are visible among the waves off the point. Paddling may be required when rounding one promontory, then it is a stroll along the sand to the remains of the **Gabbiano restaurant**, victim of a winter storm. As the beach is usually impassable here, turn inland and around through the quiet residential zone to return to the **Sabbia d'Oro** once more (total 2hr).

Return via the beach below Capobianco

WALK 19
The Stones of Selinunte

Time	2–3hr
Distance	6km/3.7 miles
Grade	1
Start/finish	Selinunte main entrance
Access	The nearest useful public transport terminal, Castelvetrano, is served by train and AST bus from Marsala, as well as train or Lumia bus from Agrigento. Then it's a brief trip by daily Salemi bus to Marinella. The bus stops close to the tourist office and the main entrance to the Selinunte site.
	The coastal SS 115 is needed by car-borne visitors. Some 4km southeast of Castelvetrano is the junction for the remaining 9.5km (on the SS 115dir) south to Marinella and Selinunte on the seafront.

A 'village of pillars' according to the 12th-century Arab chronicler al-Idrisi; curiously 'land of fleas' in a 16th-century document (from *pulci* in Italian, from a corrupt form of 'Pollux', if not 'Punic'); 'the most extraordinary collection of ruins in Europe' for poet Algernon Charles Swinburne late in the 19th century, shortly after Guy de Maupassant had likened the fallen columns to 'dead soldiers'. Visitors to the remains of Selinunte, a powerful if short-lived 5th-century BC city, never fail to leave with lasting impressions. It comprises eight massive Greek-style temples and double-barrelled fortifications around an extensive city site, whose toppled cutstone blocks are enlivened by overwhelming masses of wild poppies, golden chrysanthemums and purple bug-gloss.

On the lovely Mediterranean coast of southwest Sicily midway between Mazara del Vallo and Sciacca, Selinunte straddled two rivers with respective harbours, since heavily silted up and unusable and now colonised by tamarisk and rushes and home to flocks of elegant black-winged stilt birds and cormorants. The site is backed by a fertile plain, which attracted the first colonisers (from the Greek settlement of

Megara Hyblaea near Siracusa) in mid-7th century BC. The great Empedocles was said to have been called in for drainage and reclamation work, and still today the area supports productive market gardens. Unlike the situation at major sites such as Agrigento, where modern buildings cramp and encroach on the precious ruins, Selinunte has miraculously been kept free of extraneous constructions. The sole concession is to the shepherds whose flocks graze freely amongst rolling green hills as in some 18th-century pastoral idyll.

The city derives its innocuous name from the Greek *selinon*, meaning 'wild celery', still plentiful here and once used on the locally minted coins as a distinctive emblem. It experienced an intense period of glory based on trade: iron from the Etruscans, tin from the British Isles and gold from Spain were exchanged with silk and spices from the East. A nine-day siege in 409BC (not to mention a definitive version in 205BC) saw the systematic destruction of Selinunte at the hands of the Carthaginians; reports gave 16,000 dead, 5000 enslaved and 2600 fled to Agrigento. Several later unsuccessful attempts were made to restore settlement and it is believed to have hosted hermits and religious communities in late medieval times, though a Byzantine-period earthquake helped erase evidence as well as toppling surviving columns once and for all.

The site was recognised as that of ancient Selinunte by a Dominican monk in the 1500s, but no systematic excavation was arranged until the British consul at Palermo made a brief attempt in the early 1800s. However, soon afterwards his fellow countrymen William Harris and Samuel Angell launched the first campaign in 1822, followed by those of other nations. The acropolis and fortifications gradually came to light, and some reconstruction was embarked on. Key finds such as monumental temple pieces can be viewed at the Museo Archeologico Regionale in Palermo.

The walk itself, an easy stroll through a stunning area, can take up the good part of a morning if not a day. Distances between the various parts of the site are modest, so no intermediate timing has been given. Signboard explanations in four languages are set at strategic points. No refreshments – or shade apart from the odd eucalypt – are available on the site itself.

A fascinating follow-up is a drive (no public transport) to the Cava di Cusa quarry, which provided the yellowish tufaceous limestone for Selinunte. It lies 10km northwest of Marinella, not far after Campobello di Mazara. Probably abandoned precipitously during the dramatic siege, it has half-cut columns still awaiting completion and extraction, and offers a marvellous insight into ancient masonry techniques.

THE WALK

On the westernmost edge of the low-key fishing village of Marinella is ample parking and the **main entrance** (with ticket office) for Selinunte. An incongruous tunnel beneath the embankment for the erstwhile railway leads into the vast site, where the dimensions of the remaining temples are immediately breathtaking for their immensity. Here stand the three important **Templi orientali**, distinguished by letters. The first, E, dates back to the 5th century BC and has been partially reconstructed. Work on F, which has evidently been stripped, was commenced a century later. The furthermost ruins belong to what is by far the largest temple (G), one of the most sizeable constructions known in Greek architecture at 110 x 50 metres. Dedicated to Apollo, the guardian of Selinunte, it was never finished – due possibly to the destruction of the city – and many of the columns lack fluting. The tower-like column that has been raised, with its massive capital, gives an idea of the original dimensions. The horseshoe-shaped stone loops visible on the columns served to fit ropes for lifting into an upright position.

Follow the dirt road towards the *antiquarium* or **Baglio Florio**, once a farm. Ignore a turn left, and keep downhill into the shallow river valley of the Gorgo Cottone where ground cover includes pretty mauve-white-yellow convolvulus. Near the bottom at a curve, take the path left towards trees. A shady **picnic area** is traversed then a tarmac road joined, flanking what used to be one of Selinunte's harbours, long silted up. A short distance uphill past the **car park** is the seaside entrance to the site of the vast, impressive fortified Acropolis, preceded by a 16th-century tower to ward off pirate attacks. For the time being continue straight on, high over a stunning beach. A path leads down towards the other former harbour, through thick Mediterranean maquis and even the odd dwarf palm. Various water fowl can be observed, in addition to small hawks. A **footbridge**

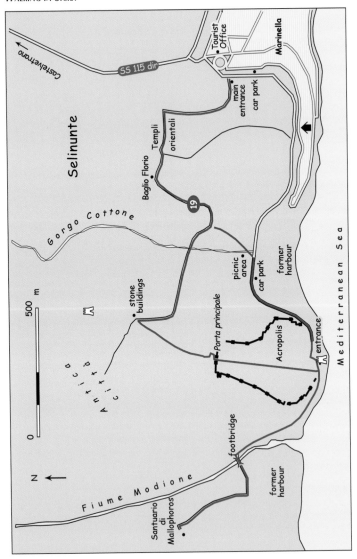

crosses the rush-lined watercourse (Fiume Modione, the ancient Selinon) you proceed through olive groves and fields to the **Santuario di Malophoros**. Its altars and temple are distinctly Punic rather than Greek in style, and were dedicated to the pomegranate-bearing divinity akin to Demeter, the Greek goddess of agriculture. The sanctuary was believed to have served as station for funeral processions en route for a necropolis to the west, while the discovery of ex voto objects suggest it was later used by Christian communities.

Wild flowers and ancient stones

Return towards the **Acropolis** and its main southern entrance. This hill site, levelled off and enlarged with embankments in ancient times, is dissected by a 9m-wide north–south road, intersected in turn by minor streets. In terms of buildings, temples dominate (labelled O, A, B, C and D) interspersed with modest ruined houses from later times, as the crosses visible on several indicate. Exit at the far northern end of the main street via the **Porta principale** (main gate). Here is a series of extraordinary multi-layered fortifications 2–3m thick and hollow in places for filling with rubble for reinforcement, and worth careful exploration. (No such artificial bastions were needed on the seaward edge of the Acropolis, as there the ground falls steeply to the beach, constituting a natural defence.)

Make your way north along the overgrown ridge through the **Antica città** (ancient city), the erstwhile residential part of the original city devastated in 409BC. As the many ruined buildings now lie buried beneath the sand, there is little to see. A clear lane is reached close to a cluster of restored **stone buildings**, not far from a medieval-looking tower. Turn down right to drop into the valley and rejoin the route used in the first part, hence back up to the temples and the **main entrance**.

Tourist Office
Selinunte
Tel 0924-46251

Accommodation
Hotel Lido Azzurro
Tel 0924-46256
Affittacamere The
Holiday House
Tel 0924-46035

WALK 20
Mozia and its Lagoon

Time	45min + extra for boat trip and museum visit
Distance	3.2km/2 miles
Grade	1
Start/finish	Landing stage, Mozia
Access	By car via the Marsala–Trapani coast road (SP 21), follow signs for Mothia. For those arriving from Palermo, a branch of the A29dir *autostrada* goes as far as the Trapani airport at Birgi, and from there you slot into the SP 21.

By public transport, slow trains stop at both Ragatissi-Birgi and Spagnuola stations, then it's a few kms on foot over to the coast and lagoon. In summer local bus n.4 from Marsala runs along the waterfront.

Small boats leave from the waterfront near the Saline Ettore e Infersa (salt pans) with their photogenic windmills, for the short trip to Mozia. Otherwise, as a more adventurous alternative, you can wade across via the underwater causeway (at low tide), starting from Birgi Vecchi!

The stretch of coastline on westernmost Sicily between the port cities of Marsala and Trapani appears flat and uninteresting at first glance. Closer inspection reveals a curious landscape punctuated by elongated man-made basins in graduated hues of white-blue-green – the famed *saline* or salt pans. Along their banks stand glistening piles of salt protected from the elements by terracotta tiles. Salt has been worked here since very early times, as documented by Arab travellers. A number of establishments still boast traditional methods and beautifully restored trademark windmills, along with informative tours for visitors.

In addition, of the sizeable inlets that indent the coast the lagoon known as Lo Stagnone (large pond) has a number of attractions which make a detour well worthwhile. First and foremost there is the lagoon itself, a surprisingly shallow body of sea some 20 sq km in size, barred from the sea by the elongated strip of Isola Grande and from the land by the salt works. A nature reserve since 1984, its waters are a haven and nursery for fish, crustaceans and water fowl, migrational and resident: on the long list are black-winged stilt, sea plover, avocet and various herons. They feed on underwater pastures of seaweed, such as the long-stranded *Posidonia oceanica* 'king of the sea'.

The majority of visitors, however, come for the diminutive 45-hectare island San Pantaleo (or Mozia, also spelt Mothia or Motya), located in the centre of the lagoon. In etymological terms the appellation may come from 'spinning mill', as indeed it was famous for its red-purple Phoenician cloth, tinted with the dye of a gastropod (snail) found in abundance there, though Mozia was also the name of a celebrated beauty from ancient times, courted by Hercules. Founded by Phoenicians from far-off Tyre as early as the 8th century BC, the settlement stood at the busy crossroads of trade routes between Africa, Spain, Sardinia and central Italy. It flourished as a stepping stone, the lagoon shallows a great advantage for defence purposes. To link it to the mainland, where numerous other outposts had grown up, a unique 2km 'highway' was constructed, still clearly visible underwater at the northernmost tip of the island. In the 5th century BC Mozia's perimeter was ringed by walls encompassing imposing gateways and lookout towers, and an internal artificial harbour sheltered ships in need of repairs.

Embarking for Mozia

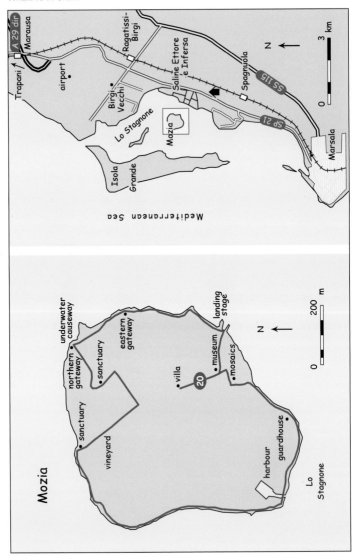

Due to Greek rivalry, in 397BC the town was besieged and all but razed to the ground by the tyrant of Siracusa, Dionysius the Elder, reportedly with the aid of the newly invented long-distance catapult. The few survivors fled to the mainland and established Lilybaeum, present-day Marsala, while the island site was re-occupied from time to time over the ages.

Englishman Joseph Whitaker, nephew of a famous Marsala wine merchant, acquired Mozia early last century in order to commence systematic archaeological excavations. These are ongoing, and the refurbished museum will soon be bursting at the seams. It already holds a varied collection of Phoenician pieces, such as balsam phials in coloured glass. The magnificent centrepiece is an elegant life-size 5th-century BC marble statue of a handsome youth, unearthed in 1979.

Though modest, Mozia is undeniably intriguing and warrants a trip for the setting alone. The towering Egadi islands are close-by, while views inland are dominated by spectacular mountain-top Erice. The walk itself is a pleasant wander around the peaceful island, reached by boat. Nothing in the way of refreshments is available, so go prepared if you intend to stay a while.

THE WALK

From the **landing stage** on the island of Mozia it's a short stroll to the **museum**, a good place to start. Close by, a grouping of houses in distinct town blocks has come to light, as well as a **villa** along a short path inland. In the opposite direction towards the water's edge a sizeable dwelling (6th–4th century BC) once stood beneath the huge shady Aleppo pines, its extant black and white pebble **mosaic** flooring depicting lions and griffins attacking helpless animals. A pathway proceeds southwest along the lagoon edge to the remains of an ancient **guardhouse** (*casermetta*) originally set in the settlement's outer wall, now all but smothered by vegetation. There are salt-loving plants the likes of fleshy glasswort and artemisia, and clumps of dwarf palms, while giant fennel plants vie with agave for height. West is the spread of Isola Grande. The curious inner **harbour** (dry dock or 'Cothon') dating back to the 5th century BC is not far away. It measures 50m by 37m, and is similar to structures found at Carthage in north Africa.

After rounding a point, you head north through lentisc shrubs and in view of other minor islands before the towering Egadi islands appear northwest. Not far around the ensuing point is the enclosed 8th-century BC **sanctuary** or 'Tofet' (20min this far). Amongst layers of cinerary urns, the remains of both infants and domestic animals, sacrifices to the principal Phoenician deities Baal Hammon and Astarte, according to the prevailing custom, were identified.

Turn right inland from here for the lane traversing a **vineyard** and lined with olive trees. Just before a set of wind generators go left at the junction for the foundations of the Cappiddazu **sanctuary** and the industrial area, the site of furnaces for ceramic vases and, possibly, a dye works.

Make your way through to the water's edge past the **northern gateway**, once equipped with an imposing defence system. Close by is the start of the 6th-century BC dual-carriage **causeway**, now submerged but easy to identify on calm days with its built-up edges akin to guard-rails. Leading across to the promontory of Birgi on the mainland, it was used until recent times by carts transporting the grape harvest, though the odd tractor evidently still crosses at low tide.

A little further around to the right stands the **eastern gateway** where the fortifications come complete with an extant staircase. It's a matter of 10min to the **landing stage** and return trip.

Tourist Office
Marsala Tel
0923-714097

Accommodation
Contrada Spagnuola:
Baglio Vajarassa
Tel 0923-968628
B&B Andrea's
Tel 328-4849399

Saltpans and windmills near Mozia

LE ISOLE EGADI (Egadi Islands)

Few foreign visitors make it over to this modest but marvellously varied archipelago off the westernmost point of Sicily, though the Italians are well acquainted with the Egadi's wondrous turquoise waters, picturesque coves and delicious seafood. Lying a leisurely hop, skip and jump from the port of Trapani, where the Tyrrhenian Sea and the Mediterranean merge, the three islands were actually long joined to the mainland: **Marettimo**, the most distant – not to mention the wildest – detached itself prior to the last ice age when **Levanzo** and **Favignana** still had a natural bridge link, affording access for Palaeolithic man as well as animals. The name Egadi means 'islands of the goats', and witnesses to their abundance were Ulysses, who hunted them on Favignana, followed by 12th-century Arab geographer al-Idrisi, who documented them on Marettimo along with gazelles. The only creatures distantly resembling a descendant are the odd shy mouflon that still nimbly navigate the island's wilds, though in all probability they were introduced by zealous modern-day hunters. A more appropriate modern denomination for the Egadi group might be 'islands of the tuna' as a good part of their history has been inextricably bound up with this deepsea torpedo. A collective hunt has been practised ceaselessly since the period of Arab domination, as have certain preservation techniques. As elsewhere on Sicily the waterfronts at Favignana and the minor land mass of Formica are graced with the elegant *tonnara* that long acted as the processing plants.

The three islands differ from one another in an extraordinary manner. Rugged, mountainous Marettimo is a paradise for walkers; quiet Levanzo offers divine rambling and an extraordinary cave with prehistoric paintings; while Favignana, the most populous and best for beaches, is perfect bicycling territory. All are composed of a mix of sedimentary rock, with a wealth of fossil-bearing tufa, limestone and dolomite, which make for both curiously eroded peaks and stupendous marine caves on sea level. Natural springs support multitudinous wild flora, and agriculture once thrived there – now in decline in favour of tourism and fishing. The Egadi have recently been declared a marine reserve, which entails some boating and spear-fishing restrictions. Clear maps with multilingual legends explaining zoning are on display at all the harbours.

The best time of year to visit the Egadi is a matter of preference: spring entails an assurance of greener landscapes and a vast range of wild flowers, with the slight disadvantage of chilly swimming; summer, of course, brings crowds; autumn can be parched but the sea much warmer; while winter may be alternately crisp and wildly windswept.

On the practical front, Favignana has all mod cons, Marettimo has them

Punta Troia (Walk 24)

to a lesser extent, whereas Levanzo is devoid of a bank for the time being. All have grocery shops.

Accommodation

Providing you don't turn up mid-August with no advance reservation, finding somewhere to stay is no great problem. Favignana has a fair range on offer, from out-of-the-way luxury hotels to camping grounds; Levanzo has the grand total of two albeit modest hotels; while Marettimo means private rooms

and the odd apartment, whose owners usually meet incoming ferries to seek out clients.

Transport to the islands

All craft depart from the harbour of Trapani, an important air, rail and bus hub. Some runs are limited to Favignana and Levanzo. The choice is between the fast hydrofoils (*aliscafi*) which have multiple daily runs year round, intensified in the summer period, or the leisurely and more economical ferries (*traghetti*), which also carry vehicles. (Private vehicles are only allowed – and are only useful – on Favignana; Levanzo and Marettimo have little in the way of roads anyway.) Stormy conditions and high seas in midwinter occasionally mean services are temporarily suspended.

Maps

The artistic sketch map handed out at the tourist offices is fairly helpful for getting your bearings, but not for walking. Several suggestions are made under the individual walks.

Tourist Office Trapani
Tel 0923-29000
Tourist Office Favignana
Tel 0923-921647

WALK 21

Favignana by Bicycle

Cycling time	1hr 30min (on foot 3hr)
Distance	13.4km/8.4 miles
Grade	1–2
Start/finish	Favignana harbour
Access	Favignana receives the greatest number of ferry and hydrofoil connections from Trapani.
Note	Don't be tempted by the track up Monte Santa Caterina and its Norman castle overlooking the harbour without checking first, as the slopes are reputedly infested with ticks (*zecche*) carried by the livestock. The numerous black snakes on the other hand are more visible but harmless.

The cry of the commanding *ràis* answered by a rhythmic chorus of chants, sounds out over the water as the fishermen heave up nets loaded with gigantic struggling tuna fish. The gleaming torpedoes, weighing a couple of hundred kilos per head, receive blows and stabs before being hauled out from a sea dyed crimson with their blood. The dramatic spectacle of the collective *mattanza* fish hunt has been repeated off Favignana year in year out with few interruptions since Arab times. It is May–June when the schools of tuna which have entered the Mediterranean to lay their eggs swim down the Tyrrhenian, keeping the coast on their left. They sweep past Calabria and follow the coast of Sicily right around to Trapani, where long nets nudge them towards Favignana and into a maze of submarine chambers. When numbers in the final *camera della morte* (death chamber) warrant it, the fishermen of Favignana tow ancient flat wooden boats to the site, then spend an exhausting morning at slaughter.

Currents, funding and willing expert hands permitting, this sole surviving *mattanza* in Sicily, is held a couple of times per season; in line with tradition, onlookers are welcome on board. Past centuries saw the tuna fishing in the hands of the Florio family of Marsala wine fame, and their cavernous and photogenic *tonnara* canning plant now stands desolate on the waterfront as the tuna are shipped directly to Trapani these days. Blanched of its redness, the fresh fish is served grilled in the restaurants, while shops offer an array of flavoursome by-products, such as dried compressed tuna roe *bottarga* (from the Arab for 'salted fish'), conserved according to techniques believed to be a legacy of the Arab/Norman heritage.

On the quieter side, the island of Favignana, a short ferry trip from Trapani, is also famous for its stunningly clear sapphire waters, a paradise for swimmers and snorkellers. The landform is gently undulating for the most part – with the exception of 302m Monte S. Caterina – and comprises calcareous tufa, rich in marine fossils and once excavated systematically for export to north Africa and other parts of Sicily as building material. Crazy columns of pink-hued and bleached rock stand in abandoned quarries, transformed into underground herb gardens and citrus orchards, invaded by gay spreading caper plants. Favignana has long attracted tourists, starting back in Greek times when, as Aegusa, it was visited by Ulysses who hunted wild goats. The island's present name came from a wind, Favonio (favourable for flowering), though 12th-century Spanish Arab traveller Ibn Jubayr called it ar-Rahib (the hermitage), a reference to a lone dweller at the castle on the mountain. The largest of the Egadi islands (19 sq km), it can get crowded late July–August, and accommodation then is best booked in advance.

Favignana does not lend itself to walking as distances are long and there is nothing in the way of shade, however the abundance of lanes makes it perfect for a bicycle tour. There is no shortage of bikes for hire, and where the going gets rough and paths narrow and rocky it's a matter of wheeling the vehicle along. The route described explores the lovely eastern half of the island, which is in contrast to the western realms that are comparatively unattractive. Both surfaced and unsurfaced tracks are followed, and numerous coves for swimming touched on. Take sun protection and plenty of drinking water unless you plan on stopping off at the snack bars for refreshments. While the island appears arid from afar, it is a blaze of colour in spring with a wealth of wild flowers, and even into summer the air is impregnated by the tang of wild furry fennel, which you'll find in your dinner, adding a unique fragrance when blended with sardines and served over pasta as *pasta con le sarde*.

THE WALK

Once you've found a comfortable trusty steed, start out from Favignana's ferry **harbour** and take the road east around the coast away from the township. Five minutes along where the asphalt bears inland, leave it for the dirt road straight ahead parallel to the coast and bordered by old stone walls smothered by caper plants and sheltering modest houses and aromatic herb gardens. At a junction

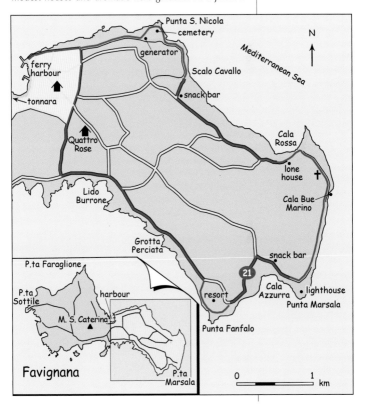

127

marked by the island's generator and fuel tanks, keep left along the coast. There's no lack of inviting coves or swimming spots, and you are accompanied by views of the neighbouring island of Levanzo and the Sicilian mainland, with the landmark mountain hosting Erice. Wild flowers such as yellow horned poppy and lilac sea rocket thrive in colourful clumps. The lane passes the rear of the **cemetery** on Punta San Nicola. Houses and tarmac are reached and paths lead into the clefts of an abandoned quarry at **Scalo Cavallo**, worth exploring. A short uphill pedal brings you to a T-junction and inviting snack bar with a shady garden. Turn left following signposting for Cala Rossa, past more small-scale quarries and a turn-off right for Lido Burrone – keep straight on (southeast). The road soon reverts to a bumpy and unsurfaced track. Ride straight on past a further fork and head for the lone, low house shaded by trees. Straight after the building, leave the track for the rocky path, left, for access to **Cala Rossa** (red cove, 30min). Bicycles can be left on the cliff top ahead, among the tiny purple iris, while you wander down the paths to the waterside for a compulsory swimming interval in the stunning crystal clear waters. As the cove is a brilliant transparent turquoise, it can only be deduced that its name derives

En route to
Cala Rossa

128

from the effects of the terrible battle fought here in 241BC when the Carthaginian fleet was defeated by the Romans, marking the end of the First Punic War.

Resume the rocky path, ignoring a fork for the point. The way soon improves to become a lane. Keep left at the subsequent forks, past an old house and shrine to a 17th-century friar. Giant 'asparagus' tips of the century plant punctuate the coastline and wild thyme grows underfoot. The next landmark is photogenic **Cala Bue Marino** ('sea cow cove'). Just after a curious old cutting leading down to the inviting waterside, you need the lane that branches left, sticking to the coastline for the ensuing wilder stretch. The way narrows, and it's often more comfortable to wheel your bike along this bumpy path, heading across the windswept headland towards the lighthouse at **Punta Marsala**, the port of the same name across the water on the mainland.

A surfaced road leads west around the point past the sandy inlet of **Cala Azzurra** and a snack bar. Keep left at the ensuing intersection via an oleander-lined avenue for **Punta Fanfalo** and its derelict resort. A dirt track leads around its sea side before rejoining the road. Marettimo looms in the distance beyond M. S. Caterina, then back on the road you pass more coves and **Grotta Perciata**, a natural rock bridge. The island's main beach, **Lido Burrone**, is next, with various eating establishments. Keep to this road for another kilometre or so, then at the sign for the water taxis turn right inland, past playing grounds and to the northern side of town for the road back to the **harbour.**

Accommodation
Hotel Bouganville
Tel 0923-922033
Quattro Rose
Tel 0923-921223
(10min on foot
from the port or call
for their minibus)
including camping

WALK 22

Levanzo and its Cave Paintings

Time	3hr 30min
Distance	10.6km/6.6 miles
Grade	2
Map	Island map (at the hotels)
Start/finish	Levanzo port
Access	The island of Levanzo is well served by both hydrofoils and ferries from nearby Trapani. See the Isole Egadi introduction for details.
Note	As the cave is locked, if you want to visit it as part of the walk you will need to arrange to meet the custodian there. An alternative is to do the outward trip by boat with the custodian, then slot into the itinerary after the guided cave visit.

In the Cimmerian recesses of the cave the guide's hurricane lamp exposes vivid scenes of sleek dolphins and tunny fish, then a hunt with wild pig, bison and a prehistoric donkey portrayed in a blend of animal fat, ochre and charcoal or scratched out with obsidian and flint implements. The paintings are from 7000–8000 years BC, but are predated by the engravings, believed to be from 12,000–13,000BC. A grand total of 29 animals and three apparently masked human figures have graced the walls of the Grotta del Genovese since prehistoric times, when the island of Levanzo was joined to the mainland by a land bridge, though the *grotto* was not rediscovered in modern times until 1994, when a Tuscan woman artist found her way in via a back-breaking corridor. Impressive quantities of animal remains were unearthed along with artefacts such as flint knives and crockery, now on display at Palermo's Museo Archeologico.

While the Grotta del Genovese is the undeniable star attraction of the island of Levanzo, it is by no means the only reason to go there. This marvellous sleepy island, with no roads to speak of, is very quiet off-season and much less visited than the other two in the Egadi group. Its already small population dwindles to 100 in winter. Exploration of its network of paths (courtesy of the Forestry Department) reveals rugged coastline with sheer cliffs – perfect shelter for interesting birdlife, including unbelievable seagull colonies – not to mention divine coves, whose turquoise water means there is no lack of swimming and snorkelling opportunities.

This modest 5 sq km limestone land mass suffers from a dearth of natural water – medieval chronicles listed it as Yabisah (Arab for 'arid' or 'dry') – evidently due to its geological composition. All the same it hosts 400 plant species including a number of endemics. The following itinerary takes in nearly the whole island, visiting several stunning coves and shady pine woods, panoramic stretches of wild coast, as well as the highlight of the fascinating Grotta del Genovese. Several up and downhill stretches necessitating good gym shoes are involved, and sun protection gear and drinking water should be carried.

THE WALK

From the **port** of Levanzo, a modest road leads east around the coast past the cemetery and becomes a broad dirt track. **Cala Fredda** is the first turquoise bay to present itself. Then, where the track climbs up left, take the path following the coast for **Cala Minnola** (25min). This charming spot is backed

Levanzo's tranquil harbour

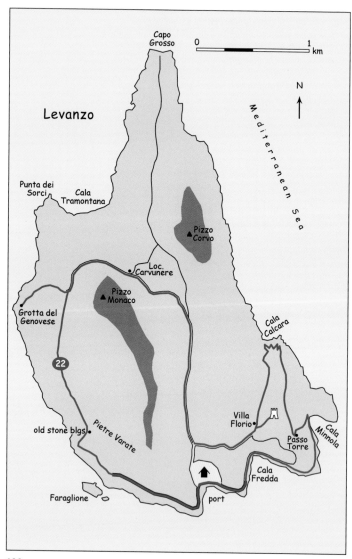

by a shady pine copse, perfect for picnics. After exploring the inviting point and environs through air scented by aromatic silver-leafed artemisia, walk up through the wood for the signed path for Cala Calcara. A good path, it climbs southeast to the **Passo Torre junction**, where you need the fork right (north) on Sentiero Calcara. It traverses a light wood, home to hordes of wild rabbits, before emerging onto an open ridge with views over the water to San Vito lo Capo, Trapani, the Marsala coastline and the diminutive island of Formica. Keep straight on at first, then gradually bear diagonally left towards the far corner of the wood. After a straight stretch heading for the point, an overgrown path that may need a little hunting around for turns abruptly down left to zigzag through shrubs such as spurge for **Cala Calcara**, hemmed in by magnificent cliffs (1hr). ▸

Note We have received reports that this route is now too overgrown to take.

Swimming completed, you need the ascent path heading up the wide valley at the rear of the bay to a lane due south between dry stone walls bordering fields of cultivated cereals. All but derelict 19th-century **Villa Florio** is passed, and through disused rambling farm premises a road of sorts is reached. Close by is the signed path for the detour to the lovely setting of curious square-based tower **Torre Saracena**, which occupies a 140m high hillock strategically overlooking the southern approach to the island (15min return).

Take the dirt road west now a brief way to a three-way intersection, where you need the right turn (north) across the cultivated central plain. A quarter of an hour on is the signed lane left (northwest) for the Grotta del Genovese.

(The road, on the other hand, proceeds northish along the elevated windswept ridge leading to Capo Grosso and the abandoned lighthouse – 1hr return).

At a pine copse and stone enclosure labelled **Loc. Carvunere**, a path breaks off in the direction of Cala Tramontana (worth a side trip), while the rocky lane climbs a little, skirting Pizzo Monaco, the highest point on the island at 278m. About 10min on, at 170m and with views over to Marettimo, the track as such terminates. There is a glimpse of a headland below west-soutwest, the site of the cave. A fairly decent path plunges down the hillside through scrubby vegetation brightened by the minia-ture iris known as the Barbary Nut. Old stone terracing is traversed and waymarking comes in the form of the

133

occasional iron pole. About halfway you veer sharp left alongside the headland housing the cave. The picturesque inlet is thick with screeching seagulls, who make no bones about dive-bombing intruders who inadvertently wander in the proximity of their defenceless, flightless scruffy grey chicks camouflaged amongst the rocks. Dark green oyster plants and moisture-seeking ferns are bunched around the entrance to the **Grotta del Genovese** (2hr 30min). It is also overhung by dripping dissolved limestone, fortunately confined to the exterior, leaving the paintings and implements unharmed inside. The innermost cavern is accessed via a low corridor, closed off by a sturdy metal door, understandably locked at all times.

After the visit, unless you're equipped for the tiring clamber around the rocks to where the track picks up at the Faraglione, climb back up the path to the lane and turn right (south) across the headland dotted with asphodels. There's a gradual descent through a circumscribed wood, before a traverse of old terracing and a couple of ingenious dry stone constructions for collecting water channelled into cisterns. Some 30min along a huddle of old stone buildings and fencing are reached, beneath the **Pietre Varate** crest and repeater. From the lowest hut a path drops seawards (past a turn-off right for a rocky bay), curving southeast towards the Faraglione island landmark. This stretch is very pretty as it zigzags down a flank akin to a veritable rock garden, dominated by clumps of lilac-pink scabious-like blooms on woody shrubs. Inclined slabs slope to sea level for divine swims, though a beach is just around the corner opposite the **Faraglione**. A narrow surfaced road takes up here for the final 15min back to the **port**.

Grotta del Genovese custodian: Natale Castiglione Tel 0923-924032. For a small fee he accompanies visitors by boat (or 4WD by road in rough weather), and is willing to meet walkers at the cave on appointment. See www. grottadelgenovese.it.

Accommodation
Pensione Paradiso
Tel 0923-924080
Pensione dei Fenici
Tel 0923-924083
Ask at the cafés for houses to rent

WALK 23

Marettimo's Coastal Path

Time	3hr
Distance	6.9km/4.3 miles
Ascent/descent	450m/450m
Grade	2
Map	Island map (from the ferry ticket office or cafés)
Start/finish	Marettimo village
Access	The most distant of the Egadi islands, Marettimo is still well served by a daily ferry and several hydrofoils a day in high season. See the Isole Egadi introduction for more information.

Cluttered around its humble harbours and facing inland as though to put up a permanent wall to the sea front, the unpretentious, drab village of Marettimo has little of the character of similarity to a quintessential Mediterranean settlement. But then the island itself is in a class of its own, and quite unlike the others in the Egadi group. Looming out in open sea, but visible from Trapani on the mainland despite the 21 nautical miles, it is to all effects and purposes, a massive, craggy mountain that rises out of the depths dwarfing the sole tiny settlement all but squeezed in under the rocky flanks. Relatively young limestone and dolomite (2 million geological years) soar to dramatic heights, culminating in 686m Pizzo Falcone, with sheer rock towers and cliffs, their bases weathered into spectacular marine caves lapped by turquoise water. Rugged, harsh and spectacularly beautiful best describe Marettimo, the island par excellence for getting away from it all, and a walker's paradise to boot.

In the absence of roads, a skeleton system of paths once used by hunters and herdsmen climb the ridges and valleys, now looked after by the Forestry Department. All other access around the island is by boat, the brightly painted and somewhat frail-looking, round-hulled craft traditionally used by the island's hardy fishermen, who are also in great demand for the prize lobster they procure.

A reliable series of fresh-water springs boost animal and plant life alike, and even the least flora-minded visitor cannot fail to have their senses saturated by the fragrant masses of wild herbs, such as thyme, apparently responsible in part for the island's current name (*mare* means sea, while *timo* is thyme), which replaced the name the ancient Greeks gave it, Hiera, for a sacred place. It was also called Malitimah, plausibly for unparalleled wealth, by the medieval traveller Ibn Jubayr. The list of plants reportedly totals 515 Mediterranean types, including over-sized exemplars of rosemary, tree heather, euphorbia domes, lentisc, everlasting and colourful rock roses. While admiring this stupendous array, the chances are good for an encounter with a shiny black snake, though its fierce appearance belies its harmlessness. As regards bird life, seagulls are not absent, though a considerable number of birds of prey can also be counted, their quarry often wild rabbits. A small number of elusive mouflon survive here, a wild sheep native to the Mediterranean.

In terms of the people – a core population of 300 hardy souls – a great sense of community prevails, and this is warmly extended to visitors who find themselves all but adopted by host families. The absence of hotels means accommodation is a simple apartment or spotless shuttered room in the home of the locals. Advance booking is recommended late July–August, while at other times the owners will be waiting at the quay to offer lodgings when the ferries come in. Other facilities include a handful of grocery shops and excellent, modestly priced eating establishments.

While the walk itself is not excessively difficult, remember there is little shade along the way and some effort is required for the series of modest climbs and drops. A delightful way to vary the walk (which returns along the same route) is to hire a boat for the outward trip (taking in some of the marine caves) then walk back. Sturdy shoes with a good grip are recommended and swimming gear can come in handy.

THE WALK

Take the main street through the **village of Marettimo** past the renowned Il Veliero restaurant for the *scalo vecchio* (old port) on the northernmost edge. Turn left past Trattoria Il Pirata to the

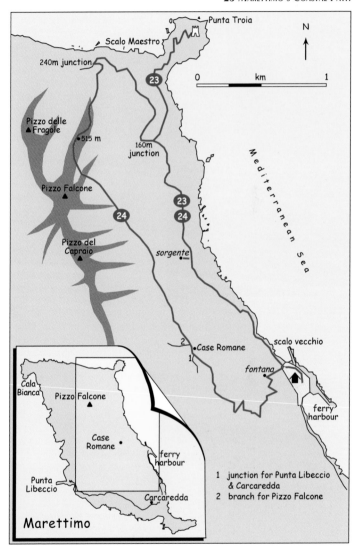

N

Punta Troia

Scalo Maestro

240m junction

23

0   km   1

Pizzo delle
▲ Fragole

• 515 m

160m
junction

M
e
d
i
t
e
r
r
a
n
e
a
n

Pizzo Falcone ▲

23

24

Pizzo del
Capraio ▲

sorgente
•

S
e
a

24

2   • Case Romane

1

scalo vecchio

fontana •

ferry
harbour

Cala
Bianca

Pizzo Falcone ▲

Case
Romane •

ferry
harbour

Punta
Libeccio

Carcaredda

Marettimo

1   junction for Punta Libeccio
    & Carcaredda
2   branch for Pizzo Falcone

Marettimo village and view to Punta Troia

Boat hire: c/o Il Veliero restaurant
Tel 0923-923195

Accommodation
I Delfini
Tel 0923-923137
La Perla
Tel 0923-923206

last houses, where a wide red track then proceeds in a northwesterly direction across the meagre grazing area for the island's surviving mule population. Amongst fragrant wind-swept pines a signpost for Castello Punta Troia confirms that this delightful coastal route leads to that distant rocky, island-like promontory Punta Troia, its light grey point merging with the ruins of a castle. Equipped with a rustic timber handrail, the path starts the first of its innumerable brief climbs through scattered rock and varied dense shrub cover. High above is a rugged mountain crest, while below is the divine deep blue sea. A very promising start.

Some 30min along, a signed fork uphill indicates a **sorgente**, a precious fresh water spring in a curious overhang featuring a miniature madonna and shaded by a huge carob tree. Back on the main path, after more ins and outs, ups and downs, a signed junction is reached (160m, 50min) for the high-level link path with the Case Romane (see Walk 24). Keep straight on towards the pointed triangular headland by firstly rounding another point then embarking on the crazy zigzags of the built-up path that plunges through a veritable carpet of yellow blooms to the neck of land. To the left is an inviting pebble beach at Scalo Maestro (but beware of tar deposits on the rocks).

The final 20min entail the winding climb to the castle itself on the **Punta Troia** cape (120m, 1hr 30min). Though there is nothing of great antiquity, despite its boast of 17th-century Spanish heritage, the setting itself is dramatic and panoramic to say the least. With seagulls wheeling overhead, the multi-storeyed constructions that creep up the rocky point are quite evocative. Used as a prison until recently, it has since been colonised by fluffy-flowered caper plants. Quite an incredible spot.

Return along the same path to the **village**.

WALK 24
Marettimo's High-Level Circuit

Time	3hr + various extensions
Distance	7.8km/4.9 miles
Ascent/descent	540m/540m
Grade	3
Map	Island map (from the ferry ticket office or cafés). See Walk 23 for sketch map of the route.
Start/finish	Marettimo village
Access	See Walk 23.

This loop route climbs along the rugged northeast coast of Marettimo, leading into a setting of craggy-ridged mountains worlds away from the typical gentle Mediterranean landscapes. Naturally there are regular reminders of the proximity of the sea, with stupendous plunging views onto turquoise coves and the chance for a swim on the final section for those who opt for the Punta Troia extension. Dense vegetation cover akin to a jungle is traversed, with pretty rock roses, heather, lentisc and dominant rosemary shrubs. Energetic walkers can extend the circuit with the ascent to the island's highest peak, 686m Pizzo Falcone (an extra 2–3hr).

All in all the route is lengthy and best embarked on at an early hour on hot days. The path is clear for the most part and rates average on difficulty, with several partially exposed passages and some steep descents. Walking boots with a good tread are essential, as are drinking water and sun protection.

THE WALK

Set out from the **village** on Marettimo heading northwest for the *scalo vecchio*. Turn up past the Trattoria Il Pirata then take the road left that climbs past the school and leads to the **fontana**, the spring identifiable by the mass of geraniums trying to suffocate it. From here bear left for a paved lane above the houses, signposted for Pizzo Falcone – Semaforo (where you turn right). The subsequent climb is constant but easy, and passes into the island's sole conifer wood for some rare shade. After a southerly stretch you head northwest, ascending decidedly, high over the settlement. Clear days mean views to the looming bulk of the other Egadi islands, Favignana and Levanzo, shadowed by Monte San Giuliano and Erice on the Sicilian mainland. A little over half an hour brings you to the signed junction for Punta Libeccio, Carcaredda and Semaforo – keep straight ahead for the nearby **Case Romane** (240m, 40min). This curious cluster of low houses, marvellously positioned, probably dates back to the 1st century, when a strategic Roman garrison was based here; the houses feature characteristic – if fragmentary – stone work.

The path for Pizzo Falcone (or 'Punta' or 'Monte' as it is alternately referred to) breaks off diagonally left now (allow 2–3hr for the return trip), whereas this itinerary continues straight ahead on the narrowing path, unpaved now and signposted for Taurro. The going quickly becomes wilder and the path is a bit exposed at times, though always clear. While constantly very high above the glittering sea, it passes beneath a series of peaks with the evocative names of Pizzo del Capraro ('goat-herd'), Falcone ('hawk') and Fragole ('strawberries'), where it touches on a maximum height of 515m above sea level. Soon afterwards it begins to cut the flank of a crest with bird's-eye views of the castle on the Punta Troia headland, and transits via a saddle (marked by a green–yellow flag) in a particularly rugged setting. The ensuing descent begins gradually, right via a scenic ridge, and is not as exposed at it initially appears. A brief clamber through a rock passage is involved at a breathtaking point close to a sheer dolomite pillar towering over the sea. The path threads its way between artistically eroded outcrops honeycombed with caves, eventually dropping left of a rocky point to zigzag down to a strategic **junction at 240m** (1hr 50min).
◀ Take the right fork.

The left variant (experts only, rough going, overgrown and exposed stretches) leads to Cala Bianca, a stunning cove on the northwestern side of the island).

Due east initially, the path leads beneath a sheer wall which shelters curious plant life such as aromatic rue and centaury, with its delicate pink five-pointed star flowers. Then it effects a magnificent swing towards the northeastern coast before a steep slippery descent to the **160m junction** with the Punta Troia route (2hr 10min).

(At this point the extension north for the castle and **Punta Troia** is feasible, as is a rewarding dip at the Scalo Maestro pebble beach, before embarking on the return route to the village. This means an overall total of 4hr 15min.)

The direct return means turning right here for the delightful coastal walk back to the village in just under an hour (grand total 3hr) – see Walk 23 for more details.

Bird's-eye view over the castello *promontory from the high path*

Accommodation: see Walk 23

Further Walks

Marettimo has marked paths for several other destinations worth exploring. Punta Libeccio (named after the gusty southwesterly wind) and its lighthouse, on the opposite coast to the village, can be reached via a lengthy high route from the signed junction near the Case Romane. After a swim, the return can be effected by way of a rough vehicle track that sweeps around the coast and back to the port – allow a full day and take a map.

Another plausible shorter walk branches off south at the above-mentioned junction and leads to Carcaredda, before dropping to the coastal track and returning to the village, all in a matter of hours.

THE GLORIOUS NORTHWEST

WALK 25
Marvellous Medieval Erice

Time	1hr 30min
Distance	4km/ 2.5 miles
Grade	1
Map	Town map from tourist office
Start/finish	Porta Trapani
Access	A funivia gondola car lift runs from the eastern outskirts of Trapani up to Erice (www.funiviaerice.it). Otherwise take an AST bus. Drivers from Trapani can choose between the SS 187 to Valderice then the signposted ascent, or the narrower but more scenic road via Casa Santa. A recently waymarked route (path n.601) via Santuario Sant'Anna allows walkers to make the 661m/5.5km climb in 2hr 20min. See www.sicilytrekkingtour.it.

Hercules was taking time off between labours, enjoying a rare stopover in Sicily with his herds when one of his prized white oxen inadvertently strayed into Erice territory. When Eryx (mythical Elymian king and founder of the town, not to mention offspring of Venus (Aphrodite) and Bute) determined to keep it for himself, the two embarked on a protracted struggle which ended in Eryx being strangled. He was buried beneath the temple of his making dedicated to Venus, based on a local Greek cult of Aphrodite, and famed throughout the ancient Mediterranean. Pilgrims and sailors would flock to the sanctuary for the animal sacrifices and the *hieròdulai*, the sacred harlots who doubled as the high priestesses.

Notwithstanding the convoluted course of its ancient origins, Erice is primarily medieval in appearance these days. After undergoing fortification by the Phoenicians and contestation by Carthage, Rome and Siracusa, it was occupied by the Saracens, who renamed it Gebel-Hamad. However, the successive ruler was the decisive hand. The Norman Roger I conquered it in the 11th century, calling it Monte San Giuliano, after the saint who appeared to the count in a vision during the siege. (The name Erice was restored in 1934.) The town grew and prospered, as testified by the marvellously intact religious and noble buildings in stone from that time. The cathedral occupies an unusually off-centre position for the town's principal religious venue, in the southwestern corner, explained by one theory as deliberate attempt to counteract the influence of the long-frequented heathen temple in the far southeastern angle. A medieval treat if ever there was one, the town has been described by Carlo Levi as 'The Assisi of southern Italy, filled with churches, convents, quiet passages and an unusual concentration of mythological memories.' The triangular layout encloses meandering cobbled streets and covered passageways, terracotta tiled roofs and swarms of chattering swallows.

The town's attractiveness is due in part to its breathtaking panoramic position at 751m above the sea on a level-topped mountain which comprises regular layers of Jurassic-era limestone over a tufaceous base. Unless enveloped in its trademark cloud, in blatant contrast to the sparkling coast, Erice affords stunning views over Trapani, the Egadi islands and a vast extension of coastline that takes in the colourful salt pans stretching towards Marsala as well as the Golfo di Bonagia (northeast), with landmark Monte Cofano and San Vito lo Capo nestling beneath Monte Monaco. The drive up is a wonderful experience in itself. The 14km road winds its way up the eastern mountain flank cloaked with soft pine woods and shrubs of fragrant broom.

The walk itself – a must – amounts to a pleasant stroll in and around the town. Inviting alleyways, courtyards and gardens beckon the leisurely visitor. Modest ups and downs are included. From the northernmost point, Porta Spada, an additional marked 4.5km loop (n.602) with 250m height gain is now feasible outside the walls via three churches. See www.sicilytrekkingtour.it. It is perfect as a day trip from Trapani, an excellent transport hub, where accommodation and meals are cheaper. Though Erice was renowned for its health-giving springs in olden times, the town's fountains are now dry, so take your own drinking water!

In addition to its medieval delights, international reputation as a nuclear scientific congress centre, ceramics, handmade rugs, 360° views and cool air, Erice has developed the local art of pastry-making, and countless cafés offer

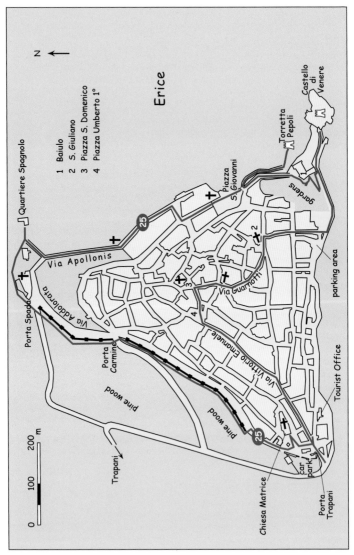

Erice

1 Baiulo
2 S. Giuliano
3 Piazza S. Domenico
4 Piazza Umberto 1°

panoramic terraces where you can try all sorts of delectables made with almonds, pistachios, dried figs, sultanas and citrus fruits. The originals are reputedly those made by the convent and known as 'Dolci di Badia'. Restaurants serving traditional Trapani dishes are not in short supply either.

THE WALK

Get off the bus or the gondola at the main car park of Erice (751m), close to **Porta Trapani**, one of its three ancient gateways. Enter the town precincts via the cobbled street, keeping left for the graceful 14th-century **Chiesa Matrice**, whose facade is embellished with a lovely rose window. Opposite is the *campanile* (bell-tower) with its elegant gothic arches, erstwhile watch-tower and even prison.

Leave the town's inner realms for the moment and follow the signs for Porta Carmine, which take you along the lane north flanking old walls on the edge of the shady pine wood that encloses the township. A shady path can soon be joined outside the actual wall. **Porta Carmine** is an arched gateway, part of a stretch of old walling with 8th–6th century BC remnants embedded in it, and even the odd inscription in Punic script can be found. From here either continue down the path or just inside the gateway take the wide flight of stone steps (Via Addolorata) shaded by taller walls. This leads to peaceful **Porta Spada** and a cluster of old churches. The graceful arches of the gate here offer lovely views of the sea and flowered hillsides. The path drops below a rocky point to a marvellous lookout, before climbing around to the isolated outcrop hosting the former **Quartiere Spagnolo** (Spanish quarter). The buildings are derelict but the views across the Golfo di Bonagia, Monte Cofano and beyond are brilliant.

Go up the lane and onto Via Apollonis, so named for the *piscina* (pool) at a small church en route. Flanked by colourful broom, mallow and poppies, this road leads back to the town in the direction

Porta Spada

This distinctly Arab-looking church dates back to the 12th century, though it underwent repeated reconstruction over the centuries.

of a Moorish church. You curve up to tarmac, and branch left for the **Chiesa S. Giovanni** set amongst shady trees. ◄

Go straight through the square (Piazza S. Giovanni) and take the narrowing path left through the overgrown wood for the eccentric **Torretta Pepoli**, set against the lower reaches of the castle. It was the work of 19th-century town mentor Count Pepoli, who was responsible for the magnificent gardens above. Return along the path to join the flight of steps leading to the spread of the beautifully laid-out English-style gardens and another medieval towered edifice, originally the residence of the Norman governor, the Baiuolo. Straight after it cut down the ramp left for access to the so-called **Castello di Venere** (castle of Venus) on its prominent isolated point, and originally accessible solely by way of a suspension bridge. Formerly the site of the ancient acropolis, it too affords wide-ranging views. The actual castle here dates back to 12th–13th centuries, and incorporates a great deal of ancient material. At the summit of the entry stairs, the old door is directly overlooked by the family crest of Charles V, not to mention a deadly slit opening for molten lead and other 'welcoming' gestures. The massive defensive walling on the left of the door dates back to Phoenician times. The inner realms, an open area, is believed to have been the site of the famous temple of Venus. A well and remnants of a Punic dwelling and Roman mosaics from a spa have been unearthed.

Once out of the castle premises, take the lower road west below the gardens. Just before the parking area turn right up steps which then become a narrow road leading two blocks up to **Chiesa di S. Giuliano**. Go left here along the tight cobbled lane (soon Via Guarnotti) curving up past the Chiesa di S. Pietro, joined by a bridge passageway to its former monastery (nowadays part of the Centro Internazionale di Cultura Scientifica 'E. Majorana'), past pretty houses and restaurants to **Piazza S. Domenico** and the 15th-century church of the same name. On the right corner is the renowned Pasticceria del Convento.

Tourist Office
Erice
Tel 0923-869388

Accommodation
Villa San Giovanni
Tel 0923-869171
Antico Borgo
Tel 0923-860145
B&B Agorà
Tel 0923-860133

Go left along Via Antonio Cordici past souvenir shops to the main square, **Piazza Umberto 1°**, with the *municipio* and museum of local interest.

From the square, Via Vittorio Emanuele (left) (also known as the Via Regia) leads back down past more enticing cafés and pastry shops to **Porta Trapani**, where you started.

WALK 26

*Riserva Naturale
di Monte Cofano*

Time	3hr (1hr less with a car)
Distance	11km/6.9 miles
Ascent/descent	250m/250m
Grade	2
Start/finish	Cornino
Access	AST buses from Trapani via Bonagia stop at the lower part of Custonaci, less than 2km from Cornino, where the walk starts. The other bus to Custonaci via Valderice, along with the S. Vito run, passes through the upper main part of the village, meaning an extra 2km on foot. Runs are rare on Sundays and public holidays. Drivers from Trapani will need the coastal road via Bonagia. The turn-off for Monte Cofano (and consequently Cornino) is below Custonaci. From San Vito lo Capo, on the other hand, take the main road south for Purgatorio and Custonaci, then downhill for Cornino.

The hermits who dwelt in the caves around Monte Cofano were famous in the 1800s for freeing the possessed of their demons. Powerful mysterious forces have clearly long been at work on this majestic limestone headland jutting out between Golfo di Bonagia and Golfo del Cofano to the north of Trapani. A chapel and shrine adorn its seaward cliffs, and a 'miraculous' episode from the Sicilian Vespers in the 13th century saw revolutionary forces beat the French occupiers around little-known Passo di la Zita in the cliffside. Nowadays the miracles come in the guise of the Riserva Naturale di Monte Cofano, which will ensure the survival of this uncontaminated angle of paradise from roads and the encroachment of the voracious neighbouring marble quarries, which, on the other hand, spell the economic mainstay of the region. A surprising number (325) and variety of floral species have been identified here, including many rare and even endemic types. Birds of prey are reportedly at home on the towering limestone crags, while the odd colony of rare monk seals was known to sojourn along the rocky coast until recent times. Two superb late medieval watch towers stand out on the promontory, along with an old *tonnara* (fish processing plant), witness to the formerly thriving industry. Earlier still Phoenician vessels plying between Palermo and the Egadi islands had a port of call in the area. Sites on Monte Cofano have provided a surprising wealth of evidence of prehistoric settlement, as a visit to Palermo's Museo Regionale Archeologico can attest. One of these, the Grotta Mangiapane, near the hamlet of Scurati, was the source of a great quantity of flint and worked stone from the late palaeolithic era. The unusual cave also shelters a miniature hamlet, a cluster of stone houses gathered in a dramatic gaping cleft, the venue of a yearly living nativity scene (*presepio vivente*) and occasionally a living folk museum (*museo vivente*).

The walk itself entails a circumnavigation of 659m Monte Cofano's headland on good, fairly clear paths, with a couple of swims easily slotted in en route. It concludes with a rewarding traverse of a 200m pass that affords some marvellous views all around this lovely coastline. In contrast to the justly famous Riserva Naturale dello Zingaro (see Walk

Monte Cofano

27), walkers are unheard of here, and only the odd fisherman and shepherd encountered. Sunday picnickers don't usually stray far from the beach or their cars.

It is easily arranged as a day trip from either Trapani or San Vito lo Capo. Any time except mid-summer is suitable, though the proximity to the sea is usually a guarantee of a breeze. The vegetation is obviously at its best in spring. The shops in the villages en route to the reserve can satisfy picnic needs, otherwise the café/restaurants at Cornino can be used. Car-borne walkers can start the route at Cala Buguto then return for their vehicles from the junction at the foot of the quarries.

The Walk

From the **bus stop** and Cornino–Custonaci junction, turn seawards (northwest) for the scattering of rustic seafood restaurants and snack bars that make up the fishing hamlet of **Cornino**. The landmark promontory Monte Cofano extends into the divine turquoise waters of the Golfo di Bonagia, while to its right, in dramatic contrast, the ridge is being sliced into by the quarries. Turn right along the seafront for **Cala Buguto** with its pretty sandy beach, then the **parking area** (30min).

A clear trail well used by fishermen follows the rocky coastline indented by countless inlets. However, you soon need to leave it to make your way inland to a prominent boulder and **ruined house** to join a rough red-earth vehicle track heading north-northwest. The vegetation is a thick, low, compact mat of dwarf palms and pungent wild thyme, while straggly caper plants have draped themselves over all available stone surfaces. The track narrows and climbs slowly across steeper flanks to imposing **Torre del Cofano** (45min), erected in the 1600s as a watchtower. High above the beautiful turquoise sea a clear path rounds the headland. Keep left at a fork for a brief drop to an unexpected **chapel**, followed by a passage around the Arabic-sounding point **Passo di la Zita** (also known as Punta del Saraceno) – a beautiful spot. Ahead northwest is another photogenic headland, Monte Monaco, which dominates the seaside resort of San Vito lo Capo. Veritable cushions of aster with striking yellow petals bedeck the pale limestone walls, while oregano, rock roses, spurge and yellow thistles brighten the lower reaches.

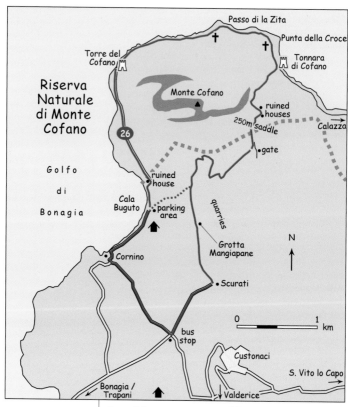

Around the next point (**Punta della Croce**) is a huge fig tree sheltering an old shrine to San Nicola di Bari, patron saint of fishermen and sailors.

Abandoned terracing precedes a rise then a short drop to the impressive **Tonnara di Cofano** (1hr 30min), a massive squat tower once part of an extensive fish processing plant. There is a scattering of modest holiday houses and a couple of suitable spots for a dip. (From the here a dirt track leads east around the coast, dotted with swimmable coves, to Calazza and on to Macari – a total of 7.3km – an alternate exit point and bus stop for the line to San Vito lo Capo.)

From behind the tower, follow the wall topped with barbed wire then head south across arid rocky terrain where the odd carob tree survives – your destination of the saddle is clearly visible alongside Monte Cofano. A clear path soon appears, zigzagging up the right side of this ample valley, where you find yourself brushing against waving stands of soft grass. After 20min a ruined house is encountered, with wonderful views east to the Monte Passo del Lupo chain. Continue climbing in the same direction to another modest building then turn sharp right, heading back towards Monte Cofano itself. A clear path is joined for the final stretch to the actual **saddle** (250m, 2hr), where pasture gives way to rock on the edge of the quarries. Ahead, overlooking the Golfo di Bonagia, the hill town of Erice is outlined on Monte San Giuliano (in all likelihood enveloped in its trademark cloud) while the island of Levanzo lies out to sea.

A descent track bears left towards a gate, but before reaching it a path breaks off right (southwest) through scruffy terrain. At a low building further down, keep left at a fork onto a wider track. This leads to flatter ground. At the subsequent junction keep left (south) around the base of the ridge and the quarries. (To return directly to Cala Buguto, keep straight on past a housing estate then right along the seafront to the car park.) Not far along is **Grotta Mangiapane**, followed by the hamlet of **Scurati**. Left (southwest) leads back to the **bus stop** where the walk started (3hr total).

Wonderful views on the Cofano walk

Tourist Office San Vito lo Capo
Tel 0923-972464 (summer and holidays only)
Trapani
Tel 0923-29000

Accommodation
Custonaci: B&B Baglio Mangiapane
Tel 0923-971859
Scurati: Hotel Cala Buguto
Tel 0923-973953

WALK 27
Riserva Naturale dello Zingaro

Time	5hr
Distance	16km/10 miles
Ascent/descent	600m/600m
Grade	2
Start/finish	North entrance
Access	Drivers can approach the area from Palermo via the A29 *autostrada*, exit for Castellammare whence Scopello. From Trapani for San Vito Lo Capo, start out on the SS 187, then follow minor roads via Custonaci and Castelluzzo. The north entrance is 11km from the resort of San Vito Lo Capo on a clearly signed minor road. This in turn is reachable by either daily Russo bus from Castellamare del Golfo, or the weekdays-only AST service from Trapani. Some hotels may run a shuttle bus the 11km to the reserve entrance. Walkers using public transport are better off using Scopello; the south entrance is 2km from the charming village. Scopello is accessible by AST bus from Castellammare del Golfo, in turn served by AST or the Russo bus company, as well as train from Palermo or Trapani.

Some of the most beautiful coastline in Sicily is ensconced in the vast sweep of the Golfo di Castellammare. Its crystal-clear sapphire waters are accessible by way of inviting idyllic white sand and pebble coves, edged by bands of lush vegetation and overshadowed by stunning limestone cliffs and reliefs. A 7km stretch is safely established as the Riserva Naturale Orientata dello Zingaro. Sicily's very first protected nature area, it came into being after a 1980 march of nature lovers made the headlines and put paid to the construction of a coastal road that would have gored its destructive way through this magnificent angle of paradise to link the resort villages of Scopello and San Vito Lo Capo on an isolated headland.

The area totals 1650 hectares, rises to a maximum elevation of 913m above sea level, and hosts a grand total of 700 plant species (20 of which are endemic or rare), 39 species of nesting birds and miscellaneous animals. Spring walkers will be delighted by the glorious cloak of green and yellow of the Mediterranean maquis species, along with superb wild orchids. A number of native plant species were once cultivated by the former inhabitants of the scattered hill hamlets: olive, carob and manna ash, visible with gashes in its trunk for gathering the sugary sap. On the other hand, tannin for leather preparation was extracted from the leaves and bark of the sumach shrub. Still widely practised in the area is the art of weaving baskets and making rope and brooms from dried strands of the fan-shaped fronds of the dwarf palm, which grows in massive clumps throughout the reserve. A final mention is due a sturdy plumed grass (*Ampelodesmos tenax*), *disa* in Sicilian dialect, whose fibres were used like string and horse-hair, while pasta was wrapped around its woody twigs to give maccheroni its characteristic shape!

The pride of the reserve in terms of bird life are the rare pairs of Bonelli's eagles at home on the limestone crags, though visitors on the upper path can expect to see the fast-flying peregrine falcon, the majestic buzzard or smaller kestrel, without forgetting the Sicilian rock partridge camouflaged on stony terrain. Regarding animals, wild rabbits are fairly common, their numbers kept in check by foxes, then there's a harmless black snake and the potentially dangerous viper, whose diamond markings are its characteristic warning sign. Porcupines leave behind striated quills, while the odd wild boar betrays itself through its chaotic rootings and digging. Legendary playful monk seals were a common sight off the coast up to the 1970s, but fishing and tourism have apparently driven them away, despite the offshore limit for all motorised craft. Plans are underfoot to instate a marine reserve.

The walk described here starts out from the quieter northern entrance of the Riserva dello Zingaro, though Scopello in the south with plentiful accommodation makes a perfect entry point, particularly for those travelling with public transport. This is a marvellously varied route, strenuous at times, through stark surrounds and dramatic scenery. In midsummer there may be a fire danger and restrictions on walking, as the tinder dry maquis burns with ardour; new growth is astonishingly vigorous and fast and lost

Turquoise coves in the Zingaro

cover quickly replaced. Path routes can be modified by fire damage as well as torrential rain and ensuing landslips, so allowances should be made for variations indicated by provisional signage.

Copious amounts of drinking water (and of course food) are essential for the walk as supply points inside the realms of the reserve should not be relied on. Sun protection and swimming gear are recommended, and footwear should include comfortable light-weight boots. In hot weather it is best to limit the walk to the coastal section with its delightful coves, as the upper realms involve a number of ascents and descents on shadeless terrain. If possible avoid public holidays and Sundays as the bays and picnic areas get crowded. For further information see www.riservazingaro.it Tel 800-116616 or 0924-35108.

A modest fee is exacted for entrance to the *riserva*, and an interesting brochure (in English) on sale (though the map is fairly useless). A good range of accommodation is available at both Scopello and San Vito Lo Capo, and includes camping grounds. Moreover for adventurous self-caterers, atmospheric *rifugi* huts located at Contrada Sughero inside the reserve, can be requested October–May.

THE WALK

From the **north entrance** (75m), you are plunged straight into the wonderful Zingaro atmosphere as the path immediately leaves behind any idea of 'civilisation' and leads high above the sparkling sea with wide-reaching views right across the Golfo di Castellammare, and there are promising wild hills inland. Massive bushes of scented rosemary, along with dwarf palms and wild gladioli, precede the first junction (15min), from where you need the uphill branch for Borgo Cosenza. A desolate broad gully is climbed in a westerly direction, and drinking water encountered some 25min up at 210m. ▶

Despite tall, soft grasses and shrubs, there is little shade and the going can be hot.

Riserva Naturale dello Zingaro

N

0   1 km

After 1hr 10min the path reaches a shoulder (450m) where you fork left for **Borgo Cosenza**. This isolated hamlet is still used occasionally by shepherds, and in fact goats, bee hives and fields of cultivated cereals are not an unusual sight. A 150-year-old grindstone for grapes has been found here. Just past the buildings a sign for Loc. Sughero shows the way (southeast) in gradual descent on a narrow path over the light, limestone-based terrain studded with the surprising crimson and pink star-shaped flowers of stonecrop, not to mention the odd red paint splash. Below

Walking in the Zingaro reserve

is a beautiful cove. At the fork (and link to the coastal path) near scattered huts, keep straight on in continuing descent to the nearby hamlet of **Sughero** (cork, 1hr 50min, 270m), a huddle of buildings (several beautifully restored for use by visitors), shaded by ageing almond and a spreading carob tree. (Here, too, a path branches off heading for the coast – your last chance!)

After crossing a shallow gully, the path climbs high to dizzying reaches on the southern slope of Pizzo Passo del Lupo (wolf) through patchy oaks along with rock roses and orchids again. You ascend to 360m above sea level on **Pizzo del Corvo** (crow) over sheer cliffs that plunge to the aquamarine sea, and Scopello comes into view. Sizeable birds of prey also appreciate these heights.

Not far along fork downhill for the clear

zigzagging path that drops all the way down to a small museum and the **visitor centre** (105m, 3hr), above inviting Cala della Caprera. (The path south from here leads via an incongruous tunnel, a reminder that the road-building project was actually well underway when the protests were launched, to the **south entrance** and **Scopello**.)

Go left on the more popular and spectacular stretch north now, where the cliffside path links a divine series of coves at the foot of imposing sheer cliffs. Cala della Disa owes its name to the afore-mentioned grass. Clumps of fan-shaped dwarf palms, domes of tree spurge and wild fennel accompany the path.

Further on are impressive agave alongside prickly pears, turpentine and mastic trees on a shady stretch leading to the scatter of dwellings known as **Zingaro**, with a number of manna ash trees. More attractive inlets follow, and after rounding a point the picturesque Torre Uzzo comes into sight. One of the links with the Sughero hamlet on the slopes above is passed, while the path descends gradually with a wooden balustrade on the approach to the amazing cavernous **Grotta dell'Uzzo** cave (70m, 4hr 30min). It sheltered Palaeolithic and Mesolithic man 10,000 years ago, and still serves as a sheepfold and as a nesting site for noisy swarms of swallows and pigeons.

There are orchards of almond trees, pomegranates and the curious prickly plant of the nightshade family, bearing poisonous shiny yellow plum fruit, around the long-abandoned district of Uzzo. At this point a pleasant alternative is to leave the principal path for the lower route hugging the coast past the Cala della Torre dell'Uzzo and close to the former tuna works, **Tonnarella dell'Uzzo**. (However walkers who started out at Scopello should stick to the main track so as not to miss the fork for the climb to Borgo Cosenza.) The main path is rejoined through the rosemary bushes for the final stretch back to the **north entrance** (total 5hr).

Tourist Office
San Vito lo Capo
Tel 0923-972464
(summer and hols)

Accommodation
San Vito lo Capo:
Pensione Sabbia
d'Oro
Tel 0923-972508
Tannure
Tel 0923-974240
Scopello:
B&B Casale Corcella
Tel 368-3654482
**www.casalecorcella.
com**
Pensione Tavernetta
Tel 0924-541129
**www.albergola
tavernetta.it**
Affittacamere
Mazzara
Tel 0924-541135

PALERMO SURROUNDS
WALK 28
Palermo's Monte Pellegrino

Time	2hr
Distance	7.7km/4.8 miles
Ascent	400m
Grade	1–2
Map	1:50,000 'Palermo. Montagne della Conca d'Oro' (Palermo Tourist Office)
Start/finish	Casa Natura/Santuario S. Rosalia
Access	The AMAT city bus n.806 (destination Mondello) from Piazza Sturzo in Palermo's northwestern reaches, transits daily via the Parco della Favorita. Ask to be let off at the Casa Natura, a short distance (1.2km) before the Reserve Headquarters (*Sede Riserva*). For the return you need daily AMAT bus n.812.
	Those arriving by car will need the Palermo–Mondello road (Viale di Diana) through the Parco della Favorita. Parking is possible at the Casa Natura. However you will need to re-descend to the Parco della Favorita afterwards, meaning an extra 45min. **Note** This stretch of road is one-way, and a nearby parallel road covers the opposite direction.

The massive limestone headland of 600m Monte Pellegrino that towers over the northernmost edge of Palermo was said to be the most beautiful promontory in the world for Goethe. On the other hand, D.H. Lawrence saw 'a huge, inordinate mass of pinkish rock, hardly crisped with the faintest vegetation, looming up to heaven from the sea'. Considering the proximity of Sicily's chaotic capital city, it is nothing short of a miracle that the wooded reserve has survived relatively intact with a host of interesting plant and animal life. Thanks are due in part to the Bourbon King Ferdinand III, who established a 400-hectare royal game park and experimental agricultural centre at its foot in 1799. Though with shrunken proportions nowadays, the Parco della Favorita still occupies the elongated wooded area in the shade of the southwestern flanks of Monte Pellegrino. The sovereign was also responsible for eccentric constructions such as the richly decorated Palazzina Cinese (Chinese pavilion) in the park grounds, now a museum.

Since 1996 the mountain itself has been safeguarded as the 1020-hectare Riserva Naturale Orientata Regionale Monte Pellegrino (www.riservamontepellegrino.palermo.it). It is riddled with caves (134 in all), such as Grotta Niscemi, inhabited since prehistoric times, as witnessed by artefacts in Palermo's Museo Archeologico Regionale. The promontory has also played host to several key episodes in the history of Palermo: the first was in 3rd century BC when Hamilcar Barca, the famous general of Carthage (and father of Hannibal), made it his impenetrable stronghold during the First Punic War. He spent three long years attempting to wrest the city back from the Romans, as well as sending out naval expeditions to regain his country's Sicilian possessions from Rome.

However, of eminently greater significance in local lore were the travails of Santa Rosalia, Palermo's beloved patron saint. Born in Norman times (1160), she was allegedly betrothed to a noble but, desiring a life of meditation, fled to the wilds of Monte Pellegrino to lead the exemplary life of a hermit. Centuries later (1624) she appeared to a hunter in a vision and the cave was discovered housing her mortal remains, which a procession bore back to the city. Palermo was at the mercy of a devastating plague at the time, and Rosalia beat the top specialists in bubonic plague – St Sebastian and St Roch – in miraculously bringing it to a halt. She is revered by all as protector, and her cave and the adjacent sanctuary are flooded with devout pilgrims on September 4th.

A great deal of conjecture surrounds the meaning of the name of the mountain; while *pellegrino* means 'pilgrim' in Italian, one of the foremost theories links it to the peregrine falcon, a popular bird for falconry and favourite of King Frederick II. Another explanation is that the name derives from *peregrinus*, the term used by the Romans to designate 'enemy', in the wake of the episode involving the Carthaginians. To top it off, other contenders are the Arabic *gebel grin* for 'nearby mount', as well as *piddirinu*, namely 'isolated' in local dialect.

The walk does not involve any particular difficulty, although 400m is covered in ascent. Thanks to the good bus service it makes a rewarding and relaxing day trip from the bustle and haze of the city. It is advisable to carry drinking water in all weather, though a variety of snacks and meals is available at the sanctuary at the end.

THE WALK

From the bus stop on the main road a wide track leads in to the low-set **Casa Natura** (86m), former royal stables (*scuderie reali*), now a modest museum for equipment used in the royal agricultural experiments. Keep left of the building past the Torrione, a tower-like pavilion, and take the path through eucalypts towards the base of the rock face. You soon enter narrow cleft Valle del Porco ('pig' – presumably the wild boars from the days of hunting). The vegetation is unexpectedly lush and rich, with typical Mediterranean species – such as the domed-shaped spurge shrubs and oregano – and dwarf palms and prickly pear cactus clinging to the steep rock sides of the gully. It echoes with deafening bird

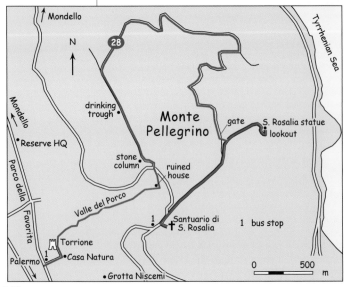

song and makes for a dramatic contrast to the throbbing city visible in the distance with its high-rise buildings. The odd red paint marking shows the way, which includes the occasional scramble, but nothing of consequence.

Continuing northeast, the path climbs to the left side of the valley and traverses a lovely shady pine wood. Proceed towards the **ruined house** that soon appears and take the stone-base track left to the nearby tarmac road (380m, 45min). ▶ Cross straight over and through a gate, then take the lane immediately left through another gate. This track curves right (north-northwest) – keep left at the ensuing fork, past a **stone column** and into a lightly wooded reforestation zone. It is planted with the drought-resistant Aleppo pine and hardy eucalpyts, and punctuated with a number of dolina depressions, characteristic of the limestone landscape. A **drinking trough** is followed by yet another fork, where you keep straight on before going right at the next junction. In gradual descent north-northeast then decidedly east, there are soon hints of promising sea views. As the vegetation becomes lighter and the track a little rougher, the distant island of Ustica comes into view due north. Giant wild fennel plants line the way, their woody stalks plastered with tiny snails collected for consumption by the locals, who will also be out after rain with their baskets in search of the delectable edible fungi that grow around the plant.

The right branch leads directly to the Santuario di S. Rosalia.

Several wide curves lead south and upwards onto a plateau akin to a vast graveyard due to a series of blanched limestone outcrops. The purple rosettes ringed by the crinkly dock-like leaves of the striking and poisonous mandrake plant are common here. The statue of Santa Rosalia soon comes into view southeast from a grazing area. A short stretch of pine wood follows. After a green gate leave the track and cut across the field left to the nearby road as it climbs in the direction of the huge figure. Tarmac for 10min will see you at the extraordinarily panoramic lookout dominated by the **statue of Santa Rosalia** (458m, 1hr 40min). The edge of Palermo with its gulf is backed by the long spread of the coast to Capo Zafferano and beyond, not to mention the mountainous hinterland.

Backtrack down the quiet road past the point where you joined it and continue on a little further to a fork left. Preceded by a string of souvenir stalls, snack stands, modest

Tourist Office
Palermo
Tel 091-583847

Accommodation
Mondello:
Conchiglia D'Oro
Tel 0931-450032
Palermo:
Hotel Cortese
Tel 091-331722,
Ballarò market
area, 10min from
the station

restaurants and the **bus stop**, is a flight of steps leading up to the **Santuario di Santa Rosalia** (429m, 2hr). A baroque convent and chapel dating back to 1625 have been grafted onto the rock face to shelter the cave where the saint spent her time in meditation. The large numbers of votive objects attest to her widespread popularity, while the stalactite-studded ceiling and walls have been blackened by centuries of candles from devotees and illustrious visitors including Goethe and royalty. The water dripping from the rock is believed to be miraculous and is thus channelled carefully away.

The return to Palermo by bus follows an immensely panoramic road high over the golden sand beach of Mondello, well worth the short detour for a dip.

Santuario di Santa Rosalia

WALK 29
Monte Iato

Time	2hr 30min
Distance	7km/4.4 miles
Ascent/descent	450m/400m
Grade	2
Map	1:50,000 map/brochure 'Percorsi storici e naturalistici della Valle dell'Iato' (from S. Cipirello museum or Palermo Tourist Office)
Start/finish	Municipio, San Cipirello /San Giuseppe Iato
Access	Monte Iato stands 30km southwest of Palermo. Both the starting point, San Cipirello, and nearby San Giuseppe Iato, the finish, are served by AST buses from Palermo. By car there's the handy freeway SS 624 'scorrimento Palermo–Sciacca' – leave it at the San Cipirello exit. **Note** The upper part of the Parco Archeologico (Perciana entrance) can also be reached by road, appropriately signposted east from San Cipirello.

Feasible as a day trip from Palermo unless you prefer to stay locally, this recommended circuit combines two rural townships and an archaeological site on a windswept mountain top. The elevated Parco Archeologico on the 40-hectare plateau of Monte Iato is approached by way of a straightforward ascent along a bare panoramic flank, while the ensuing return makes use of an evocative medieval way via a surprising side gully.

The ancient city known as Jaitas to the Greeks, Ietas to the Romans, Giatas to those in the early Middle Ages and now as Iato, actually boasted origins dating back to the 9th century BC, courtesy of the Elymian people. However, its heyday came in the 4th century BC when the major monuments were erected, notably a 4400-seat theatre (unearthed in 1971), agora, sanctuary and several elegant Hellenic-type dwellings. In the wake of Carthaginian occupation, the Romans took over the city for several centuries and brought considerable stability, before all slid into insignificance and decay. A sizeable fortified settlement flourished there during the Arab period from AD827, and evidence has come to light pointing to peaceful rapport between its Christian and Muslim residents, including intermarriage. In the early 13th century the town was a leader in the revolt against the Swabian domination, and that factor, combined with its strategic position dominating one of the essential access routes to Palermo, attracted the attention of King and Emperor Frederick II, who subjected it to a 'drawn-out' 20-year-long siege, along with neighbouring centres, before categorically razing it to the ground in 1246. Many starved to death; there are accounts of the discovery of emaciated infant skeletons in an evident anaemic state on the mountain site, as there was little left but grass for sustenance. The few Muslim survivors were given the choice of conversion or deportation to Puglia. Since that period the site has sporadically been frequented by shepherds and farmers, generations of whom have spent painstaking years clearing the stony rubble of bygone eras into orderly mounds, followed by the archaeologists who sift through those heaps. Excavation is ongoing under the supervision of the University of Zurich.

While the ruins themselves cannot hold a candle to those of Selinunte for example, the position itself is marvellous, with far-reaching views, and the experience is augmented by the solitude and desolation of the lofty site, in stark contrast to the lush fertile valley it dominates. On the other hand, the rather grim aspect of the adjoining townships touched on by the walk can be partially explained by the hasty reconstruction after the disastrous 1838 landslide from Monte Iato which buried a good two-thirds of San Giuseppe. Another factor was the area's long forced subjugation to a powerful local Mafia boss, finally put behind bars in the '90s; the district was even out of bounds to walkers. Nowadays these quiet backwaters are experiencing a modest degree of prosperity from recently established vineyards which produce a very drinkable table wine (San Cipirello) thanks largely to the construction of the nearby Lago Poma reservoir in the early 1970s. That took place in the wake of a bitter drawn-out struggle spearheaded by a grass-roots movement to 'legalise' the water supply and dam the River Iato for irrigation purposes.

Spring and autumn are the best periods for a visit and provide an escort of wild flowers. Winter, on the other hand, can mean both crystal clear visibility and bone-chilling winds sweeping the bare mountain ridge, whereas the mid-summer months are generally far too hot for the shadeless climb. **Note** Before setting out, it is a good idea to check with the San Cipirello museum that the Militi entrance is open.

Good accommodation is available in the vicinity, otherwise head for Piana degli Albanesi (see Walk 30).

THE WALK

The bus terminates close to a war memorial, not far from the **Municipio** building at San Cipirello (394m). Cross the elongated square Piazza Vittorio Veneto (northwest) and proceed along Via Garibaldi, past the inviting bakery that produces fragrant sesame rolls. Via Roma is soon encountered –detour briefly down left for the museum (10min), which features a pair of impressive two-metre limestone caryatid statues from the stage of the Greek theatre on Monte Iato. Moreover it's advisable to check here that the Militi entrance to the archaeological site is open – the staff will contact the custodians.

Back up Via Roma, it's a matter of minutes to the limited roadside parking area facing a flight of steps signed uphill for route n.3 for Monte Iato. At the top of the steps a narrow road curves left to the base of an old stone building known locally as the **Militi** (465m), as it once belonged to the Carabinieri, though since relegated for use as a stable. Turn right for the path that quickly leaves houses and chicken coops behind, climbing east across open hillside to the gate in the perimeter fencing around the Parco Archeologico (25min).

The clear path continues climbing gradually due east, marked by the odd wooden post topped with yellow and dark green paint. Behind is the glittering expanse Lago Poma and the distant Golfo di Castellammare. The sparsely grassed limestone terrain has been colonised by scented narcissus, striking purple thistles and slender white asphodel.

▶ A signed junction (650m, 45min) is set at the **'Vauso 'a morte'**, a slab of rock where in olden times coffins would be laid to rest temporarily while the bearers got their breath back en route to the former sanctuary of San Cosmo, to the east, for burial in the floor of the church.

The views south take in the extensive rolling hills and vineyards, almost reminiscent of the Chianti zone.

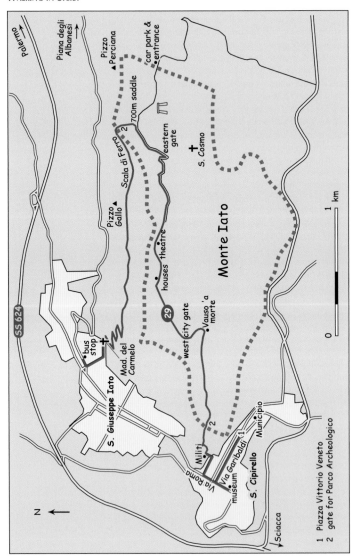

Piana degli Albanesi

Palermo

Pizzo Perciana ▲

car park & entrance

SS 624

700m saddle

Scala di Ferro

2

Pizzo Gallo ▲

eastern gate

✝ S. Cosmo

Monte Iato

bus stop

Mad. del Carmelo

S. Giuseppe Iato

houses theatre

29

Vauso 'a morte

west city gate

2

S. Cipirello

Militi

Via Roma

museum

Via Garibaldi

Municipio

Sciacca

1 km

0

N ←

1 Piazza Vittorio Veneto
2 gate for Parco Archeologico

Path n.3 breaks off uphill (north) for the ascent to the erstwhile fortified site. Bearing right (northeast) via the former **west city gate**, you enter the city proper, dotted with stone mounds. Make your way towards the uppermost ridge and fence (link with route n.2 to/from San Giuseppe Iato via a shady pine wood – Percorso Camposanto Vecchio). Not far over are the remains of the first house, then the more impressive second two-storey exemplary, complete with ancient bathroom, red stuccoed walling, terrazzo flooring and a peristyle (an erstwhile spacious colonnade-enclosed courtyard), along with water tanks and adjoining dye-room – over 1600 sq m in all. Next are the **theatre** and agora, punctuated with stumps of fluted columns and ancient debris (850m, 1hr 15min).

Next head for the guardian's building on the southern edge of the plateau and the stone track that winds down eastwards past more excavations and out of the main city site by way of the original **eastern gate**. The underlying knoll east is the site of a Hellenistic necropolis, and the vast outlook from here encompasses the neighbouring outcrop culminating in Pizzo Perciana. At a broad **saddle** (700m) with a bench, the dirt road continues right to the car park and only motorised entrance to the Parco Archeologico. However you need the concrete ramp up left leading out through the fenced zone to the northernmost limit of Monte Iato for the worn rock passage **Scala di Ferro** ('iron staircase', 1hr 40min). Once crowned by a stone arch, this evocative if brief tract once provided key access to the city for those arriving from Palermo. This sheltered northern aspect of Monte Iato is thick with a riot of vegetation, ranging from cyclamens and red valerian to young conifers from a reforestation project and unbelievably massive sprawling ivy plants.

Ignore a signed junction (for a roadside car park below), and on for the saddle south of modest Pizzo Gallo, chaotic with jackdaws. The decent path is a series of ups and downs, and the views now extend to Lago Poma and the gulf once more.

Once the path joins route n.2 (Percorso Camposanto Vecchio), it descends through trees. Keep straight on at a 4-way junction, then left at the next fork for the modest church **Madonna del Carmelo**. Turn left down Via Bellini, then right to make your way down the steps and concrete

Scala di Ferro passage

Museum
San Cipirello
Tel 091-8573083
open daily
9am–1pm, extended
to 6pm Tues, Thurs,
Sat – same for the
Sito Archeologico

Accommodation
Agriturismo near
S. Giuseppe Iato:
Casale del Principe,
Contrada Dammussi
Tel 091-8579910
Feudo Chiusa,
Contrada Chiusa,
Tel 091-8572747
Agriturismo near S.
Cipirello: Casale
dello Jato, Contrada
Percianotta
Tel 091-8582309

ramps to the main road through **San Giuseppe Iato** (470m, 2hr 30min). (The bus for Palermo stops outside Bar Terzo.)

Should you need to return to San Cipirello to collect your vehicle, go to the next street down, Via Umberto, and either catch the bus or take the shorter route on foot as the road soon becomes Via Roma in San Cipirello, as per the early stage of the walk (allow 20min extra).

WALK 30

Piana degli Albanesi

Time	3hr (2hr 30min with a car)
Distance	7.5km/4.7 miles
Ascent/descent	550m/550m
Grade	2
Maps	1:50,000 map/brochure 'Percorsi storici e naturalistici della Valle dello Iato', or maps 'Palermo Montagne della Conca d'Oro' or 'Corleone. Bosco della Ficuzza' (from San Cipirello or Palermo Tourist Office)
Start/finish	Bus stop opposite S. Demetrio church
Access	There are plenty of weekday buses to Piana degli Albanesi from Palermo's central railway station, courtesy of Prestia & Comandè. Piana degli Albanesi can be easily reached by car from several other walk locations, namely Ficuzza (Walk 31) and San Giuseppe Iato (Walk 29) via Portella della Ginestra. Otherwise from Palermo drivers should embark on the secondary road via Altofonte. Vehicles can be left on the outskirts of town, at the map-board at Chiesa dell'Odigitria, which means cutting 30min off the walk.

Piana degli Albanesi (plain of the Albanians), a sprawling, nondescript township set in a basin in the hilly hinterland of Palermo, was founded in the mid-15th century by Albanian nobles fleeing Turkish domination and persecution. This was not the only example of its kind, as an estimated one quarter of the population of Albania at that time settled in southern Italy as well as Dalmatia. The refugees received a warm reception as earlier anti-Arab campaigns had left the countryside all but deserted and the archbishop-proprietor was duly concerned about the dearth of labourers to work his land. The settlement originally called Hora (city) then Piana dei Greci (Greeks), became Piana degli Albanesi in 1941. The inhabitants continue to think of themselves as Albanians and even today speak an ancient version of their language. This is encouraged by the Greek Orthodox

Church, whose extended Byzantine-style rituals bring the town alive at Easter, when richly decorated traditional costumes are proudly paraded.

The surrounding ample, fertile basin-cum-plain is intensively cultivated thanks to the capacious dam constructed in 1923 and comprising a hydroelectric power station. Lago di Piana degli Albanesi has since taken on the added function of an important watering stop-over for migratory birds and has been declared a reserve under the protection of the World Wildlife Fund for Nature.

Masses of broom above Piana degli Albanesi

The walk itself strikes out across broom-laden hillsides for a circuit around the dominating mountain La Pizzutta, rarely visited. It was from the southern reaches of this rugged stony outcrop on 1 May 1947, in turbulent post-war

Sicily, that the enigmatic outlaw-cum-separatist-cum-Mafia ally Salvatore Giuliano, together with his band, opened fire with machine guns onto a group of festive peasants celebrating May Day and land reforms at Portella della Ginestra. The massacre left 11 dead and 54 wounded. The pass is aptly named for the unbelievably scented thickets of broom (*ginestra*) that smother the mountain sides here, making spring the best time to visit. Any later than May is inadvisable as it can get pretty muggy. Autumn on the hand (late September onwards) means enhanced visibility, while winter more often than not brings snow. The walk has been classified average on the difficulty scale as waymarking cannot always be located, making for difficulties in orientation magnified by the thriving undergrowth which, in combination with lack of passage to keep the way open, means overgrown paths; both long trousers and a compass are a good idea. In 1998 the zone was declared Riserva Naturale Orientata 'Serre della Pizzutta', and is managed by the Forestry Department. A total of 45 endemic plants have been identified, including the rare yellow *Viola ucraina*; the local Museo Civico has helpful displays.

Grocery shops in Piana degli Albanesi will make up picnic supplies with their renowned wholesome local bread, and those with a sweet tooth can indulge in the *cannoli* pastry tubes stuffed with rich sweetened ricotta.

Though the walk is feasible as a day trip from Palermo, accommodation is on offer at Piana degli Albanesi at a couple of B&Bs as well as scattered *agriturismi*. Portella della Ginestra can be used as an alternative access point, as a signed path climbs to the Neviere.

THE WALK

The bus drops you off in the main street of **Piana degli Albanesi** (640m) at a small park and cenotaph opposite the church of **San Demetrio**. Proceed uphill following the red and white SI (Sentiero Italia) signposting via Piazza Vittorio Emanuele and the richly adorned 17th-century church of the Madonna dell'Odigitria (not to be confused with the upper church where the actual trail starts). The road narrows to traverse the older, more interesting, part of town, and alleyways branch off to snake their way between clusters of neat old houses set at curious angles. After another church (S. Vito Martire) and a junction, keep straight up on Via Odigitria and a flight of steps and continue past drab newer housing and abandoned factories on the denuded slopes. Modest **Chiesa dell'Odigitria** is preceded by a map-board and signposting for walkers (770m, 15min, car parking).

Path n.17 forks left (southwest) below the church through a scraggly olive grove to a concrete lane coasting below rugged La Pizzutta. Waymarking comes in the form of squat wooden poles adorned with yellow and green paint stripes, though as you move onto a path the markers tend to be swallowed up by the overwhelming forest of

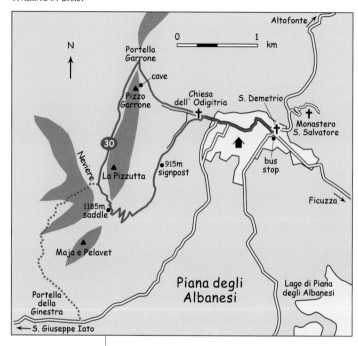

golden broom that all but smothers the mountainside. The spread of the lake below the Kumeta mountain, due south, comes into view. Keep a constant southerly direction in gradual ascent, and you'll hopefully reach a modest rise and clearing (20min from the church). The path then drops briefly across a small watercourse and resumes uphill again, at which point you branch right to leave the main path and battle your way through thick undergrowth west-southwest towards a fence and visible **yellow signpost** on the lower edge of a pine copse (10min, 915m). A brief clear stretch leads left (south) before the start of the climb, aided by more frequent marker poles now. A barbed wire fence bordering a diminutive pine plantation needs crawling under to reach the ample curves of an old overgrown mule track that zigzags its way west towards a clear saddle. The grassed terrain here includes flourishing thistles, wild roses and red valerian. The lovely ample **1185m saddle** (1hr 30min), separating La Pizzutta from curiously named Maja e Pelavet (the name a reference to heifers), comprises oblique slabs of light rock colonised by brilliant pink and purple stonecrop. To west-southwest is the level-topped Monte Iato, site of an ancient Greek city.

Variant

Those with time to spare and an adventurous spirit are advised to head south from here transiting via the pronounced pass to the neighbouring peak, Maja e Pelavet, whose crest and 1279m peak afford a bird's-eye view of Portella della Ginestra and its memorial.

Following the markers, go north-northwest to another saddle preceded by a deep grassed-in hollow, part of the snow/ice manufacturing business practised in this area in the not so distant past. At the nearby pass, in fact, stands a ruined stone house and more 'bomb craters' (ice and snow stores once reinforced with circular stone walls continuing underground), the **Neviere**. Stocked up during the winter months, the ice would be transported to the capital in summer for the consumption of the well-to-do in the form of refreshing *granite* and ices. Don't bother attempting to battle your way through the impassable barbed wire fence, as the path proceeds on the eastern flank of this new valley. Keep just above the fence (north-northeast) and faint stretches of path occasionally make themselves seen at the base of the rock wall. Consistent zigzag drops follow (some 200m in all) around otherwise impassable rock outcrops. The path hugs the flank and there are close brushes with colourful rock flowers and shrubs. A final short ascent leads to **Portella Garrone** (1000m, 2hr 20min) with a couple of stone huts and a World War Two bunker, which could serve as emergency shelter in bad weather.

Clear red and white SI waymarking leads over the ridge and in descent southeast past a pine plantation, where a detour wanders up to a limestone cave Grotta Garrone, which hosts unusual ferns. From the ensuing pass, a rough dirt track leads quickly down to the **Chiesa dell'Odigitria** and the map-board. Return to the main street and **bus stop** the same way as the ascent (total 3hr).

Accommodation
Affittacamere
Fileccia Vita
Tel 091-8571763
B&B Sant'Antonio
Tel 091-8571293
Portella della
Ginestra Agriturismo
Tel 091-857 4810
or 328 213 4597
portelladellaginestra@
liberaterra
mediterraneo.it
www.liberaterra.it

This lovely *agriturismo* occupies a property confiscated from the Mafia by the State and turned over to a cooperative to encourage local employment.

WALK 31
Bosco della Ficuzza

Time	2hr
Distance	8km/5 miles
Grade	1–2
Start/finish	Palazzina Reale, Ficuzza
Access	AST run a Mon–Sat bus from Palermo to Ficuzza. The more frequent Corleone run is also useful – get off at the obelisk at the Ficuzza turn-off for the final 1.5km to the village.
	By car from Palermo you need the main road (SS 121) for Agrigento. After 15km from Villabate, take the exit for Marineo, then the SS 118 for Corleone. Soon after Lago di Scanzano is the turn-off for Ficuzza.

Only a short distance from chaotic Palermo, in a gentle hilly region some 700m above sea level, is the peaceful wood of Bosco della Ficuzza. It lies in the shade of a towering, elongated limestone mountain, Rocca Busambra, which ostensibly protects it from devastating African winds. The area was once a vast royal hunting reserve, established by the Bourbon King Ferdinand IV in early 19th century; about a third of the original spread (9000 hectares) remains – now a nature reserve under the watchful eye of the Forestry Department. Due to extensive damage during the war, when it was torched to flush out enemy forces, the prevalent trees are relatively young, however cork, holm and downy oaks make for dense cover, with the occasional chestnut and ash as well as a scattering of conifers. Moreover, thanks to the carefully regulated hunting practices of the past, a good number of animals have survived, and dawn or dusk observers will be rewarded by deer, foxes and even the shy porcupine. Wild boar, once appreciated by the king, have evidently been reintroduced. Wild rabbits are widespread and help feed the numerous birds of prey that prefer the safety of the isolated reaches of the mountain overhead. There are rumours of Egyptian vultures in the vicinity, and Ficuzza's wildlife rehabilitation centre nurses wounded specimens.

The walk takes in the curious Pulpito del Re, the king's pulpit – a rock outcrop akin to a massive throne with carved steps where, it is said, the king would recline in comfort and have his beaters parade boar and deer so he could pick them off without excessive exertion. The return route follows the winding (rail-less) scenic route of a former narrow gauge train line that functioned from Palermo all the way to Burgio, near Agrigento, up until 1959. Back at the village of Ficuzza there is the added attraction of the Palazzina Reale (royal palace), home to a remarkable colony of spotless starlings. Originally a hunting pavilion constructed 1802–6 for the king by the architect Venanzio Marvuglia, it became property of the Italian state in 1871 and is open to the public.

On the whole, spring is the best time for the walk because of the plentiful wild flowers, and April–May visitors should look out for the rare white peonies in clearings. Wide tracks are followed all the way, making the route suitable for all. Food and drinks can be had in Ficuzza.

While plausible as a day trip from Palermo, it is a pity not to stay in this beautiful area longer to savour the peace and quiet and watch the wildlife come out at dusk. Ficuzza's railway station has been beautifully converted into an atmospheric restaurant and guesthouse, otherwise see Walk 32.

The Palazzina Reale in the shade of Rocca Busambra

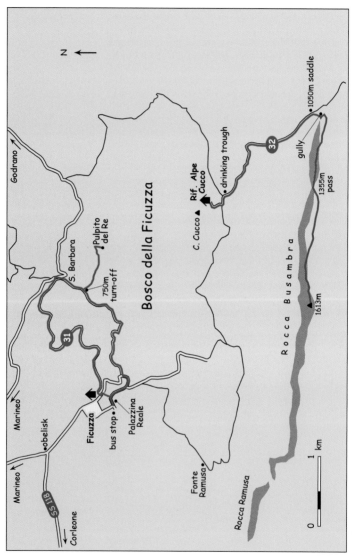

THE WALK

Start with a visit to the well-preserved **Palazzina Reale**, around which the village of **Ficuzza** (680m) has grown up. Facing the palace entrance, go left (east) along the road towards a shrine on the edge of the village. The road curves right (southish) and leads uphill briefly to a Y-junction – take the left fork (right is signposted for Rif. Alpe Cucco). At the ensuing junction you need the right turn (east) along a quiet, unsurfaced forestry track parallel to the massive run of the Rocca Busambra. This means light mixed wood, heaps of scented broom shrubs, wild crimson gladioli and views down over the Lago di Scanzano and its pastoral plain. After gradual climbing, 35min from Ficuzza a modest rise is attained, flanked by a noteworthy sandstone outcrop and a track off to the right, barred to unauthorised vehicles (**750m turn-off**). This leads over a sandy rock base into shadier wood sporting rock roses, peonies and asphodel. Not far in the track peters out at a saddle, and sharp right is a clear path for the final stretch to the **Pulpito del Re**, the curious sandstone rock for the king as armchair hunter (815m, 45min).

Return to the **750m turn-off** and continue right downhill, past some notable cork oaks, to the **S. Barbara** intersection with the asphalt road to Godrano. Just before the actual road, let yourself in through the barbed wire gate on the left (red paint stripes), then walk hard right and follow the fence downhill (go through the first opening) into a shallow gully, an overgrown railway cutting. It soon becomes a dirt track leading west at first. No rails as such are visible, but a plethora of clues remain to the presence of the railway, including old 'Attenti al treno' signs further around. It winds its easy-going way through the pleasant wood noisy with doves and woodpeckers, and there are occasional views through to the lake again and northwest over to the mountains over Piana degli Albanesi. Ficuzza comes into view as you cross a high-arched bridge. Masses of golden chrysanthemums and giant fennel line the track, not to mention oregano and butterflies galore. Once at the **old railway station** (now a guesthouse), directly below the village, follow the track to the rear of the building and across a road for the final flight of steps to **Ficuzza** (2hr total). Bar Cavarretta has great photos of the old steam trains.

Accommodation
Antica Stazione
Ferroviaria di
Ficuzza Tel
091-8460000

WALK 32
Rocca Busambra

Time	4hr
Distance	11km/7 miles
Ascent/descent	650m/650m
Grade	3
Map	For sketch map of the route see Walk 31.
Start/finish	Rif. Alpe Cucco
Access	For Ficuzza, see Walk 31. Then it's 5km on a partially surfaced road to Rif. Alpe Cucco, whose friendly staff will pick up carless walkers if required; otherwise allow 1hr 30min on foot, all uphill.
	Sturdy vehicles can be used to drive via the rough dirt road to the 1050m saddle on the initial stage of the walk, reducing the time by almost 1hr.

The magnificent isolated limestone massif of Rocca Busambra is the undisputed master of the rolling uplands that include notorious townships such as Corleone. Rumours have it that the mountain's multitudinous profound natural cavities and fissures were infamous until very recently as the final hidden resting places of unfortunate Mafia victims, while the underlying wood, Bosco della Ficuzza, provided cover for stolen cattle. Reminiscent of a scaled-down version of the Civetta massif in Italy's Dolomites, Rocca Busambra's desolate rambling ridge stretches east–west for almost 6km. It receives few visitors but affords shelter to a noteworthy colony of coral-beaked choughs not to mention a number of birds of prey, the likes of the golden eagle, the peregrine and lanner falcon, which feed on the wild rock doves and wildlife in the thick tree cover at a lower level.

The walk itself is particularly rewarding if somewhat tiring. The desolation of the windswept or sunbaked upper reaches can be enjoyed in peace and quiet. Set out early in the morning during the late spring–summer period as it can get hot in ascent and there's no shade on the mountain. Sturdy boots, plenty of water and sun protection are essential, and a compass is strongly recommended as a path is rarely visible. Any time of year is suitable except for winter, when snowfalls are common.

Comfortable Rifugio Alpe Cucco, justifiably renowned for its delicious country-style cuisine, is set back from the base of Rocca Busambra overlooking a vast rolling landscape; it takes its name from a nearby hill-cum-hummock Cima Cucco or *gufo* ('owl'). For more accommodation see Walk 31, as well as information on Ficuzza and its wood (Bosco della Ficuzza).

THE WALK

Take the dirt road that passes in front of **Rif. Alpe Cucco** (950m) and head left (southeast), away from Ficuzza, ignoring the downhill fork for Godrano. You climb gradually past a **drinking trough** for the numerous cattle then into a light wood of oaks brightened by wild roses, cyclamens, asphodels and veritable armies of wild fennel. The echo of woodpeckers, pigeons and cuckoos is all around. After 25min, approaching the eastern extremity of Rocca Busambra, the track levels out at a long **1050m saddle**, and a curious tower-like structure (Pizzo di Casa) can be seen ahead. (It is

Rocca Busambra

possible to drive this far.) You soon come across a number of openings in the barbed wire on your right, marked by faint red paint stripes on the curb. Once through the fence head straight across the pasture area (due south) aiming for the ample saddle above in the crest. There is no path as such. Make your way through the oak trees via the myriad cattle tracks to the base of the rock for the clear zigzag path that climbs a brief rocky gully. It emerges onto a pasture slope, where you keep left for a minor red-earth ridge and huddle of trees.

From here the faint path heads right (southwest) to a low rise, from where you strike out due west across the vast pasture basin dotted with wild pear trees to the crest that is the eastern continuation of Rocca Busambra. En route you'll encounter a barbed wire fence, passable by way of a short detour. Soon an immense slope with masses of yellow asphodels is traversed, then the actual ridge gained. It offers wide-reaching views, swooping swallows and porcupine burrows scattered with their brown and cream needles. Do beware of the pit holes (minor sink holes) where rainwater has dissolved the limestone. Several obstinate shrubs will need negotiating on the final stretch before an easy drop and a clear-cut **pass at 1355m** that precedes the central and more desolate section of Rocca Busambra (1hr 30min).

View from Rocca Busambra over Bosco della Ficuzza

You now tackle the vast, sloping 'rear' flank of the mountain. A path of sorts appears briefly as you transit through thick vegetation which all but suffocates orchids and baby iris. After a passage through a barbed wire fence, set your sights on a lone cairn, and proceed west across a curious and vaguely hostile landscape with uneven heaps of rocks separated by hummocks of grass or low shrubs. Ground-nesting rock partridge are likely to fly off grumbling in their guttural cry when disturbed. To reach the top of the mountain keep westwards, clambering diagonally up the steep slope towards the crest. Even if you miss the actual **1613m peak** of **Rocca Busambra** (2hr 15min), not easily identifiable from the back with its modest cross (soon after the antenna), the views are magnificent from any point on the ridge and the vast extension of the Bosco della Ficuzza can be appreciated. The mountain itself curves westward, culminating in Rocca Ramusa. On a clear day the view ranges far and wide, taking in Piana degli Albanesi, Corleone and Prizzi due south with its lake, and even the far-off Aeolian islands. Myriad cushions of rock flowers punctuate the northernmost face of the mountain, anchored into the multitude of crevices, while the acrobatic choughs glide around effortlessly.

Final slope of Rocca Busambra

The descent and return to **Rif. Alpe Cucco** follows the same route as the ascent, and takes around 1hr 45min, making a total of 4hr.

Accommodation
Rif. Alpe Cucco
Tel 091-8208225

181

LE MADONIE (MADONIE MOUNTAINS)

Apparently named after a noble family, the Madonie – or 'Mons Marones' as Strabo the Greek geographer referred to them – are attractive, rambling mountains that account for a 48km wide tract of central Sicily, their northern border dropping to the Tyrrhenian coast. Except for an untamed core, long frequented by itinerant shepherds as well as many a *mafioso* in hiding, the Madonie are dotted with quiet old townships and farming communities, where the legacy of Arab and Norman times persists in narrow winding alleyways, medieval churches or the odd crumbling castle. The uplands are spread with marvellous varied woods of beech, chestnut and myriad oaks, such as cork and holm varieties, inevitably recent but well on the way to recovery after the ravages of the war years. Towering above are sheer limestone cliffs that reach a high point of 1979m in the case of the central Carbonara massif. The Madonie are made up of ancient rock, formed during the Triassic era (220 million years back) and rich in marine fossils; it is second only to the neighbouring Sicani, which boast 260 million, Permian. This geological make-up also means widespread karst landscapes and characteristic phenomena, such as 400 funnel-shaped dolina basins known as *quarare*, and naturally little in the way of watercourses.

The survival of the flourishing vegetation on the upper reaches is guaranteed by frequent dense mists. In fact, though the Madonie account for a mere 2% of the surface area of Sicily, they boast a healthy half of the 2600 plant species found on the island. Amongst these are several endemics, such as the *Abies Nebrodensis* (Nebrodi fir), a relic from the ice ages. It is relatively squat and compact compared to alpine types, and now limited to 31 well-monitored exemplars in the Vallone Madonna degli Angeli (see Walk 37) that are successfully reproducing, albeit slowly.

The Carbonara massif, on the other hand, features veritable meadows of yellow asphodels mingled with the curious *basilisco*, or *Chachrys ferulacea*, a member of the fennel family and endemic to this restricted zone of the Madonie. Both are signs of over-grazing and are apparently nature's revenge, as both are unappetising for livestock, which is thus obliged to seek out greener pastures elsewhere, allowing the meadows to recuperate. The presence of the *basilisco*, however, is a guarantee of finding a flat-capped, pale-fleshed mushroom of the same name, highly prized in gastronomic circles, that sells for up to 60 euros per kilo (about £40 sterling)! Other curiosities include the exquisite insect orchids and white or pink peonies.

Despite the intrusion of man, his roads and flocks, a fair array of wildlife has survived in the shape of roe and fallow deer, foxes and a host of winged creatures, including birds of prey such as eagles, thanks to the abundance of rabbits, hares, wild mice and the hazel dormouse. Plans are underfoot to reintroduce the Egyptian vulture. Of the 30 insect endemics, one curious example is the Sicilian Red Apollo butterfly, which is to be found only in the Madonie uplands.

As from 1989 a good part of the mountainous area comes under the Parco delle Madonie, a regional body that is coming to terms with managing almost 40,000 hectares of mountainous terrain with the Forestry Services. Due to the altitudes, snowfalls can usually be expected from November well below the 1000m mark, unless Sicily's typical summer near-drought conditions are protracted. On the other hand late falls are referred to as '*L'ultima varva di San Giuseppe*', 'the last beard of St Joseph', whose feast day is March 19, only two days prior to the official start of spring.

While snow does not necessarily preclude walking, it can hamper orientation; winter visitors are advised to come equipped with cross-country skis or snow shoes. Late spring–summer can be simply divine in view of the masses of wild flowers and full range of green tones, though conditions are excellent through to autumn, when the beech woods are especially enchanting in copper and russet, and crisp conditions enhance visibility. The only time anything resembling crowds can be expected at popular points such as Piano Battaglia and Piano Sempria are summer Sundays and the month of August, when coastal dwellers seek relief from the sweltering conditions and head upland to picnic.

Visitors to the Madonie should be suitably equipped for extremes of weather at all times of year. Layered clothing is recommended, warm jacket and waterproofs, as well as shorts, sunglasses and hat. Pretty Petralia Sottana (from *pietra lilium*, lily of rock) located at 1207m on the southern flanks, with good accommodation and facilities, makes a lovely base for the walks on the northern flanks such as 35, 36 and 37. Both the helpful tourist office and Park HQ keep the 1:50,000 walking map 'Carta dei Sentieri e del Paesaggio: Cefalù-Madonie', a joint effort involving the Palermo Tourist Board, the Madonie Park, the Palermo Province and the Forestry Authority. The township can be reached by daily SAIS coach from Palermo.

Parco delle Madonie, headquarters Petralia Sottana Tel 0921-923327 or 0921-684011, www.parcodellemadonie. it. Petralia Sottana Tourist Office Tel 0921-641811

Accommodation

Hotel Madonie Tel 0921-641106, old family-run establishment with a breathtaking roof-top restaurant; B&B La Meridiana Tel 0921-641537

The Carbonara massif from Portella Colla (start of Walk 36)

WALK 33
Cefalù and its Rocca

Time	The town – 1hr; the Rocca – 1hr 40min
Distance	The town – 1.6km/1 mile; the Rocca – 3.8km/2.4 miles
Ascent/descent	Rocca – 250m/250m
Grade	1
Map	Town map from the Tourist Office
Start/finish	Piazza Garibaldi
Access	Cefalù is a 1hr trip by SAIS coach or train (main Messina–Palermo line) from Palermo to its west. It is something of a transport hub, with bus lines radiating out to neighbouring seaside localities as well as the Madonie villages. Those travelling by car will need the A20 Palermo–Messina *autostrada* and the Cefalù exit, otherwise the coastal road SS 133. Drivers are warned that parking is restricted close to the centre.

The enchanting town of Cefalù, on Sicily's glorious northern coast, has a past intertwined with fanciful myths and colourful historical figures. Unknown to many, the Greek goddess Artemis (Diana to the Romans) used to bathe in a sheltered bay below the headland where her worshippers erected a temple. At a much later stage in history, 12th-century sovereign King Roger II had the town's magnificent Norman-style cathedral constructed in recognition of his fleet's delivery from a violent storm. Both structures are visited on the following walks.

Cefalù nestles beneath a majestic limestone headland known as the Rocca, towering several hundred metres over the coastline, and which itself hosted a good part of the town for lengthy periods. A Greek colony to start with, Cefalù began life around the 5th century BC as Kephaloídion, a reference to the head shape of its trademark promontory, and a curious presage of their inextricable destiny. This marvellous natural massif site has sheer impenetrable rock flanks on all but the landward western side, where a sloping gully provides access. It was frequented for religious purposes in prehistoric times, of which activity copious evidence has been found in the numerous caves which honeycomb the rock, then became the main town site following the fall of Rome's western empire. Overseen by an impregnable castle, the upper settlement flourished, along with churches, storehouses, ovens, underground cisterns and, naturally, extensive multi-layered fortifications.

As betook a large part of Sicilian coastal settlements in the 9th century, Cefalù was taken by the Arabs, who left their unmistakable mark and an exotic atmosphere. On the subsequent arrival of Roger II in 1063 the bulk of the town moved back downhill and reconstruction proceeded on a grand scale, including the landmark duomo in 1131, as part of the move to encourage the spread of Christianity to counter the well-established Islamic faith.

Charming, picturesque and hospitable, Cefalù makes a good base for forays into the neighbouring Madonie which back this coastal strip. The town caters to a broad range of tourist needs, and has a stunning stretch of golden beach on crystal clear water, backed by multi-starred hotels. The listings below are in the old town centre. The varied cuisine starts naturally with seafood, but also includes rich meat dishes from the mountainous interior, and a delicious range of *antipasti* involving luscious local mushrooms, aubergine and capsicum, to be accompanied by the excellent vintages from the inland region. The *pasticcerie* (pastry shops) will not escape notice with their mouth-watering displays of rich almond and pistachio dainties alongside creamy speciality ice creams.

The itineraries below entail an easy stroll around town then a rewarding uphill exploration of the Rocca, an easy 250m climb, marvellous panoramas, wildflowers and zooming swallows, and perfect picnic spots. Sandals are fine, as long as they have a decent grip.

The pastel roofs of Cefalù en route to the Rocca

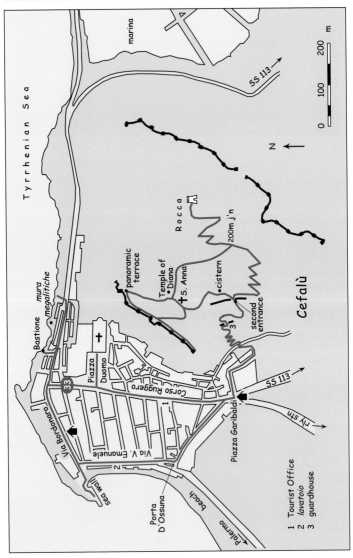

THE WALK

The Town (1hr)

Find your way to **Piazza Garibaldi** on the southern edge of the historic inner town. This was the site of Porta di Terra, namely the town gateway on the land side, and boasts megalithic stone foundations at the base of the present clock tower. The main shop-lined thoroughfare, **Corso Ruggero**, named after King Roger, leads northwards into the peaceful restricted-traffic zone, and is the venue of the pre-dinner evening stroll, or *passeggiata*, when the town's population turns out in full force dressed to the teeth. In contrast, narrow parallel streets runs downhill towards the sea flanked with slender houses, their façades hidden behind loaded lines of fluttering laundry. On the left, the medieval building just before the helpful **tourist office**, is the Osterio Magno, plausibly King Roger's residence. Past the information centre for the Madonie Park, is the town square, **Piazza Duomo**, flanked by the 18th-century bishop's palace and crowned by the twin-towered cathedral. Following the Eastern tradition, the interior of the central dome is dominated by an unbelievably gigantic and particularly severe figure of the Pantocrator (the all-ruling Father) in glittering Byzantine-style mosaics, completed by a chorus of angels and saints in the company of the Virgin set on lower levels in a befitting smaller scale.

Continue along the last leg of Corso Ruggero to the T-junction with Via Bordonaro, and walk right for about 100m past remains of **mura megalitiche**, ancient fortifications and to steps leading down to the rocky seashore. Back the other way (west) at Piazza Crispi is the **Bastione**, a raised platform where lovers and others hang out to enjoy the sea views. Further on are a number of eateries boasting terraces hanging out over the sea, such as the Trappitu, whose cavernous interior houses an ancient oil press. At the northwesternmost corner a picturesque bay complete with fishing boats opens up in the shelter of a **sea wall**, which affords a view onto the backside of the town, as it were, with the Rocca as backdrop.

Proceeding south along Via Vittorio Emanuele, named after the last kings of Italy, exotic-sounding Via Mandralisca is passed, along with its historic but over-rated museum. Close by now is the fascinating and photogenic medieval **lavatoio** ('wash house'). Below street level this extraordinary structure features troughs sculpted out of the rock floor, still fed by a gushing freshwater spring.

At end of the street, after the **Porta D'Ossuna** gateway and out of the town proper, is the expanse of the magnificent golden beach.

To return to the start, take any way uphill back to **Piazza Garibaldi** (1hr) and the Rocca itinerary.

The Rocca (1hr 40min)

From **Piazza Garibaldi** (16m) a sign for *'Pedonale Rocca'* ('pedestrian route') indicates the stepped way Via Giuseppe Fiore. Ahead is the promising vision of the pale rock flanks of the massive Rocca, dotted with prickly pear and ranks of ancient stone walls. ◄ Underfoot, in contrast, the steps are edged with dark grey fossil-filled stone, the limestone of the promontory. At the top of the steps, go to the **ticket office** then embark on the zigzagging climb through parkland replanted with conifer. You follow the sheltered cleft in the western side, which long acted as the sole point of access to the otherwise inaccessible Rocca. You pass through the first line of defensive walling incorporating a **guardhouse** (95m).

Check locally on the Rocca opening hours as they vary.

Fortified entrance to the Rocca

Views gradually open up over the town, seemingly chaotic from this angle, a jumble of warm orange-tiled roofs and glimpses of pastel facades, not to mention the fringe of stunning turquoise water and golden beach. Only minutes later is a small cistern preceding further fortifications and the **second entrance** (150m). Keep right here for a short leg south, before the wind upwards through scrubby vegetation and bright yellow daisies, heading for the central knoll.

At a **200m junction** at a clump of olive trees (where you fork off on the way back), follow signs for the tight zigzags covering the final steep stretch to the innermost sanctum of the Rocca, namely the **Castello** (270m, 1hr). Here more walls and several underground cisterns have survived the ravages of time, along with the ruins of the 12–13th century castle, second in importance in the whole of Sicily at the time, with its own contingent of 30 special guards. Evidence has been unearthed of even earlier constructions dating back to the Greek period. But it will be the views that grab your attention at first – 360° from the Aeolian islands northeast, to Palermo and its coastal spread, and inland to the Madonie mountains.

Return to the **200m junction** and turn right in descent following signs for the archeological site, which bring you out at the so-called **Temple of Diana**, a megalithic sanctuary dating back to pre-Hellenic times, possibly 8–9th century BC.

Walk on downhill towards the paved way to reach the walls and a superb **panoramic terrace** (130m) from where the entire spread of the town as well as the twin-towered cathedral are at your feet. From here the way continues to a further lookout corner then you need to retrace your steps before forking right back up to the church of **S. Anna** (150m). Here it's right past medieval stone ovens then a massive underground cistern covered with impressive stone slabs, to the **second guardhouse** (150m) passed during the climb. Here fork downhill and return to **Cefalù** (1hr 40min) the way you came up.

Tourist Office
Cefalù Tel
0921-421050

Accommodation
Hotel La Giara
Tel 0921-421562
www.hotel-lagiara.it
Locanda Cangelosi
Tel 0921-421591
**www.locanda
cangelosi.it**

WALK 34
Isnello to Gratteri

Time	3hr 30min
Distance	8.5km/5.3 miles
Ascent/descent	550m/450m
Grade	2
Map	1:50,000 'Carta dei Sentieri e del Paesaggio: Cefalù-Madonie'
Start/finish	Isnello/Gratteri
Access	An AST bus connects Cefalù with Isnello, while Gratteri and Cefalù are linked courtesy of the F.lli La Spisa company. By car from the SS 113 along the coast, you'll need the minor roads to Isnello either via Collesano or Gibilmanna, while Gratteri is also accessible by way of Lascari.

This is a fairly strenuous walk that crosses a medium-altitude mountain ridge to link two quiet farming communities. Wild open terrain is traversed and wide-ranging views take in the stark limestone reaches of the southern Madonie mountain range as well as the Tyrrhenian coast. The villages themselves provide quite a contrast: medieval Isnello (the name from the Arabic for 'donkey') is set on a series of ancient terraces in a deep, sheltered valley, while Gratteri occupies an elevated site surrounded by thick woods, its charming traffic-less streets of Arab design weaving their way around the mountain top. Both have ruined castles along with a handful of interesting churches decorated with works of art, and though a mere matter of kilometres as the crow flies from the animated coast, they are worlds away in terms of pace and lifestyle. This is not to say that time has stopped still – shepherds and farmers here are more likely to be at the wheel of a Toyota four-wheel drive than on a donkey. However, tourism is very low key and the passage of walkers, foreigners or otherwise, inevitably arouses curiosity.

The chances are good of spending a whole day without encountering another soul apart from the occasional herder or forestry worker. Bird life in the form of hawks and other birds of prey is plentiful, and on the flora side the open stony terrain is a preferred habitat for pale spring varieties of candytuft and scented narcissus, not to mention the masses of scented broom shrubs which transform entire mountainsides.

Little waymarking en route is to be expected, and a good sense of direction – not to mention a compass – is needed on the middle section, especially in low cloud, as the paths peter out momentarily. Take food and plenty of liquid supplies, particularly in hot weather. The walk is feasible as a day trip from Cefalù using the buses, though accommodation in the form of private rooms is available in both Isnello and Gratteri.

THE WALK
At **Isnello** (550m), where the bus drops you a little way inside the southwestern part of town, walk back up the main road past the minuscule tourist information office then the inviting bakery. Viale Impellitteri, named after an illustrious migrant son who became mayor of New York, then leads past an inspired modern bronze sculpture of a mother and child on horseback, after which you turn right down a lane, prior to an iron cross. Just before it curves past the **cemetery** (on your left), cut across the field diagonally right to the watercourse and cross it to reach the fenced forestry area. This conifer plantation is entered by way of a gate, and a lane leads uphill. At the first curve, turn right past a small **chapel**. This wide track climbs steadily in wide curves through the thinning conifers and dry terrain, relieved by occasional spring blooms if not the striking purple flowers of the poisonous mandrake plant. Wild rabbits give themselves away dislodging stones.

Nearly half an hour uphill, on the upper edge of the conifer wood just as the track begins to bear right into a broad gully, a faint path breaks off to the right, marked by a cairn (**655m junction**). This means you stay on the main southern flank of the limestone massif Monte Grotta Grande which overshadows Isnello. This path, clearer soon, climbs in perfect zigzags affording lovely views of the township below, with its ruined castle on the brink of a precipice. South-southeast is the broad, imposing grassed ridge that culminates in Pizzo Carbonara, at 1979m, the highest in the

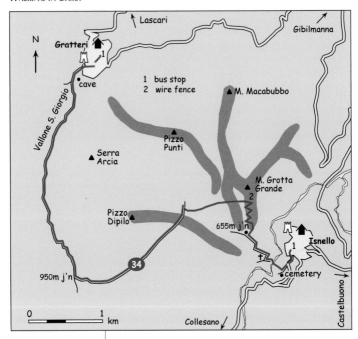

Madonie, which sprawl in many directions, crowned with hilltop settlements.

The going is easy and pleasant on mostly grassy terrain. At 855m, after a total of 50min, keep right at a fork, then a short while later, when the path peters out, make your way uphill (north) heading for the ridge. On encountering the **wire fence** at about 1000m (1hr 10min), follow it around left. (It is also feasible to detour off right to the nearby flat top of 1064m Monte Grotta Grande for the views.) In about 10min, after crossing the top of a valley that divides the two main peaks of Monte Grotta Grande and Pizzo Dipilo, you find yourself on a lane through a grazing zone. At a rise, take the stile right into a pasture corridor for goats and cut up the hillside towards the red dirt road akin to an unsightly gash in the eastern flank of Pizzo Dipilo. You join the track at 1090m, after a total of 1hr 30min, and can rest assured that from here on it's more straightforward.

Turn left (southwest) at this point, coasting around Pizzo Dipilo to a broad saddle 1km along, in all likelihood in the company of goats. The track descends gradually, a tin shed in the shade of a prominent tree the only useful landmark in the vicinity. Birds of prey are occasional visitors on this lovely wild stretch.

After a further gate, the track becomes a little rougher and drops markedly into light wood dominated by holm oaks. Not far along is a **950m junction** (total 2hr 5min), distinguished by a hut and the usual gate. Ignore the track that disappears south over the rise, and keep right (north) through a dense plantation of cork and holm oak, brightened underfoot by cyclamens. To your right is the sheer light limestone flank of Pizzo Dipilo, while ahead north is the sparkling sea. The track descends quickly now in wide curves, and clearings are crammed with aromatic herbs, the likes of mint and oregano. As the wood is left behind, the track climbs briefly past a turn-off right then a drinking trough on the side of a lovely elongated pastoral valley known as the **Vallone San Giorgio**. A concrete ramp dips past a Parco delle Madonie sign to a junction and a cave in the limestone flank of Serra Arcia. Go straight ahead up the rough tarmac road, which shortly brings you into the back entrance to the village, only actually visible when you reach the shoulder.

This is the old picturesque part of **Gratteri** (657m), well worth exploring. Past the church follow the narrow street downhill. It's worth detouring left for the evocative (8th-century) castle underpass which leads around to the adjoining church of the Matrice Vecchia, work of the barons of Ventimiglia and which dates back to 1350. It once boasted a marble casket with four thorns attributed to the crown of Christ, since transferred to the 19th-century Chiesa di Madre Nuova in the more recent part of town.

Back on the descent route continue straight on cutting through the labyrinth of alleyways, the legacy of the Arab period. A small square is soon reached, where you take the street signed for 'no vehicle entry', to the left of the steps. It quickly brings you out onto a street lined with cafés, and the **bus stop**.

Accommodation

Gratteri:
Affittacamere
Tedesco Salvatore
Tel 0921-429633
Isnello: *Affittacamere*
Bonafede Manzella
Vincenza
Tel 0921-662179

WALK 35
Pizzo Carbonara

Time	3hr
Distance	5.8km/3.6 miles
Ascent/descent	370m/370m
Grade	3
Map	1:50,000 'Carta dei Sentieri e del Paesaggio: Cefalù-Madonie'
Start/finish	Start of *Sentiero Geologico*, Piano Battaglia
Access	Despite the plethora of good roads that climb to Piano Battaglia, unfortunately none are used by public transport in the walking season. Drivers have various options: from the coast a well-signed road climbs via Collesano and Piano Zucchi, otherwise from the uplands and the SS 120 turn off at either Polizzi Generosa or Petralia Sottana for the final ascent.

The lush fresh beech woods that cloak the rolling uplands of the Madonie mountain range are the most southerly in the whole of Europe. Alternating with a wilderness of stony limestone karstic 'wasteland' pitted with dolina depressions and a multitude of marine fossils, they are easily appreciated from Piano Battaglia. This ample high-altitude basin (alias 800mx2.5km *polje*) owes its name to a landmark sanguinary battle when 1000 Normans on horse-back annihilated 20,000 Saracen forces in the Middle Ages. Until recently the area was the focus of a struggle of a different nature: between those in favour of further exploitation for the winter ski season – massive parking lots and multiple roads currently serve a single mountain equipped with a ski lift and a handful of pistes – and the defenders of the threatened wilderness, now safeguarded under the auspices of the Parco delle Madonie.

This itinerary starting at Piano Battaglia, entails the ascent of Pizzo Carbonara, the Madonie's highest peak (it lords it over the second-in-line, Pizzo Antenna, by some two metres!), which is also the highest non-volcanic summit in

Sicily, or the second peak in Sicily after Etna. In clear conditions it offers a wealth of breathtaking panoramas. However the Carbonara massif is unfortunately infamous for being subject to thick mists that come rolling in without warning, making orientation troublesome for walkers as landmarks are few and far between. While the walk is not excessively difficult, a sense of direction (and a compass) do help, as paths are followed only on the initial and return stretches. It is extremely inadvisable to start out on the walk in weather that is anything but perfect. Moreover snow patches are to be expected early summer, and may necessitate substantial detours.

The upside of the frequent mists is that the vegetation – endemic types and beech included – flourishes on the cloud-borne moisture, essential in the absence of surface water, which drains underground out of the reach of plant life in this karstic landscape. The bottom line for walkers is: carry your own drinking water.

Accommodation is available year-round at Piano Battaglia at comfortable establishments: the so-called Ostello della Gioventù (youth hostel) and rambling Rifugio Marini, currently undergoing much-needed renovation. There are no food shops at Piano Battaglia though snacks are always available.

THE WALK

At the northeastern extremity of **Piano Battaglia** (1605m) and the *Sentiero Geologico* signboard, follow signs towards observation points PO1 and 2. A lane is followed briefly, then a clear path strikes out northeast over soft grass. After PO2 as the *sentiero geologico* curves right downhill towards a massive sinkhole, ignore it and keep straight ahead in the direction of a clear saddle. The path cuts the southeastern flank of the central Carbonara massif, while south is Monte Spina Puci, the local name for the endemic astragalus (milk-vetches) found here. You climb gradually in wider curves through veritable meadows of yellow asphodels mingled with the curious endemic basilisco, a fennel-like plant. A beech copse and **ruined hut** precede a **1687m fork** in Vallone di Zottafonda. Turn left (northwest) along a modest ridge sporting a Parco delle Madonie signpost. You are now well and truly in the wild, undulating sprawl of the

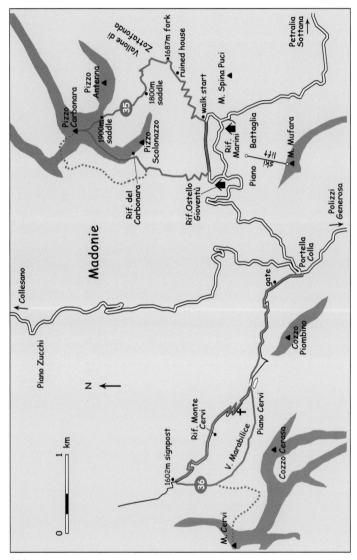

Carbonara. West is Pizzo Scolonazzo, while second-highest peak Pizzo Antenna (aka Principessa) looms due north above the chaotic slopes scattered with fragmented rock and splashes of green, where beech trees have settled into the numerous dolina depressions where soil has accumulated. The terrain is brightened by grape hyacinths, mouse ear, a midget type of euphorbia and low-growing Greek medlar, a type of hawthorn.

On the Pizzo Carbonara path (Pizzo Antenna right)

The path climbs gently north-northwest through shady beech, occasional red paint spots then odd cairns serve as waymarking. Even the least geologically minded walkers will not fail to be impressed by the wealth of fossilised marine remains such as corals, sponges and shells, in the rock base. About 30min from the 1687m fork is a **1800m saddle**, affording a glimpse of Etna. Closer-at-hand is Pizzo Antenna, which is now skirted north-northwest. It's across level stony terrain populated with hardy beech at first (ignore a path that breaks off left) then you climb gently high over a dolina, at the foot of Pizzo Carbonara at last. A minor **1900m saddle** is touched on. With no path as such (faint

197

A fairly clear but longer, red-marked path n.2 leads northwest then south from the peak; it joins up with the route described below close to Rif. del Carbonara, and is preferable in low visibility. ◀

red paint splashes), cut northwest up the rocky mountainside for the 10min climb to the ridge above. Then it's a mere 5min right (north-northeast) to the modest peak on **Pizzo Carbonara** (1980m, 1hr 30min), and a heap of stones bearing a makeshift wood cross. Just a tad visibly higher than its neighbours, this windswept point affords a vast panorama in clear conditions, taking in the sparkling coast as far northwest as Palermo, east-southeast to Etna and across the sea to the Aeolian islands. ◀

Now backtrack briefly and follow the ridge marked by cairns and barbed wire via a modest peak. Head southwest downhill. Despite the lack of a path at first, orientation is no problem, as you are actually following the rim of a massive depression, down left, and what's more the next destination is the hut visible south-southwest. A little clambering is required, and beech shrubs occasionally need detouring. Several stone markers for council borders are passed before a faint path can be perceived along the narrowing ridge. It soon leads to **Rif. del Carbonara** or Biv. Scolonazzo (1903m, 2hr). Though the hut is locked, an overhang in the entrance could offer temporary shelter. Again, the outlook is simply marvellous. A detour uphill leads to Pizzo Scolonazzo and a somewhat incongruous monument to a dog named after Argus, the hound of Odysseus. You see straight down to Piano Battaglia from here, not to mention Monte Mufara, with its ski piste.

Back at **Rif. del Carbonara** a faint path drops southwest to quickly join a broader route left (east-southeast) that meanders through beech thickets and traverses immense expanses of basilisco before dropping to the roadside above **Piano Battaglia**. Turn left to retrieve your vehicle at the walk start, or right for Rif. Ostello della Gioventù (1hr 15min return time).

Accommodation
Rif. Ostello della Gioventù
Tel 0921-649995, CAS
Rif. Marini
Tel 0921-649994, CAI

Further Walk

A 2hr *Sentiero Geologico* has been marked from Piano Battaglia to Portella Colla. Start out from the Battaglietta sink hole (*inghiottitoio*) heading southwest following the helpful bilingual signboards. Unfortunately the concluding stretch is along asphalt.

WALK 36
Piano Cervi

Time	2hr 15min
Distance	9km/5.6 miles
Grade	1–2
Map	1:50,000 'Carta dei Sentieri e del Paesaggio: Cefalù-Madonie'. See Walk 35 for the sketch map of the route.
Start/finish	Portella Colla
Access	See Walk 35 for Piano Battaglia. Portella Colla is 3.5km southwest from Piano Battaglia, at the intersection between the roads for Collesano and Polizzi Generosa.

Envisage a perfect flowered meadow, edged by a fresh beech wood and complete with a lake, set in a basin at 1500m amongst gentle mountains. This quintessential peaceful picnic spot, Piano Cervi in the heart of the Madonie mountains, is a must. It was long appreciated by four-hoofed visitors according to its name – *cervo* is Italian for deer – and can be reached by way of an easy path. The walk, a glorious circuit suitable for the whole family, entails climbs of little consequence. Good paths or forestry tracks are followed, so trainers are sufficient. Both deciduous woods and clearings are traversed, with interesting vegetation bands and a good range of wild flowers.

THE WALK

Before starting out from **Portella Colla** (1420m), take time to admire vast, elongated Monte Quacella which sweeps east-southeast in a magnificent curve. Signposting for n.11 points along the wide forestry track that leads northwest, with a marvellous outlook onto the pale Carbonara massif northeast. Through a gate below the modest Cozzo Piombino relief, you enter shady wood consisting predominantly of maple and beech and sheltering such natural treasures as cyclamens and stunning clumps of rare white peonies. About 20min in, a signposted path leaves the track to short cut through to a shallow rise, surrounded by slopes carpeted

Pagliaio on the Piano Cervi path

with white asphodels and the fennel-like basilisco. Ahead now is the pretty, grassy basin-plain known as **Piano Cervi** (or, confusingly, as Piano della Battaglia, 1530m), boasting an unpretentious lake which either dries up in summer or freezes in winter. Cut straight over the forestry track and across the flowered meadow of thrift and crane's-bill, making a bee line for the beech wood on the opposite edge of the clearing. West now is Monte Cervi, identifiable by a castle-like rock formation on its right. You pick up path n.11b and proceed into lush **Vallone Marabilice**, climbing almost imperceptibly. At a clearing in the beech directly below the rock outcrop on Monte Cervi, bear right for a lane. ◄

A worthwhile extension branches off left here for the zigzagging 200m ascent of 1794m Monte Cervi.

The route soon joins n.11 then turns right (southeast) at a wider forestry track and **signpost** (1hr 10min, 1602m). The curious low rock flank on the right is layered with nodules of flint. Northwest is the looming shape of Monte Castellaro. You pass through reforested areas planted with cedars and Austrian pine, alternating with beech, before reaching a locked hut, **Rif. Monte Cervi**, property of the Sicilian Alpine Club. Straight after it is a lane to a *pagliaio*, a characteristic shepherds' hut roofed with dried grass and feasible for emergency shelter.

The main track proceeds past a **crucifix** to reach Piano Cervi once more. You need the path and track back to **Portella Colla** retracing the outward route (2hr 15min total).

Accommodation
see Walk 35

WALK 37
Vallone Madonna degli Angeli

Time	2hr 15min
Distance	8.3km/5.1 miles
Ascent/descent	400m/400m
Grade	2
Map	1:50,000 'Carta dei Sentieri e del Paesaggio: Cefalù-Madonie'
Start/finish	Information board, forestry track turn-off.
Access	8.3km north of Polizzi Generosa, and 3.3km below Portella Colla is the bilingual information board announcing the start of the Madonna degli Angeli *sentiero natura*. Parking is roadside. There is no public transport here.

The Vallone degli Angeli ('valley of the angels') in the central Madonie is a carefully protected and monitored nursery for a group of humble conifers that have survived unchanged for 10,000 years. The *Abies nebrodensis* (Nebrodi fir) has evidently been there since the end of the last ice age. But the story began long before when the boundless glaciers of the Würm period forced the silver fir to abandon the Nordic countries and move southwards towards relatively milder climes and the Mediterranean. Through genetic mutations it adapted into the Nebrodi endemic (so-called as the combined mountain ranges of central-eastern Sicily were referred to as Nebrodi in ancient times). Understandably used for building material and local needs, it suffered the ravages of time then inexplicably became sterile last century. And just as mysteriously recommenced reproducing 15 years ago, much to the joy of the Forestry Department. Currently a total of 30 exemplars are flourishing, and have recently become the object of a European Union LIFE Natura project. Other seedlings are being encouraged to develop in special nurseries. The local dialect name is *arvulu cruci cruci* for the cross-like arrangement of its branches.

In addition to the attraction of the revered trees – hundreds of years old though a mere 15 metres tall – the walk passes through beautiful woodland and along panoramic ridges, studded with fascinating flora. It follows a broad but stony forestry track then clear paths with frequent waymarking as per the *sentiero natura*.

THE WALK

From the roadside **information board** (1247m) go through the gate into a plantation where broom shrubs have been twinned with the Nebrodi fir saplings, fixing nitrogen in the soil for their consumption. The track climbs easily, leading northeast then south with wide-sweeping views towards the Sicani range. It rounds a corner to enter Vallone degli Angeli itself and soon reaches the signed **path start** (1350m, 20min), opposite Monte Scalone (south). You drop a little towards the valley floor through an interesting mix of beech and ilex oak, unusually tall for this altitude. Not far up the other side the first sizeable exemplar of *Abies Nebrodensis* is encountered; the path now detours the tree, circled by a low stone retaining wall, so as to avoid damage to its offspring. Steadily southeast, accompanied by pretty cyclamens, peonies, song birds and boar scratchings, the path crosses a stream and traverses beautiful beech wood. Waymarking

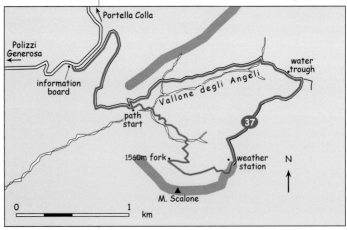

comes in the shape of low-set poles marked 16b. The occasional clearings were once used by charcoal burners. You zigzag out of the wood on the flanks of M. Scalone. Ignore the **1560m fork** (50min) right (for Polizzi Generosa) and continue on n.16. Past several majestic isolated Nebrodi firs, you ascend east towards the ridge, a spring and a plantation of black Austrian pine.

At the 1600m mark near a small **weather station**, a good track lined with pink thrift is joined left (north, 1hr 15min). The marvellous views take in M. Quacella north-northwest. After a rise, you begin descending gradually through beech, then go left at the ensuing track, n.16. A water trough (drinkable) is passed, then forestry hut. Occasional tracts of the track are concreted. The rocky sunbaked flanks are home to exquisite flowers such as a blue endemic type of flax. The signed **path start** (passed earlier) is soon passed, and you return along the track to the **information board** and road.

Accommodation
see Walk 35.

An exemplar of Abies nebrodensis *in the Vallone degli Angeli (photo: Professor Schicchi)*

WALK 38
Piano Sempria Sentiero Natura

Time	1hr 30min
Distance	4.7km/3 miles
Ascent/descent	325m/325m
Grade	2
Map	1:50,000 'Carta dei Sentieri e del Paesaggio: Cefalù-Madonie'
Start/finish	Rif. Crispi
Access	A car is essential as the walk start is 10.5km from the township of Castelbuono (SAIS bus from Palermo via Cefalù).

Drivers from Castelbuono (reachable from the SS 113 coast road via the SS 286) will pass through San Guglielmo, following clear signposting, before winding up through the thick mixed oak wood on a narrow, rough, but motorable road.

Bushy holm oaks modelled by the elements into topiary forms, historic downy oak trees that date back to the 12th century, and gigantic hollies whose tight-knit cluster has resulted in a lightless corridor likened to a Gothic cathedral, are the natural highlights of this unpretentious *sentiero natura*, a marked nature trail in the Parco delle Madonie. The range of unusual natural phenomena encompassed in such a short length of path is quite remarkable, with added attractions in the form of superb panoramas from Cozzo Luminario and the delightful, hospitable chalet Rifugio Crispi, run all year round by the Sicilian Alpine Club (CAS). (Cross-country skiers are welcome in winter.) These are the northeastern reaches of the rambling Madonie mountains, cloaked in extensive thick Mediterranean wood and overlooking the township of Castelbuono. The quiet township is worth a stop for its 14th-century castle-cum-mansion with intricately decorated wood-panelled ceilings.

The walk is both highly recommended and straightforward, and entails a gradual climb. The only warning concerns orientation, which can be tricky on the upper reaches in low cloud, despite the frequent path markers and six numbered Observation Points (PO) along the way, handy for reference.

THE WALK

Rif Crispi (1250m) is set at Piano Sempria in an enchanting position, shaded by a couple of massive ancient oak trees. Pizzo Carbonara, the highest peak in the Madonie, is visible to the west. The start of the *sentiero natura* is signposted from the refuge and winds straight up into the apparently impenetrable wood of holm and downy oak, holly and butcher's broom. After crossing the forestry vehicle track

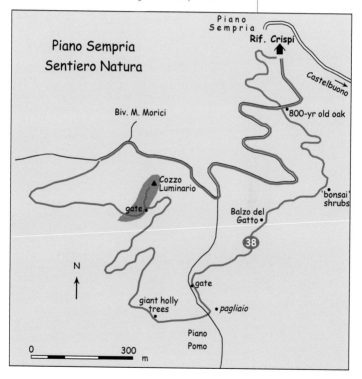

it encounters a huge specimen of downy, moss-covered **800-year-old oak** (PO1), the most ancient and gnarled of all. The path climbs gently southeast and crosses a fire break, before entering an orderly beech wood (PO2), long subject to careful cutting so as to ensure growth. Not long after a charcoal burners' clearing is an open stretch of mountain-side dotted with asphodels, dog roses and the odd orchid, in the company of holm oak shrubs curiously sculpted into stunted topiary forms by incessant tearing and nibbling by goats and sheep combined with exposure to the wind. The forestry workers refer to them as 'bonsai' shrubs. Close by is PO3, a wonderful lookout on the cliff edge with views to the Nebrodi mountains (east), Monte Etna (southeast), and Monte San Salvatore (south).

Nearby, the **Balzo del Gatto** (crag of the cat, PO4) is a cleft pass in light limestone rock, said to have been shaped by the charcoal burners who came this way with their mules. You are plunged into beech and chestnut before an uphill stretch to a forestry track. Left via a **gate** leads through to an asphodel-dotted clearing and the picturesque **pagliaio**, or shepherds' hut, of wood and straw (*paglia* in Italian) reconstructed by the Forestry Department. While

'Bonsai' shrubs on the sentiero natura

206

rudimentary, it can be used for shelter. From the main track you clamber over a stile and follow the pole-marked path right, across **Piano Pomo** (1261m, PO5) to the amazing thicket of **giant holly trees**. The tallest reach 15m in height and 4m in circumference, and the oldest surpass 300 years – while less unusual for Europe's northern regions, they are a record for Italy. The likeness to a cathedral nave is striking, with the trunks as columns and the foliage forming an intertwined canopy that prevents light from entering, making for a gloomy interior. A carpet of ferns and even the odd white peony outside complete the picture.

The path proceeds northwest at first past a number of very old, bushy, downy oaks, then starts a 200m climb as light mixed wood takes over on the clear slope brightened with thorny broom, rock roses and cyclamens. A **gate** precedes a lookout (PO6) then the modest rise that doubles as the peak of **Cozzo Luminario** with its cross (1hr, 1512m). From here there are sweeping views over west to the Carbonara massif, northeast down to the township of Castelbuono, with the sea to the north.

Back at the **gate** and marker, follow the poles right (west) for a short stretch before curving down a grassy slope in a northeasterly direction to join a lane. Keep right. A short way downhill is a turn-off left leading to a locked CAS hut, Biv. M. Morici. The main track drops through pasture then a dense beech wood to a Y-junction. Keep left on the forestry track, which winds quickly back down to **Rif. Crispi** and Piano Sempria (1hr 30min total).

Tourist Office
Castelbuono
Tel 0921-671124

Accommodation
Rif. Crispi
Tel 0921-672279, CAS

I NEBRODI (NEBRODI MOUNTAINS)

Long gone are the fawns for which the Nebrodi mountains were originally named (*nebros* in Greek), not to mention the elephant, hippopotamus and rhinoceros discovered in fossilised form. Similarly extinct as from this century are the wolf and griffon-vulture. The good news, however, is that since 1993 this sprawling medium-altitude mountain range has been a protected area – the Parco dei Nebrodi. Italy's most extensive, it clocks in at 85,687 hectares, extending east–west for 70km, virtually parallel to the northern coast of Sicily, and embraces a total of 21 local council areas in three different provinces, ranging in altitude from a matter of metres above sea level to the 1847m of Monte Soro.

Light years from the 'typical' sun-scorched Sicilian landscapes featuring scraggly prickly pears and olive trees, the wild Nebrodi mountains are thickly wooded with extensive yew, oak and beech, now the domain of roaming flocks of sheep, goats, cows, black pigs and docile horses, along with the occasional reticent shepherd plus retinue of dogs. Less obvious are the thriving populations of foxes, native wild cats and rabbits, as well as the elusive crested porcupine, whose tell-tale black and white quills are a common sight littering the pathways. The scattered lakes host the European pond tortoise, the kingfisher and a multitude of water fowl, both resident and migratory, while on open rocky terrain the quail often can be sighted. In all the birds total 150 species, including the eagle and several Sicilian endemics. The underlying backbone of limestone covered by Tertiary era soils provides the base for interesting vegetation, with a blend of Mediterranean types.

Walkers should not expect to find a classical park situation with information centres and marked trails, but a vast wilderness where exploration is possible for days on end without meeting another soul. There is a labyrinth of dirt roads, the heritage of age-old stock routes, now used by Toyota-mounted herders or forestry rangers. For the time being there is little in the way of waymarking, mountain refuges or bivouac huts, as apart from sporadic cross-country skiing, outdoor leisure activities such as walking are little practised. The area is well suited to horse-riding and mountain-biking.

In addition to the delightful mountain chalet at the start of Walk 40, visitors can stay in the handful of towns or villages on the outer edges of the park that offer food and lodging.

The two moderate walks given here are intended to give a taste of the Nebrodi: the first follows a ridge in the heart of the park, while the second covers a picturesque valley on the easternmost edge. Both are feasible with either private or public transport.

Parco dei Nebrodi headquarters at Caronia Tel 0921-333211 www.parcodeinebrodi.it

WALK 39
Biviere di Cesarò

Time	Biviere – 4hr; Alcara Li Fusi – 4hr 30min
Distance	Biviere – 18km/11.2 miles; Alcara Li Fusi – 23km/14.5 miles
Ascent/descent	Biviere 250m/250m; Alcara Li Fusi 1000m descent
Grade	1–2
Start/finish	Portella Femmina Morta
Access	All drivers will need the SS 289, which virtually bisects the Nebrodi park area north–south. Those approaching from the north and the Tyrrhenian coast will find it branching off the main coastal road (SS 113) a short distance west of S. Agata Militello, which has its own exit from the A20 Messina–Palermo *autostrada*. From the south the SS 289 runs through Cesarò and can be joined at Bronte on the SS 284, for example. The starting point, Portella Femmina Morta, is located 33km from S. Agata Militello and 18km from Cesarò. By public transport, the ISEA company has a daily year-round service that connects S. Agata Militello with Cesarò, Bronte and Catania. Cesarò can also be reached from Randazzo and Taormina on the Interbus run. Alcara Li Fusi is served by Sberna from S. Agata Militello.

This walk takes you on a wander through wild, thickly wooded rolling hills, where the order of the day is encounters with roaming shy wild pigs, sheep and the elegant, dark reddish Sanfratello horses left to graze freely. Starting out from a quiet mountain pass set at 1500m in the heart of the Nebrodi mountain chain it passes through beautiful beech wood and takes a panoramic ridge leading to a fascinating inland lake, the Biviere di Cesarò. This is a strategic refuelling stop-over for vast flocks of migratory birds, a real boon for enthusiasts. A good number of species actually make the lake their nesting and breeding station, creating a resident population that includes coots, kingfishers and grey herons, along with the pond turtle.

Biviere di Cesarò

For the geologically minded, the terrain is composed of flysch, a combination of layers of clay and limestone rich in fossils from when the zone was at a submarine level. Thus a wide range of soils, and a corresponding variety of flora, such as concentrations of wild peonies on clear rocky zones, along with orchids and roses.

Thick mists are not uncommon here, though wide tracks are followed all the way and the route is straightforward. Any time of year is suitable, even midsummer when these cool heights are a haven for those fleeing the scorching lowlands. While November is the busiest time for winged visitors, at this time of year two-footed types may have to deal with particularly crisp conditions and possibly ice. These medium-altitude reaches of the Nebrodi are generally blanketed in snow from around December to March, much to the delight of cross-country skiers and toboggan enthusiasts. The starting point, Portella Femmina Morta (pass of the dead woman), is supposedly a reference to a mysterious female figure said to have perished in the snow in some bygone era. Walkers in any season should be equipped with picnic supplies, drinking water and binoculars.

The enchanting hotel-cum-chalet known as Villa Miraglia, set among the squirrel-ridden wood close to the walk start, is highly recommended. Its renowned rustic restaurant serves hearty local dishes such as home-made maccheroni pasta tubes with a rich tomato and meat sauce, followed by *castrato*, choice grilled lamb. The hotel is a museum of Sicilian craftwork, decorated with old painted cart boards, puppets and some marvellous ceramics.

The walk can be extended into a rewarding traverse (see below) by proceeding down to the village of Alcara Li Fusi, set below the limestone outcrop of Rocche del Crasto, home to rare eagles. In addition to accommodation and a bus service, it offers visits to some interesting limestone caves, such as the Grotta del Lauro. Moreover, summer visitors will have the privilege of participating in the ancient 'Muzzini' festivities, held religiously on June 24, and the chance to appreciate the village's colourful home-woven cloths known as *pizzari*.

A worthwhile detour can be made to Monte Soro, at 1847m the highest point in the Nebrodi mountains. It is accessible by way of a good, if narrow, 5km surfaced road from Portella Femmina Morta – allow 2hr return time on foot. The summit affords wide-ranging views.

THE WALK

From the main road and the scenic opening at **Portella Femmina Morta** (1524m), take the lane to the right of the surfaced road leading to Monte Soro, in the *riserva naturale orientata*. You head northeast through beautiful beech wood which alternates with grassy clearings affording lovely views of the northern aspect of distant Mount Etna. A little over 15min is **Portella Calaudera** (1562m), where you cross over the Monte Soro road onto a rougher stony track dropping quite steeply at times. Here the majestic beech is interspersed with clumps of holly and scented bushes of wild rose, providing shelter for a wide variety of both bird and animal life, including noisy jays and woodpeckers. The only other frequenters of this dense wood, known as Sollazzo Verde, are likely to be Sunday picnickers and forestry workers.

The next landmark is pleasant man-made **Lago Maulazzo** (1444m, 45min), created in the 1980s by the

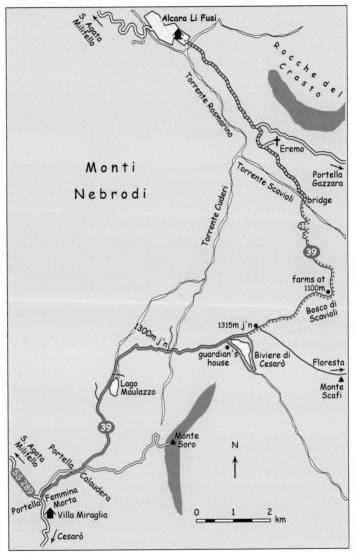

Rocche del Crasto

Forestry Commission for pastoral purposes, is set on the northwestern slopes of M. Soro.

The track follows the lake's left bank and its fencing, past a junction (link right to M. Soro), and heads gradually downhill (northwards) alongside a stream. Open pasture and beech wood continue to a shepherd's hut and junction (1300m), where you keep right over a watercourse, Torrente Cuderi. After a longish shady stretch eastwards of gentle ups and downs, the horizon north starts to open up with the first glimpses of the impressive 1315m limestone formation Rocche del Crasto that dwarfs the township of Alcara Li Fusi.

In a while you pass the lake **guardian's house**, (ignore a track left), and cover the remaining metres to the reserve that encompasses the **Biviere di Cesarò** (2hr, 1276m). The magnificent body of water opens up abruptly to your right, backed by the unmistakable volcanic form of Etna southeast. One of the stiles lets you in to the lake zone itself and the path around the water's edge, to the right or left at will.

Tourist Office
Alcara Li Fusi
Tel 0941-793130

Accommodation
Alcara Li Fusi:
Albergo Castelturio
Tel 0941-793788
B&B Nicolò
Tel 347-2927684
Cesarò:
Albergo Nebrodi
Tel 095-696107
B&B Saint Carlos
Tel 095 697063
Portella Femmina
Morta: Villa Miraglia
Tel 095-7732133

Basin-like Biviere di Cesarò, set below the northeastern flanks of Monte Soro and the western edge of Monte Scafi, accounts for some 18 hectares, and is edged in on the southwest by more beeches, holly and the occasional yew tree. The water itself hosts an extraordinary variety of reeds and rushes, the stuff of impressive floating islands and perfect retreats for nesting waterfowl; then there are delicate flowering plants such as pondweed, responsible for adorning the surface with a light rose-tinged sheen. Moreover, in the summer months a stronger red hue appears, courtesy of a micro-alga. The lake has long been a crucial watering hole for flocks of sheep as well as the winged visitors. A couple of hours can easily be spent exploring its perimeter and watching birds or the multitudes of bright butterflies, and enjoying the breezes that cool the banks.

Return to **Portella Femmina Morta** the same way (a further 2hr).

Extension to Alcara Li Fusi (2hr 30min)

Leave **Biviere di Cesarò** and continue on the main track a short distance east along the ridge to a **1315m junction**. Take the left branch (northeast) down between fields of cereals and lean pasture (while the right fork proceeds east, eventually reaching Floresta). Trees are few and far between at this point and Alcara Li Fusi is soon in sight. After a sole house, the track veers right (east) into shady wood, the Bosco di Scavioli. Further around a couple of **farms** are passed (1100m), then you swing north. Some time later, after a series of seemingly endless curves, the **bridge** over Torrente Scavioli is eventually reached, followed by a quiet 5.5km surfaced road northwest towards the township, out of sight for the time being. Stick to this lower road, ignoring turn-offs, (unless you wish to climb to the Eremo di San Nicola at 595m). Through picturesque gardens and paddocks, you reach the modest town of **Alcara Li Fusi** (420m) and its marvellous 18th-century fountain, la Fontana dei setti cannoli, which spouts delicious cool water year-long, as the residents recount with pride. The Motta, the old part of town, has narrow, well-kept medieval streets, a scattering of churches and the remains of a castle which acted as the outpost of fortifications dating back to the Arab period.

WALK 40
Floresta to Randazzo

Time	3hr 15min
Distance	15km/9.7 miles
Descent	500m
Grade	2
Start/finish	Floresta/Randazzo
Access	Randazzo, at the northeastern base of Monte Etna, lies on the SS 120. It is also on the Circumetnea train line that connects Catania with Giarre-Riposto, and is served by SAIS buses from convenient tourist points such as Taormina via the Alcantara. SAIS is also responsible for the Mon–Fri line to Floresta. At the time of writing, the early afternoon bus to Floresta gave sufficient time to do the walk. Floresta is on the SS 116, due north of Randazzo.

A delightful stroll through woods and cool valleys in the easternmost part of the Nebrodi mountain chain, this peaceful walk follows an ancient route, long transformed into a country lane on the first stretch, and then a track through a Forestry Department reserve. It runs parallel to the early course of the celebrated Fiume Alcantara, which later flows through a renowned sculpted basalt gorge, the spectacular Gole dell'Alcantara, in the proximity of Francavilla on the lower northern edge of Etna (see Walk 4). The descent is gradual and problem free, and accompanied by constant views of unmistakable, dominating Monte Etna.

The itinerary commences at the sleepy village of Floresta, its name a reference to 'forest'. It is said to have been settled by bandits fleeing from the Spanish authorities, though other sources date its foundation to the 17th century, when population increases led to emigration to the mountainous recesses of the interior. Floresta's claims to fame are as the highest-placed village in Sicily on the watershed of the Nebrodi, a month or two of snow every year, and a lively, large-scale livestock fair in late July.

In contrast is the walk's destination, the somewhat stately township of Randazzo. It harks back to the early Middle Ages, as clearly demonstrated by its surviving medieval heart. The first settlers were probably Greeks, retreating from the ninth-century Arab invasion, and were followed by Latin people and Lombards, each of which built up a separate district, maintaining distinct language and customs right up until the 16th century. This explains why the town today has three major churches. Randazzo's geographical location – on the lower southern skirt of Etna in addition to the northernmost border of the Nebrodi range – is embodied in its architecture: dark volcanic stone is set side by side with the limestone that characterises the Nebrodi, and to great effect. The old district, with its basalt-paved alleyways and picturesque arches, merits a visit. The 12th-century Castel Svevo, formerly a prison infamous for its gory tortures, has a low-key archaeological museum and a collection of gigantic traditional Sicilian puppets. In its more recent history (1981), Randazzo had a close call with advancing lava – the main road from the east together with the railway line were cut off, but luckily the flow ended up at the river, missing the town by a matter of metres. Visitors flock to Randazzo mid-August for the Festa dell'Assunta when a 20m tall tower-like *vara* construction, with 25 children precariously hanging on, is transported through the streets. Randazzo makes a good base for visits to both the Etna and the Nebrodi, as it is well served by public transport, and offers a range of accommodation and food, such as renowned pistachio-filled pastries, good walking fare. Floresta, on the other hand, offers little more than a shop or two, café and trattoria, though its flavoursome *provola* cheese and cured sausages are worth tasting.

Virtually any time of year is feasible for the walk, with the exception of the mid-winter months when snow could be a problem, not to mention mid-summer when temperatures soar.

THE WALK

From the bus stop in Floresta's quiet **Piazza Umberto I°** (1275m), walk west along the main street to the traffic mirrors on the first corner, then turn down as per signs for the *cimitero*. Old and not-so-old houses are quickly left behind as you venture out into pasture land. Take the narrow surfaced road right just before the **cemetery** for the descent into lovely woodland thick with dog roses. The quiet road follows a stream, the Fiume Alcantara, a short distance downhill from its source. At this stage it is lined with poplars, broom and huge wild fennel plants.

A sizeable farm is followed by a **1080m junction** (35min), where the road becomes a dirt lane. Keep left through the idyllic broad grazing valley known as the **Piano Grande**, frequented by cows, donkeys and the elegant dark red coated horses from San Fratello in the northern Nebrodi. Heading southeast now, you coast close to the water course shaded by willows, below light grey cliffs and the photogenic outcrops of Punta dell'Inferno and Punta Randazzo Vecchio high above. In a delightful shady stretch after a gate are the scant ruins of the **Mulino di San Giacomo** (mill) and concrete water tanks. It's a matter of metres now to the junction (1065m, 1hr), where you go left to cross the river by way of a small concrete **dam**-cum-bridge, and enter the Forestry area.

The massive triangle of the volcano has reappeared. The track, widened for the purposes of reforestation and fire control, begins a gradual ascent east at first. Here is drier wood, where young conifers alternate with downy and holm oak, chestnut and Mediterranean maquis, along with huge purple orchids. Gigantic wild fennel sprout in every conceivable clearing. 20min from the river crossing you traverse a tall shady wood with a spring (1145m, ignore the fork off left). Still climbing, southish now, you pass another fork and keep right. The

track levels out and Randazzo is soon visible in its broad valley. After another spring (Fontana del Primitivo) is a great scenic curve coloured with masses of broom and oversized thistles. Seeing the Sicilian rock partridge is not unusual on these open stretches, scuttling back into the undergrowth with chicks in tow. A slight descent leads to the well-kept Forestry buildings of **S. Maria del Bosco** (1090m, 1hr 45min), complete with a chapel, drinking water and picnic tables set under the trees. The views are of course lovely, with Monte Colla west over the valley.

From here on, the route continues in a similar vein, following the ins and outs of the Fiume Alcantara river valley with the water course appearing and disappearing from time to time. There are occasional copses of eucalypts, cypresses and poplars, and herds of shy pigs will often surprise you. The rumblings of Etna are within earshot, while the successions of lava flows on its southeastern flank are clearly distinguishable.

A total of 2hr 45min (945m) will see you at a **stile/gate** as you leave the Forestry area, and a good track proceeds downhill through more pasture country. Randazzo is a stone's throw across the valley now, literally engulfed in swallows. Its ancient gateways are embedded in the lower walls and its three monumental churches stand out from the skyline. After 20min you join the tarmac road for two hairpin bends to the river, then after the **bridge** take the lane sharp right. This old access route leads below remnants of defensive wall and turreted fortifications, and into the township. After the steps, turn right for the striking 13th-century Chiesa di S. Maria, then left down the dark basalt-paved Corso Umberto I° for Piazza Loreto in **Randazzo** (750m, 3hr 15min).

Tourist Office
Randazzo
Tel 095-923841

Accommodation
Randazzo:
Hotel Scrivano
Tel 095-921126
www.hotelscrivano.
com
B&B Ai Tre Parchi
Bed and Bike
Tel 095-7991631
Mob 329-8970901
www.aitreparchibb.it

LE ISOLE EOLIE (Aeolian Islands)

Glassy black obsidian and bleached pumice stone characterise **Lipari**, intense green conjures up **Salina**'s woods and caper gardens, then there's the sulphur yellow found on **Vulcano**'s lunar crater, and the cinder black beaches and fiery red eruptions on Stromboli. While united by volcanic origins, these four of the seven Aeolian islands could not be more different (the 'missing' three islands are Panarea, Alicudi and Filicudi). Laid out in a Y-configuration corresponding to three massive intersecting fractures in the Tyrrhenian Sea off the north coast of Sicily, they are actually the summits of a submerged chain of mountains. The closest to the Sicilian mainland is Vulcano at 25km, while the most distant, Stromboli, clocks in at 75km.

As the name suggests, the group has been home to the god of winds, Aeolus, since at least ancient Greek times, and is a perfect place to go during a sweltering Sicilian summer, as temperatures rarely exceed the mid-20s thanks to the cooling breezes. April through to October is the most suitable period for visits, though those with no tight time limits may enjoy the mild conditions during winter (13°C in January), when they may be windswept. Heavy seas are not unusual and ferry connections can be disrupted for days on end. In spring the air is balmy and heady with the scent of myriad wild flowers. January receives the most rain, and the hottest month is July.

The islands were probably first valued for their naturally occurring obsidian in prehistoric times, while later promotion came from Homer's descriptions of the wonders in *The Odyssey*. There have also been several interesting cinematographic works – the 1949 *Stromboli* by Roberto Rossellini, starring Ingrid Bergman, and Michael Radford's poignant *Il Postino* (*The Postman*) set on Salina.

Beaches are not extensive due to the sheer nature of the coastlines, so private boat services provide opportunities for swimming and diving, as well as the recommended round-island trips which include marine caves.

Before the advent of tourism, the islands subsisted on fishing, trading and agriculture, though after the early 1800s there was vast migration to Australia and the US. For instance, Alicudi's erstwhile population of 2000 has dwindled to 100. Some emigrants have since returned home, and it is not unusual to be addressed in Oz English in the shops.

Local products continue to include meat and fish, but it is the capers and grapes that have become famous – the latter for the sweet dessert wine *malvasia* from Salina and Lipari, produced as far back as Greek times, and renowned in medieval times as a muscat. However, so low are present-day production levels (and so extortionate are prices) that most of the *malvasia* sold on the islands is a slightly inferior quality imported from the Sicilian mainland. Capers, on the other hand, abound in two varieties: the classical caper, the pre-flower or bud type, then the elongated fruit known locally as *cucunci*.

Accommodation

Visitors won't normally encounter difficulty in finding somewhere to stay outside the late July–August period, when advance booking is advisable. In addition to the broad range of hotels on Lipari, the other islands have modest *pensioni* in addition to private rooms, whose owners usually wait at the harbour to meet incoming boats and offer lodgings.

Wild camping is forbidden throughout the Eolie, but there are camping grounds on Lipari and Salina.

Transport to the islands

The port of Milazzo on the northern coast of Sicily is the main base for passenger-vehicle ferries and hydrofoils to the Eolie, and the timetable is intensified from June to September. Milazzo, in turn, can be reached by train (then local bus to the port), by coach from a number of towns in Sicily, or by car via the A20 Messina-Palermo *autostrada*.

Additional hydrofoil runs are arranged daily in summer from Naples, Cefalù and Palermo, and there is also a Naples–Milazzo overnight ferry which calls in at Stromboli, Panarea, Salina, Lipari and Vulcano several times a week all year round. A further hydrofoil service from Reggio Calabria and Messina operates for a good part of the year. The

Sunrise near Panarea

The island-volcano of Stromboli

ferries are considerably slower than the sleek hydrofoils, but also much cheaper, more scenic and less likely to induce discomfort should the sea be rough. Hydrofoil services are also subject to cancellation under prohibitive meteorological conditions.

Visitors are allowed to take their own vehicles onto Lipari, Salina and Vulcano (outside the July–October period), though it is neither necessary nor recommended. Buses and taxis cover the limited distances involved.

Maps
Several fairly decent commercial maps of the Eolie are available at news stands and miscellaneous shops on the islands as well as the mainland port of Milazzo. At the time of writing the most up-to-date was the 1:25,000 'Isole Eolie o Lipari' by Arte Photo Graphic Oreste Ragusi, which also includes multilingual descriptions.

Tourist Office Lipari Tel 090-9880095 www.aasteolie.info acts as the main information point for all the islands and the web site has links to all transport timetables.

WALK 41
Vulcano's Gran Cratere

Time	2hr 15min
Distance	7km/4.3 miles
Ascent/descent	380m/380m
Grade	2
Map	1:25,000 'Isole Eolie o Lipari', Arte Photo Graphic Oreste Ragusi
Start/finish	Porto di Levante
Access	Virtually all the ferries and hydrofoils that run between Milazzo on the Sicilian mainland and the main island of Lipari stop at Porto di Levante on Vulcano.
Note	A modest fee is charged for access to the crater. Tickets can be purchased at the start of the path.

The world's very first volcano in etymological terms, Vulcano is also one of the islands in the enticing Aeolian group. The ancient Greeks, who speculated on the nature of volcanic eruptions, believed that the island was the workplace of lame Hephaestus (or Vulcan, according to the Romans), their deity for fire and blacksmith to the gods themselves. The dark smoke issuing from the crater announced that his forge was operating, with the help of the massive Cyclops, whereas the actual volcanic explosions were thought to be him hammering on the anvil.

The volcano here was long active, inspiring awe and reverence all through the ages. Its image was well exploited by the church as the gateway to hell. 'Enemies', the likes of several Frankish sovereigns, were reportedly bound and cast into the fiery crater, while the king of the Goths, mounted on a white steed, was hounded over the rim by the Pope in person! The rumblings of the volcano were said to be the torments of souls in hell, and the flames that issued from the crater the suffering of the sinners. A resident hermit told of the cries of the demons when a soul escaped them on the strength of prayers and alms from the faithful on earth, and when the account filtered back to the Benedictine monastery at Cluny in France, the abbot declared a special day be instituted – 2 November, All Souls Day.

Modern-day visitors will find the volcano on Vulcano essentially dormant, its only sign of life the bellowing clouds of sulphur-ridden, rotten-egg gas emitted from the fumarole vents on the crater rim: a dramatic and evocative sight. Scientists, however, are keeping the crater under constant surveillance as gas discharges are reportedly escalating. Live images of the volcano (filmed from the island of Lipari) can be obtained at www.ct.ingv.it.

Early in the 19th century an extensive industry for the extraction and processing of sulphur, alum and boric acid was established by a Bourbon general, along with large-scale construction of roads and factories. The Scottish entrepreneur Stevenson took over mid-century and purchased the entire island. He had a decent track built up the mountain flank and huts for the workmen inside the actual crater, however it all ended in 1888 with a massive, fiery, explosive eruption that lasted 19 months.

The Gran Cratere can presently be visited with ease on a well-graded path. The yawning ulcer-like pit is still an awesome sight and involves a moderately easy trek. Anyone who feels up to a gentle hour-long climb should embark on this itinerary. Drinking water is recommended as are decent

Great views from Vulcano's crater

non-slip shoes or light walking boots as the way can be very slippery if wet. Small children will need constant supervision on the upper rim as, though the path is good, there are steep drops on either side. It's advisable to avoid inhaling the sulphur-laden gases emitted by the *fumarole*.

In short, it is a must for everyone. If you only manage an ascent to a single volcano, make it this one. It is by far the easiest and safest (compared to Etna and Stromboli) and, despite the lack of ongoing lava flows, offers myriad volcanic phenomena, not forgetting the marvellous views from the 390m top.

One follow-up to the walk is a wallow in the radioactive mud in the caramel-coloured pools on the beach, a matter of minutes north of the port. A Fellini-esque scene assails the senses. The mud can evidently cure a surprising array of ills if applied with constancy, and is best followed by a refreshing cleansing dip in the sea, where warm bubbles surface from submarine *fumarole*. Close by is a curious headland composed of a rainbow of volcanic debris.

The northern extremity of Vulcano consists of the modest promontory of Vulcanello, a 123m cone formed by a submarine eruption in 183BC and joined to the rest of the island by a slender isthmus, which is submerged by high tides. The area now hosts a sprawl of upmarket accommodation for the peak-season tourists who inflate the skeleton population of 250 to 10,000, rather too many for safety at such close quarters to an active volcano, according to experts.

THE WALK

From the landing stage at Vulcano's **Porto di Levante** (10m), in the looming shade of the volcano, take the main road southwest. The area backing the beach on your left once housed the industrial zone, beneath the Forgia Vecchia. You pass an *alimentari* (grocery shop), recommended for lunch supplies, and begin to circle the broad eastern flank of the volcano. Signs for '*accesso al cratere*' soon appear along the roadside, and 15min along is a prominent pine and start of the wide path for the crater and the ticket booth. The setting is desolate, gravel and black sand barely anchored by sparse grass and scraggly broom, very little cover for the nervous rabbits. The initial arm of the leisurely winding way goes northeast, followed by longer, straighter climbs over shallow

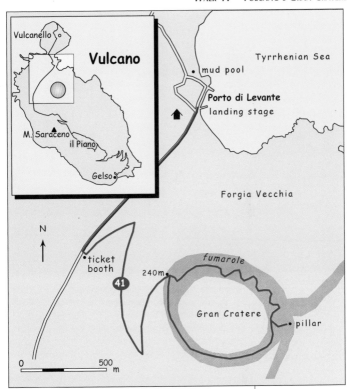

gullies towards a curious pink clay corridor modelled by rainwater runs. The air is heavy with the stench of nearby *fumarole*, surrounded by yellow sulphur deposits. ▶

At **240m** (50min) is the edge of a lunar rock desert and marvellous viewing point to the neighbouring islands. Take the centre path for the ensuing climb to the actual **Gran Cratere**, enveloped in steamy-looking vapours and overpowering sulphurous gas released by gashes in the rim. The temperature of these fumarole vents has been known to attain 400°C (in 1987) – approach with due respect! The crater itself is inviting, however a descent can be extremely dangerous, particularly on a windless day, due to the lethal

Rest stops give you the chance to appreciate the clear cone shapes of the minor Vulcanello formations behind on the promontory.

The Gran Cratere, Vulcano

concentrations of CO_2 that settle in its depths.

Winds and odour permitting, cross the jaundiced ground on the crater rim pitted with vents and bright yellow crystals and proceed southeast for the steep, tight zigzags up the shoulder. A junction is passed before the highest point of the rim is reached, marked by a **pillar** (391m, 1hr 15min). (An alternate, if longer, route is to circle the crater via the southern edge as per the descent route.) A panoramic and windswept point frequented by acrobatic wheeling crows, it affords far-reaching views that extend to the Sicilian mainland. Closer at hand are the island's surprisingly dense woods, not to mention Monte Saraceno to the south. However, it is the dramatic gaping crater below with its striking colour contrasts that holds your attention. A perfect circle 500m in diameter and 200m deep, it is reminiscent of a set from a sci-fi film, and you almost expect the floor to open up to release a flying saucer.

For the descent, return to the nearby junction and turn left to circle the airy southwestern rim. 15min will see you back at the **240m junction**, then it's a further 30min to the road leading back to **Porto di Levante** (1hr return).

Tourist Office
Tel 090-9852028
(June–Oct)

Accommodation
La Giara
Tel 090-9852229
Buganville
Tel 0909853090

WALK 42

Lipari's Castello and Southern Headlands

Time	Castello – 40min;
	main walk – 2hr 40min
Distance	Castello – 1.1km/0.7 miles;
	main walk – 9.3km/5.8 miles
Ascent/descent	Main walk – 200m
Grade	Castello – 1; main walk – 2
Map	1:25,000 'Isole Eolie o Lipari', Arte Photo Graphic
	Oreste Ragusi
Start/finish	Marina Corta
Access	All ferries and hydrofoils bound for the Aeolian islands come to Lipari (see the Isole Egadi introduction). Visitors who arrive by ferry or hydrofoil will need to cross the township south (10min on foot) to reach Marina Corta where the walks start.

Originally known as Meligunis, this island was renamed Lipari, a possible derivation from the ancient Greek for 'fertile' if not from Liparo, first mythical king of the island. Settlement by colonisers of Sicilian stock dates far back to Neolithic times (around 4000BC). The arrivals are believed to have been attracted by the rich deposits of obsidian: harder and sharper than flint, the prized glassy black material of volcanic origin was in great demand when fashioned into all manner of implements and ornaments. On the other hand, the mining of pumice, of identical composition to obsidian, was essential to the island's economy until recently. Obsidian is expelled by a volcano in its final stage of eruption, when the temperature has dropped and the slow cooling process means the dissolved gases remain entrapped in the lava. Spongy pumice, in contrast, is formed when the volcano is much hotter and the material is exuded as a liquid. So rapidly does cooling take place that the gases are released in a rush, forestalling crystallisation and thus resulting in the frothy structure. It was much in demand as an abrasive for

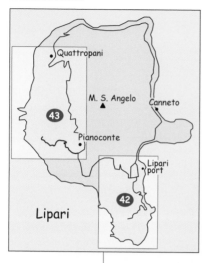

cleaning purposes, ballast for railways and a lightweight aggregate in pre-cast masonry. A vast chunk of northeastern Lipari has been excavated for pumice, resulting in some unsightly desert-like landscapes that are punctuated by rusting machinery relics painted white by the invasive dust. The good news is that residue on the sea floor enhances the beautiful aquamarine hue of the transparent sea.

As was the norm in this part of the Mediterranean, Lipari had its full share of visitors, conquerors and raiders in the shape of Greeks, Carthaginians, Romans, various Barbarians, Saracens and Normans. Virtually everyone moved into the so-called Castello, the heart of the township of Lipari, a raised natural rock platform dominating the twin harbours. One early occupant was plausibly King Aeolus, captain of the winds, who transformed it into a stronghold encircled by an unbroken wall of bronze. He made the hero Ulysses the gift of the famous oxhide bag with all the winds but one useful one imprisoned in it. As the story goes, the bag was subsequently loosened by a curious sailor, and they were blown mercilessly off course.

Another prominent character in the history of Lipari, who had the habit of reappearing at key times, was the early Christian martyr St Bartholomew, or San Bartolo, as he is known locally. Although he met his gruesome end (flayed then decapitated) in distant Armenia, his stone coffin miraculously washed up on the shores of Lipari on 13 February, AD264, and he is venerated as the protector of the islands. During the Arab invasion in AD838, the saint's remains were flung into the sea, this time thoroughly dismembered and mixed with those of other holy men. Not easily discouraged, the saint appeared in a dream to a handful of monks who were instructed to make haste to the sea and gather his bones, which were bright and luminous, shining in the dark water like stars. The body has since been transported to Benevento for safekeeping, however Lipari's cathedral boasts a fragment of arm and a thumb. San Bartolo's protection was invoked in 1693 when Sicily was subjected to widespread earthquake devastation – and there was not a single victim on the islands. He similarly intervened on behalf of the islanders during a terrible famine, guiding a phantom ship loaded with foodstuffs to their aid, as well as lending a helping hand during times of plague.

Lipari is the most populous of the Aeolian islands, with 8500 permanent inhabitants, and acts as a transport hub and administrative centre. Moreover its excellent range of accommodation and facilities make it a convenient base for visiting the other islands.

The initial section of the walk is a stroll round the historic *castello*, a natural stage where the history of Lipari has been played out; it is occupied by the excellent archaeological museum and a good hostel. The main walk touches on superb lookout points over the rugged southwestern extremities of the island and affords marvellous views onto the massive crater of Vulcano. Plenty of drinking water and a sun hat are essential, and the lack of shade makes it unsuitable for the peak of summer.

Lipari's fortified castle

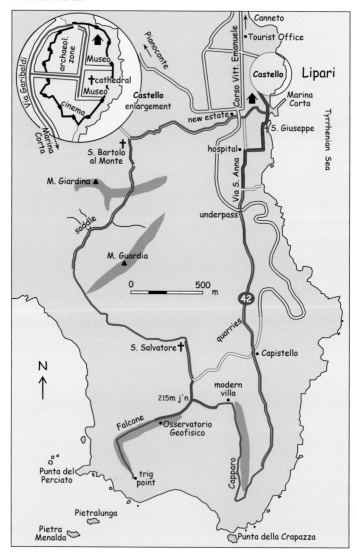

THE WALK

The Castello (40min)

Start at **Marina Corta**, which features a picture-postcard harbour of fishing boats alongside the old church erected for the *anime del purgatorio* ('souls in purgatory'). From the waterfront and statue of San Bartolo in the shade of the natural massif, or castle, take broad Via Garibaldi (northwest), that climbs in the shade of the imposing ramparts constructed by the Spanish in the wake of the devastation wrought by the Barbary pirate Khayr ad-Din alias Barbarossa (Redbeard) in 1544. Past the rows of craft shops and recommended traditional restaurant La Cambusa, the paved street runs the entire western flank of the fortified platform – ignore the main stone staircase access for the time being. At a small square below the northern corner, take the stepped lane right for the original entrance to the Castello. An intriguing covered passageway leads via a series of ancient walls (dating back to the fourth century BC) and slit openings which afford attractive glimpses of the town and its coves, and into the erstwhile stronghold. Alongside the well-placed youth hostel are the numerous rooms of the excellent *museo archeologico*, (a prison for political detainees under both the Bourbons and the fascists). Opposite are circular huts from the Bronze Age and remnants of the roadway from the period the Castello served as the Greek acropolis, side by side with 18th-century churches (archaeological zone).

A little further on is the cathedral dedicated to San Bartolo. Adjacent is the former Bishop's Palace, erstwhile Benedictine monastery. The southernmost extremity of the Castello is taken up by an open-air cinema, popular on summer evenings. Close by is a line-up of stone sarcophaguses from the Greek–Roman periods, unearthed in the lower part of town. There are a number of panoramic walkways via the ramparts and pleasant shady rest areas.

Leave the Castello by way of Via del Concordato, the majestic flight of steps opposite the cathedral, and return to **Marina Corta**.

The Main Walk (2hr 40min)

From **Marina Corta** follow the waterfront south away from the Castello and take a lane (Salita San Giuseppe) to the picturesque church of **San Giuseppe**, perched on the cliff edge. A brief uphill stretch into the old part of town, with

231

its typical narrow alleyways, leads to Hotel Villa Meligunis, where you go left onto Via Maddalena. The second on the right, Via Dante, brings you to the entrance for the archipelago's **hospital**, hence left onto Via Sant'Anna and into a quiet, country-like atmosphere. In a short while, where a narrow road turns down left for Hotel Carasco, you keep right (10min). This passes beneath the main road south from Lipari, sustained by a tall stone wall, and quickly becomes a sunken lane all but smothered by caper plants, broom and rock roses. It passes through a deep-cut valley, whose craggy outcrops are frequented by sizeable birds of prey. Ignore the odd turn-off for small quarries, and you'll emerge on tarmac at **Capistello** (120m, 25min), for the first splendid views over to Vulcanello, the northernmost promontory of the island of Vulcano.

Take the concrete ramp in descent south on the opposite side of the road (signposted for the Osservatorio). An ensuing climb leads past modest whitewashed holiday houses overgrown with vivid bougainvillea. Far-off Stromboli, with its plume of smoke, and Panarea come into view, as does mainland Sicily. The way narrows to a good path, lined with artemisia and rock roses, high over the sea heading towards the channel between the two islands, backed by the looming shape of Vulcano and its vast smoking crater.

Some 45min from the township you reach a lookout (103m) over **Punta della Crapazza** and a number of rock pinnacles rising out of the sea. Where the path turns down left, leave it for the faint trace right (northwards) straight up the crest (**Capparo**). A clear path quickly appears, flanked by

Marina Corta, Lipari

an old stone wall, through windblown heather and scraggly broom, the hideout of wild rabbits. At the top, on the edge of a private property (low-set **modern villa**), keep left around the perimeter fencing to pines then the concreted access lane. This veers around west to a junction (215m) – take the left fork for the white buildings of the **Osservatorio Geofisico** (226m). A marvellous spread of islands comes into view, and you take in Alicudi and Filicudi northwest, and Salina with its twin volcanic peaks north-northwest.

After the buildings a path strikes out southwest, through shoulder-high shrubs and aromatic herbs, across the headland ridge known as **Falcone**. Bear left over eroded Punta del Perciato to a **trig point** (215m, 1hr 20min) with marvellous views over the rock pillars in the sea, Pietralunga and Pietra Menalda, as well as an inviting black sand beach far below (boat access only). On a clear day the unmistakable towering form of Etna can be seen due south. ▸

Backtrack past the observatory to the **junction at 215m** and take the left fork. As the main road drops towards Capistello keep straight on for the lane heading north past houses to the tiny old church of **San Salvatore**. From there it's the lovely narrow old path left (west) overgrown with rushes. It follows a side valley in the shade of Monte Guardia, then coasts northwards through a wild area high over the rugged western coastline. Scattered huts and a concreted section past a vineyard precede a crossroads in a **saddle** between Monte Guardia and Monte Giardina. Lipari and its impressive Castello complex come into view now on the eastern coast. Keep straight on (north) following the vehicle-width track through light wood for the gradual descent towards the township.

At the photogenic whitewashed church of **S. Bartolo al Monte** (157m), turn right down the dreadfully steep lane, which thankfully soon returns to its original form as a picturesque paved winding mule track. At the bottom of the hill, you join the tarmac in a smart **housing estate**, and follow the road briefly right to its abrupt end. Via steps you drop into a sunken lane (or stormwater channel), which transits via an underpass to become Via Roma. This weaves its way downhill through the old part of town to emerge on the waterfront at **Marina Corta**. ▸

Accommodation
B&B Diana Brown
Tel 090-9812584
www.dianabrown.it
Affittacamere Enzo
il Negro
Tel 090-9812473
Ostello IYH (youth hostel)
Tel 090-9811540;
March–Oct

The ground here is scattered with fragments of glassy black obsidian from some long extinct volcano.

The harbourside cafés here specialise in luscious *granite* ices flavoured with coffee or fresh strawberry and peach, and served with a topping of thick cream. What better way to conclude the walk?

WALK 43
Lipari's San Calogero Spa

Time	1hr 45min
Distance	5.5km/3.4 miles
Ascent/descent	100m/240m
Grade	2
Map	1:25,000 'Isole Eolie o Lipari', Arte Photo Graphic Oreste Ragusi
Start/finish	bus stop, Quattropani/S. Calogero
Access	From the township's main bus stand at the northern extremity of Corso Vittorio Emanuele, near the car ferries, take the daily Urso bus via Pianoconte to Quattropani for the start of the walk. For the return, a bus runs from San Calogero to Lipari (Mon–Sat, May–Sept), otherwise continue on foot through to Pianoconte for the daily bus – see extension.

An unusual aspect of the popular island of Lipari is covered on this route along the dramatic cliffs on the western coast. Banks of long abandoned terracing high over the windswept coast precede the modest but curious ancient spa named after San Calogero, the popular saint associated with spas and mineral waters and widely revered throughout Sicily. Here he is attributed with causing the hot therapeutic waters to flow from the rock flanks, not to mention banishing all the devils from the island of Lipari. Furthermore the saint miraculously extinguished flames during an eruption from the island's erstwhile foremost active volcano, Monte Sant'Angelo; on that particular occasion the township of Lipari itself was threatened by the fires and the womenfolk vowed never again to let wine touch their lips if the fires would only cease.

As concerns the San Calogero area itself, despite disfiguration by an unseemly quasi-modern structure, the spa has a fascinating extant beehive tholos structure that harks back to 15th century BC (Bronze Age), though it was restructured by the Romans in fourth century BC in the wake of an earthquake.

Clearly well frequented through the ages for the healing effects of its waters, San Calogero is reputed to be the oldest known spa structure in the Mediterranean, as well as the only example of Mycenaean architecture outside Greece; their traders, in fact, regularly dropped in at Lipari for the obsidian.

The walk itself is straightforward and warmly recommended. Don't forget sun hats and wind jackets, as well as food and drink, as there is nothing in the way of grocery shops or bars until the very end of the walk. Springtime will mean waves of perfume from the many wild flowers, while the magnificent views over the coast are available all year round.

An extension to Pianoconte is given at the end – it entails an extra 30min, 2km/1.3 miles, and 130m of uphill.

THE WALK
Get off the bus at the very last stop in the spread-out village of **Quattropani** (282m). At the nearby curve in the road, take the concrete ramp downhill (south) through houses and gardens, ignoring the side alleys. About 5min on is a shallow gully where the track turns abruptly down right. Following it, you need the second lane to the left – it immediately becomes a picturesque old path lined by a stone wall bordering what were once prosperous market gardens. Ahead is a hillside bearing traces of extensive ancient terracing, while below, the first free-standing rock pillars in the sea come into view. The occasional red and yellow dots along the way serve as waymarking as you wind downhill through a riot of colourful plants dominated by olive trees, prickly pear, aromatic herbs and fragrant flowering broom.

Twenty minutes from the village the path becomes a wide dirt track running on a level on the top of wild cliffs, the sea a plunging 50m below. Directly overhead is the lofty outcrop with the curious appellation of Timpone Ospedale. After 45min on foot take the fork right towards the coast. A heap of stones – the **ruins** of a Saracen watchtower – are passed on a curve, then it's down to windswept **Punta Palmato** (40m) and stunning views of the splendid rock pinnacles Scoglio le Torricelle and the imposing eroded cliffs. Rock and earth colours vary from dark brown to deep red, while uphill, in contrast, are pale traces from a kaolin quarry.

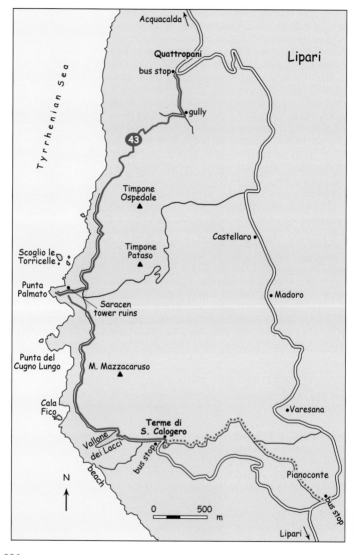

Back at the curve with the **ruins**, take the faint path that strikes out right (south) over the next grassy headland via a shallow gully with solitary dwarf palms and flowering goldy-locks. High over a wild cove it climbs to rejoin the main track just below a hut and trees in the proximity of the junction with the track that descends from the kaolin quarry behind Timpone Pataso.

Continuing south the next prominent outcrop is **Monte Mazzacaruso**, said to be where the ancient Greeks cast disabled infants into the sea, according the custom of the time. Soon the steep-sided cove of Cala Fico comes into view. Cala Fico is worth a brief detour for views of another curious rock outcrop that has separated itself from the coast to become a towering island and haven for nesting seabirds.

Shortly along the main track a number of huts and fertile olive groves are passed, then you veer left into **Vallone dei Lacci**, a shallow gully, to climb the hillside in wide curves. The lane is soon paved and climbs eastwards towards scattered houses. Through gardens of massive caper plants and grape vines, this leads past a fork (for a drop to a cove and beach) to the destination, **Terme di San Calogero** (141m, 1hr 45min). Uphill from the main building is the original spa

The rock pinnacles at Punta Palmato

construction. Reminiscent of an igloo, its sauna-like interior is fitted with stone benches, and a trickle of 60°C water still flows along the ancient channelling encrusted with calcium deposits.

Extension to Pianoconte (30min)

Briefly uphill from the ancient spa a lovely old paved mule track marked with red paint stripes heads up through the fields. It winds east for the most part and later becomes concrete-based. Ignore all the turn-offs. Several modest houses are passed, where the sparse trees are used as a drying rack for all manner of material ranging from onions and garlic to chilli peppers. After a long stretch southeast, the main road is joined at **Pianoconte** (260m, 30min from San Calogero), close to the bus stop for the return trip, while across the road is the local bar and a grocery shop.

Not far down the road at a bend, en route to Lipari, is a marvellous belvedere called Quattrocchi, which means 'four eyes', plausibly because that many are needed to appreciate the stunning coastline that presents itself, with Vulcano in the background.

Accommodation
see Walk 42

Further Walk

Monterosa, the 239m pinkish promontory to the northwest of the township of Lipari, is accessible by way of a clear track from the Marina Lunga waterfront due north of the port. As the road for Canneto turns inland for its tunnel, the track climbs alongside it before turning east for the panoramic summit. Allow 1hr 30min return time from the road.

WALK 44
Salina's Monte Fossa delle Felci

Time	3hr 30min
Distance	7.2km/4.5 miles
Ascent/descent	650m/950m
Grade	2–3
Map	1:25,000 'Isole Eolie o Lipari', Arte Photo Graphic Oreste Ragusi
Start/finish	Church of Madonna del Terzito/Santa Marina
Access	Frequent hydrofoils and slower ferries on both the Lipari–Panarea and the Lipari–Filicudi run stop at Salina's main port, Santa Marina. From there the daily Citis bus service transits via Malfa and climbs inland, via the Valdichiesa, to the saddle for the Madonna del Terzito sanctuary, where the walk starts.

The quiet island of Salina in the Aeolian group is recognisable from afar by its two towering trademark volcanoes, both long extinct, which appear to split the land mass in two. The Greeks, in fact, knew it as Didyme (twin). Salina was actually shaped over time by a total of six different volcanoes, which have bequeathed it a marvellously fertile heritage, encouraged by abundant fresh spring water. The outcome, sweet grapes for the renowned malmsey or *malvasia* wine, and capers, have long provided the mainstay along with fishing, although summer tourism has now gained the upper hand. Man has dwelt, worked, worshipped and imported ceramics on Salina since at least 2500BC, in common with the other Aeolian islands. However, apart from the lush woodland and thriving market gardens, any resemblance to a paradise is out of place, as the terrain can be terribly rough and inhospitable, of obvious volcanic composition with lapilli and rubble, making for easy erosion by rainwater and wind.

The name Salina comes from the salt pans once at Lingua, on the island's southernmost point. They have since shrunk to a triangular lake, which serves migratory birds as an R&R stopover – there have been reports of 25 pairs of

Eleonora's falcons nesting there. There are also wild geese and ducks, herons, and even swans, cranes and flamingos.

The walk ascends the mountain, or extinct volcano, Monte Fossa delle Felci, via a clear forestry track and a series of paths, with its destination a broad lookout area with unbeatable views over the islands and the Sicilian mainland. Since 1981 the area has been a State Forestry Department *riserva naturale*. The subsequent descent from the mountain follows a steep ridge down to the coast and Santa Marina, making sturdy non-slip walking shoes with ankle support a must (unless you go back the same way). A wind jacket could be handy as the peak, the highest point in the whole of the Aeolian island group, is understandably exposed to the elements. There is an extraordinary variety of vegetation, and the marvellous views amply repay all effort. Carry plenty of water and, of course, food.

The Walk

It's 5min from the **bus stop** up to the modest sanctuary and yellow-stuccoed church of **Madonna del Terzito** (313m). It stands at the foot of the immense bulk that culminates in Monte Fossa delle Felci and Monte Rivi. Take the track that runs around the building (left) to start climbing through vineyards invaded by sprawling caper plants. Very soon a signed path breaks off to the right, an old stepped way edged with dry-stone masonry. Forks are marked with the odd red paint spot or low cairn. The dirt road for forestry vehicles is crossed a couple of times as well. ◀ This delightful path passes through the broad swathe which is kept scrupulously cleared as a fire break circling the upper crown of the relief, and is visible from afar. Behind (west) is the perfect cone of bare Monte dei Porri. Some 40min, at 550m, you join the forestry track and follow it uphill briefly among Aleppo pines and the first chestnut trees before the path itself resumes, right.

An hour and 700m in altitude will see you rejoin the dirt road, left, with views having opened up to include Alicudi and Filicudi beyond Monte dei Porri now. Close at hand is a signed **Y-junction** – keep right for Monte Fossa delle Felci. North now, you are led past a forestry hut then onto the open ridge and picnic area (800m). At the ensuing four-way junction (left for the 854m top of Monte Rivi, or

Early morning means cool, shady walking through the aromatic herbs such as oregano and sage, mixed with ferns and typical shrubby Mediterranean species, which make for a luxuriant cover with tree heather, lentisc, the strawberry tree, colourful rock roses and introduced eucalypts down for the alternative descent route to Santa Marina), keep on south along the wide cleared ridge to reconnect with a vehicle track. Via shady wood, with lovely views north of smoking Stromboli and even the Italian mainland on a good day, you eventually reach a saddle (930m) and a marvellous open position close to some antennas. Turn sharp right up the final stretch of track to the cross on the 960m 'peak' of **Monte Fossa delle Felci** (1hr 45min). This is the northernmost edge of the ancient crater rim. Its 500m diameter and 100m depth notwithstanding, it is a little difficult to discern as it is choked with trees, heather, juniper and, of course, ferns, hence the name – *felci* is Italian for ferns. ▶

Back down at the junction near the antennas, go right and follow the rocky ridge (the former crater rim) via a series of huts and shrubs south to its very scenic end (5min). This lookout affords spectacular views over Lingua, the southernmost point of Salina.

These heights usually feature swallows, crows and birds of prey such as the hovering kestrel. The islands of Lipari, Vulcano, Alicudi and Filicudi are clearly visible, plus the coast of Sicily itself.

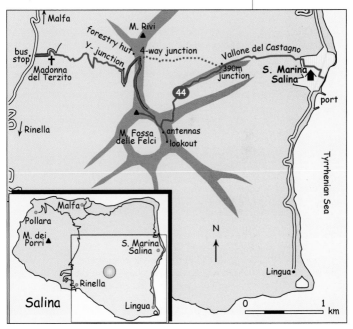

Accommodation
Santa Marina:
Hotel Bellavista
Tel 090-9843009
Lingua: *Affittacamere*
A Cannata
Tel 090-9843172

Retrace your steps along the ridge, and just after the antennas is a fork downhill (marker pole) for the descent path. Stepped at first, the going is steep and can be slippery if wet, due to the clay underfoot. You are mostly sheltered by light wood, including birch, under which cyclamen bloom. The path wastes no time in dropping, crossing a wide track and intersecting another path, but you keep relentlessly downhill with the occasional view to Santa Marina and the port. The vegetation becomes drier and fencing starts, and your situation becomes clearer – on a ridge, **Serro Favarolo**, between two plunging gullies, Vallone del Castagno to the north, beneath the southeastern flank of Monte Rivi, and Vallone di Batana to the south.

One hour in is a prominent **390m junction**, where the alternative path via the Vallone del Castagno from the four-way intersection joins up. Keep right at the ensuing fork, then right again as you encounter the surfaced road on the outskirts of Santa Marina. The village and ferry wharves are a short walk now, and you can stagger into the peaceful, typical port of **Santa Marina** (25m) and collapse at one of the waterside cafés for a refreshing *sorbetto* (descent 1hr 30min).

From Monte Fossa delle Felci, down to the lagoon of Lingua, then Lipari

WALK 45

*Stromboli –
Ascent to the Volcano*

Time	5hr
Distance	8.2km/5.1 miles
Ascent/descent	918m/918m
Grade	3
Map	1:25,000 'Isole Eolie o Lipari', Arte Photo Graphic Oreste Ragusi
Start/finish	Scari port
Access	Getting onto and away from the island of Stromboli can be a marvellous experience in its own right. For example, arrival by the year-round night ferry from Naples means disembarking around sunrise. Ferries and hydrofoils also come from Milazzo on Sicily via Lipari and Salina, a marvellous trip. However, it is not unusual for shipping to be disrupted by rough seas and strong winds such as the *scirocco*, stranding passengers for days on end.
	The island's only transport consists of battery-powered taxis or scooters and three-wheelers, which have replaced donkeys for shifting supplies or baggage. There are no cars.

'"Look, Axel, look!"
Above our heads, not more than five hundred feet up, there was a volcano, through which, every quarter of an hour, with a loud explosion, there emerged a tall column of flame, mingled with pumice-stones, ashes, and lava. I could feel the convulsions of the mountain, which seemed to be breathing like a whale, and puffing out fire and air through its huge blowers. Below us, on a fairly steep slope, streams of eruptive matter stretched for a distance of seven or eight hundred feet, giving the mountain a height of about 1,800 feet. Its base was hidden in a regular bower of green trees, among which I made out olives, figs, and vines laden with purple grapes.'

Thus did Jules Verne's heroes emerge from the crater of Stromboli as a fitting end to their adventures in *Journey to the Centre of the Earth* (1872). However you get there, a trek up the active volcano on the remote island of Stromboli is a very exciting, unforgettable experience. This is particularly true at night-time when the explosive lava fountains are at their most spectacular against a starry background. The red hot spurts of molten rock put on quite a show, and the flickering torches of other walkers on the dark mountainside look like fireflies, completing the magical experience.

The island-volcano of Stromboli is the farthest north in the Aeolian group, and the name is derived from the Greek *Stronglyle* – 'rounded', apparently for the shape of the volcanic summit. Its unceasing smoke and intermittent fiery output of clots and sprays of incandescent lava, believed to have persisted for the last 5000 years, have earned it the nickname 'lighthouse of the Mediterranean'. About 12 sq km in surface area, the mountain-cum-island is 924m in altitude, while reaching down some 2km below sea level. Its lack of naturally occurring fresh water means supplies of tank-collected rainwater are necessarily augmented by deliveries from the mainland in summer. Today only about 400 people live here permanently, in contrast to the surprising 2700 inhabitants recorded in the late 19th century when shipping, fishing and agriculture were booming. Olive groves and vineyards were spread along the volcano flanks on terracing that is still discernible, while the coast was punctuated by a number of minor settlements. Ficogrande, now a tourist beach, was long the base for a fleet comprising dozens of majestic schooners involved in the prosperous trade of wine exports for wheat imports with Naples, Genoa, Puglia, Sardinia and as far afield

Lava fountain (photo: Libby Gallagher)

as the Atlantic coast of Spain. Faster steamships and the development of railway networks caused its decline.

The celebrated film *Stromboli*, directed by Roberto Rossellini in 1949 and starring Ingrid Bergman – without forgetting the rival production *Vulcano*, by William Dieterle and with Anna Magnani – make for riveting background viewing for their portrayal of the island (along with Lipari and Vulcano) in the immediate post-war years. Nowadays, apart from the village and port of Stromboli on the easternmost corner of the island, only the backwater hamlet of Ginostra on the opposite shore still survives with a skeleton population; a ferry berth was constructed in 2004, bringing an end to a centuries-long reliance on a tiny rowing boat that acted as the shuttle link for incoming craft.

Stromboli is understandably one of the foremost attractions on the Aeolian islands, and the ascent to the volcano popular with adventurous visitors.

Note For the time being the uppermost slopes of the volcano – above the 400m mark – are officially out of bounds to walkers not accompanied by a qualified guide. While this may seem incomprehensible when the volcano is relatively dormant, putting on its normal show of fireworks at fairly predictable intervals, recent years have seen increasingly frequent explosive episodes and eruptions – notably 2003/4 – of extreme danger. People have lost their lives here. This is mountainous terrain and unexpected bursts of volcanic activity in the dark including showers of incandescent stones, can also be frightening. The brush vegetation just below the crater can be set alight, adding a further complication. Should you be caught out in fog, rain or other adverse conditions, stay put until the weather clears, as it is easy to lose your bearings and inadvertently blunder into ravines or worse. While the guided groups have a rather low ratio of guides to visitors, the advantages are that you are with people who know the terrain like the back of their hand, supply you with a helmet, hire you a torch and are in constant radio contact with their base. Remember, it's a 900m climb.

Due to the 2003 eruptions, the classic Bastimento ridge route is not currently used by the guided treks; a new safer ascent route has been devised (see the map). Modifications may be introduced so allow for differences compared to the following description.

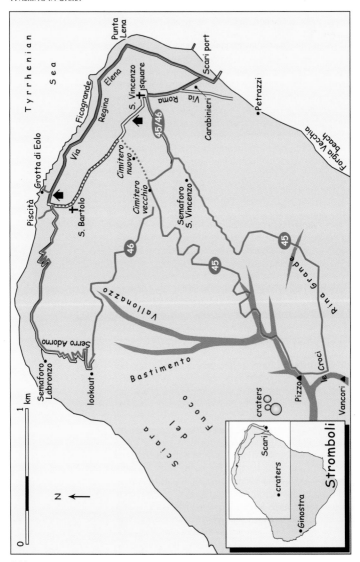

The trek can be done at any time of year if the weather is clear. The winter months can be chilly but beautiful and, of course, quiet. Snowfalls on the mountain are a 'once in a blue moon' occurrence. At any time of year all-weather gear is essential for the ascent, along with liquid and solid sustenance, and a strong torch. Gaiters are helpful to keep the volcanic sand out of your boots. Under normal circumstances it is not an extremely difficult walk, but this is a mountain with unstable terrain with steep stretches. Decent stamina and fitness are essential.

Warning: Under no circumstances is the complete circuit described here to be undertaken by unaccompanied walkers, especially at night-time when the descent routes can be difficult to pinpoint and require a sure foot.

The islands' expert guides can be contacted at Tel 090-9865768 www.magmatrek.it. For live images of the volcano visit www.ct.ingv.it, courtesy of the Italian Institute of Geophysics and Volcanology. Another helpful web site www.stromboli.net, even has a virtual climb to the summit to the delight of armchair travellers.

Otherwise visitors can enjoy a limited view of the volcano's fireworks display from the boats that moor out to sea below the Sciara del Fuoco for an evening, or from the Semaforo Labronzo bar/pizzeria, 45min on foot from the village. (See Walk 46.)

THE WALK

Leave the port of **Scari** on the lane uphill past the ferry ticket office then the Carabinieri station, to Via Roma. Continue climbing (right) past a scattering of shops and cafés to the main square, recognisable with the **Chiesa di San Vincenzo** on one side and Café Ingrid in the scenic corner opposite. Turn left on Via Soldato Francesco Natoli with red/white marking as CAI route n.13. Continue up past a whitewashed shrine to where the concrete paving terminates. A path curves right (northwest) through bushy vegetation and shortly to the **cimitero vecchio** (20min). Not far on it strikes out decidedly southwest, zigzagging its way steadily uphill through ever-diminishing plant life. Black and grey soon dominate.

Increasingly sandy terrain, which makes the going tiring, awaits before you reach the start of the final crest (865m), an old crater rim in actual fact. (This marks the resumption of the

Waiting at the summit for the next lava fountain

old route). Here you head southwest through a lunar landscape while the horizons open up with ever-expanding views.

A total of 3hr should see you at 918m on the breathtaking **Pizzo** (Sopra la Fossa or Sopra La Porta) and the helicopter landing pad, actually a good 200m over the craters, for the best views of the lava spouts and fountains. Hours can be spent watching the breathtaking sight.

For the return route, you need the branch south. It soon reaches a saddle, **le Croci**, below the island's highest point, known as Vancori (924m), then plunges down eastish over the soft, warm sand of **Rina Grande**. Despite the insidious particles that inevitably find their way into your shoes, this is a very pleasant stretch, and far beneath are the twinkling lights of the village. After a level tract some 500m below the crater rim, the way climbs briefly over rock and into thick reeds for the winding but knee-jarring drop (northeast) down a lengthy, narrow water-eroded passage where clouds of choking dust are raised. You pass close to the **Semaforo San Vincenzo** (195m, signal station) and join a concreted lane that leads through the whitewashed houses, eventually emerging at the square, for the final leg to **Scari**, 2hr from the top.

Accommodation
Barbablù
Tel 090-986118
Casa del Sole
Tel 090-986017
Pensione Brasile
Tel 090-986008

WALK 46
Stromboli Loop

Time	3hr 30min
Distance	8km/5 miles
Ascent/descent	300m/300m
Grade	2–3
Maps	1:25,000 'Isole Eolie o Lipari', Arte Photo Graphic Oreste Ragusi. See Walk 45 for sketch map of route.
Start/finish	Scari port
Access	See Walk 45
Variant	This route can be transformed into a simple 1hr 30min stroll by way of the direct Piscità route from the *cimitero vecchio*.

This varied itinerary gives an excellent overview of the island. A new path traverses the volcano's lower northeastern flanks keeping well below the 400m contour line, the safety limit set by the authorities for unaccompanied walkers. Across hillsides thick with typical Mediterranean maquis it leads to a breathtaking lookout over the Sciara del Fuoco, a vast chute where rocks and lapilli from the craters are discharged into the sea. The subsequent descent is via the historic paved mule track that dates back to the late 1940s, built to enable Rossellini's crew to film volcano footage. Back down at sea level, black sand beaches and the pretty village itself is visited, its charming traffic-free lanes and simple white houses over-hung with bougainvillea and pomegranates.

THE WALK
Start out from **Scari** (0m), the port for Stromboli, and take the lane uphill past the *Carabinieri* to join Via Roma. A gentle climb leads to the main square, dominated by the **Chiesa di San Vincenzo** (10min). Facing the church, take the surfaced lane (Via Soldato Francesco Natoli) to its left, marked by red/white paint stripes as CAI route n.13. Heading southwest, it ascends between whitewashed walls and passes a curious shrine bedecked with flowers. Evidence of a Neolithic

The white-washed houses of Stromboli contrast dramatically with the volcano

village along with Greek and Roman remains have evidently been unearthed in this zone. As the concrete ramp comes to an end below Semaforo S. Vincenzo signal station, curve right. You are plunged into delightful vegetation that includes flourishing spurge, rock roses, broom, olives and tall reeds. After ignoring a turn-off right, a brief climb brings you out at the poignant site of the windswept **cimitero vecchio** (20min, 114m), high above the settlement. Weathered majolica tiles can still be made out on the overgrown graves from 1901–2 in this old cemetery, the high percentage of infants particularly salient.

(For a shorter circuit, take the direct route to Piscità.)

A short climb follows, briefly in common with the summit route, then you fork decidedly northwest for the start of the new traverse path. It makes its way through surprisingly colourful maquis vegetation and broom, punctuated

Direct Píscità route (30min)

Return to the turn-off and continue downhill past the *cimitero nuovo*, for a flight of steps bordered by walls of red chunks of lava. This emerges on Via Vittorio Emanuele III, a glorified lane in actual fact. A left turn leads through the extended residential area and past the **Chiesa di San Bartolo**, the island's patron saint, before bearing downhill and seawards. Keep left over a minor watercourse for the beachfront at **Piscità** (40min).

by burnt patches caused by careless tourists if not smouldering material ejected from the volcano. Passing high over the settlement, the path makes a number of detours, such as dipping through the Vallonazzo, a shallow gully which channelled incandescent lava seawards during the devastating 1930 eruption, causing the death of six inhabitants. Smoke from the summit craters and underground rumblings are often perceivable. Not far west now is the **Serro Adorno** ridge and a **lookout** over the gaping Sciara del Fuoco, simply amazing. At 270m it joins a clear marked track (the summit ascent came this way until recently).

A steep descent awaits due north to a forest of reeds surrounding strategically placed **Semaforo Labronzo** (115m, 2hr). ▶

Next a broad mule track leads eastwards, its ample curves leading through grassland dotted with beautiful domes of tree spurge. You reach sea level and coast the beach of **Piscità,** where a decent spread of fine black sand and pebbles is edged by bizarre sculptured forms of lava that halted and solidified at the sea edge at some point in the distant past (the direct route from *cimitero vecchio* joins in here).

Fork left onto Via Regina Elena and take the second set of steps seawards (at the end of Via Soldato Cincotta with the Casa del Sole guesthouse). A sheltered cove is revealed ensconced in grotesque striking red-black lava shapes where bright yellow-green rock samphire has taken root. At sand level, in to the left, is the **Grotta di Eolo**, a yawning, evocative cavern, the legendary home of Aeolus, captain of the winds, so the locals recount. Back on Via Regina Elena, continue on the narrow lane between whitewashed walls overlooked by swaying palms, olives, pomegranate and fig trees. As a glance uphill at any point shows, the smouldering volcano crater is not far away.

A series of scenic cafés precedes the inviting broad sandy beach of **Ficogrande**, site of a bustling port two centuries ago. It's not far over the water to Strombolicchio, the islet – a spectacular volcanic plug of basalt – which predates Stromboli by some 200,000 years in geological terms.

Otherwise, from Ficogrande continue around the surfaced road along the seafront via Punta Lena and the Italian Institute of Volcanology premises, not to mention the broad beach, back to the port at **Scari**.

Set on an ancient volcanic terrace formed by eruptions from a mouth once located on the very spot, the former signal station long served as an aid to shipping, and was manned on a continuous basis 1874–1916. Now a bar/pizzeria it is popular for sunsets and leisurely volcano watching.

Accommodation
see Walk 45

APPENDIX A
Italian–English Glossary

acqua (non) potabile	water (not) suitable for drinking
agriturismo	country property or farm with meals and/or lodging
affittacamere	rooms for rent
albergo	hotel
alimentari	grocery shop
aliscafo	hydrofoil
antiquarium	museum
aperto/chiuso	open/closed
approdo	landing stage
area attrezzata	picnic area
autostrada	motorway
balzo	cliff, outcrop
belvedere	lookout
biglietto/biglietteria	ticket/ticket office
biviere	body of water subject to seasonal variations
borgo	village, hamlet
bosco	wood
cabinovia	gondola car
caduta sassi/massi	rock falls
cala/caletta	cove
camera singola/matrimoniale	single/double room
campanile	bell tower
camposanto, cimitero	cemetery
cancello	gate
capanno d'osservazione	hut for bird or animal watching
capo	cape, point
carta geografica	map
carta telefonica	prepaid phone card
castello	castle
cava	quarry or valley
centro	town centre
chiesa	church
chiesa madre/matrice	main church
chiusa	weir or lock
colata lavica	lava flow
comune, municipio	local council
contrada	hamlet or district
corpo forestale	forestry division
dagala	'island' of vegetation in a lava flow
divieto di caccia	no hunting

duomo	cathedral
entrata	entrance
eremo	hermitage, monastery
est	east or eastern
faro	lighthouse
fermata dell'autobus	bus stop
ferrovia	railway, station
fiumara	watercourse that comes to life after heavy rain
fiume	river
foce	mouth of river
fontana	fountain, spring
fossa	cavity, hollow
fosso	small valley or watercourse
frana	landslide
fumarola	volcanic vent which emits hot gases
funivia	cable-car
gola	gorge
grotta	cave
imbarcadero	landing stage
isola	island
lago	lake
laguna	lagoon
lido	beach
mare	sea
massaria	old-style farmhouse, originally a self-contained feudal-style community
monte/montagna	mountain
mulattiera	mule track
mulino	mill
navetta	shuttle service
nord	north or northern
orario	opening times or timetable
ostello	hostel
osteria	inn, wine bar
ovest	west or western
ovile	sheep pen or hut
pagliaio	shepherd's hut or hay stack
palazzo	palace
panificio	bakery
pantano	marsh or lagoon
parcheggio	car park
pasticceria	cake shop
pedone/pedonale	pedestrian
pensione	guesthouse
percorso	route
pericolo	danger

253

piano	plain, flat or slow, quiet
piazza	public square
pineta	pine wood
pizzo	mountain peak
portella	mountain pass
pullman	bus, coach (not train)
punta	peak or promontory
riserva	nature reserve
rocca	fortress or stronghold, mountain
ruderi	ruins
salina	salt pan
salita	ascent or laneway
santuario	sanctuary, church
scalo	port of call, harbour
sciara	lavic terrain or vast stony waste
scoglio	rock, reef
sella	saddle
semaforo	signal station for shipping or traffic lights
sentiero	path
sentiero natura	marked nature trail
serpente innocuo/velenoso	harmless/poisonous snake
sorgente	fresh water spring
spiaggia	beach
stazione ferroviaria	railway station
stazione marittima	ferry terminal
strada	road, way
strada senza sbocco/uscita	dead end
sud	south or southern
tempio	temple
terme	spa
timpa/timpone	rounded rock outcrop
tonnara	tuna canning plant or collective fishing
torre	tower
torrente	stream
traghetto	ferry
trattoria	restaurant
treno	train
uscita	exit
zecca (zecche)	tick (ticks)

APPENDIX B
Further Reading

Literary works from Sicily are valuable in building up an essential background for a visit. Recommended writers whose works are available in English translation include Danilo Dolci (*Racconti siciliani*), Carlo Levi (*Le parole sono pietre*), Leonardo Sciascia (*Il giorno della civetta*) and Elio Vittorini (*Conversazione in Sicilia*). The 1984 film *Kaos*, by Paolo and Vittorio Taviani, is a tragic and exhilarating version of short stories by prolific playwright Luigi Pirandello.

Riveting factual Mafia books in English include the excellent *Cosa Nostra* by John Dickie (Hodder & Stoughton, London, 2004), along with studies by Pino Arlacchi and assassinated magistrate Giovanni Falcone, amongst others. In contrast mythological matters are amply covered in Salvino Greco's *Miti e leggende di Sicilia* (Flaccovio Editore 1993, Italian only), while several episodes in Homer's *The Odyssey* make for curious reading.

A beautiful personal account of life in Sicily is found in Mary Taylor Simeti's *On Persephone's Island* (Vintage, New York, 1995), while Peter Robb's *Midnight in Sicily* (Harvill Press, London, 1998) explores many a murky alley in the island's affairs. J.W. von Goethe enthuses about the Sicilian climate and just about everything else in his *Italian Journey (1786–1788)*, D.H. Lawrence left poetic accounts in *Sea and Sardinia*, while a precious find for Italian readers is *Delle cose di Sicilia: testi inediti o rari*, vol. I, ed. Leonardo Sciascia (Sellerio, Palermo, 1980).

Nature enthusiasts will appreciate *Birds of Britain and Europe* by Bertel Bruun et al. (Hamlyn, London, 1992), *Mediterranean Wild Flowers* by M. Blamey and C. Grey-Wilson (Collins, 1993), or the classic *Flowers of the Mediterranean* by Oleg Polunin and Anthony Huxley (Chatto & Windus, London, 1987), not to mention the comprehensive *Guida alla natura della Sicilia* by Fulco Pratesi and Franco Tassi (Mondadori, 1985, Italian only).

Walking – Trekking – Mountaineering – Climbing – Cycling

Over 40 years, Cicerone have built up an outstanding collection of over 300 guides, inspiring all sorts of amazing adventures.

Every guide comes from extensive exploration and research by our expert authors, all with a passion for their subjects. They are frequently praised, endorsed and used by clubs, instructors and outdoor organisations.

All our titles can now be bought as **e-books**, **ePubs** and **Kindle** files and we also have an online magazine – **Cicerone Extra** – with features to help cyclists, climbers, walkers and trekkers choose their next adventure, at home or abroad.

Our website shows any **new information** we've had in since a book was published. Please do let us know if you find anything has changed, so that we can publish the latest details. On our **website** you'll also find great ideas and lots of detailed information about what's inside every guide and you can buy **individual routes** from many of them online.

It's easy to keep in touch with what's going on at Cicerone by getting our monthly **free e-newsletter**, which is full of offers, competitions, up-to-date information and topical articles. You can subscribe on our home page and also follow us on **Facebook** and **Twitter** or dip into our **blog**.

Cicerone – the very best guides for exploring the world.

CICERONE

2 Police Square Milnthorpe Cumbria LA7 7PY
Tel: 015395 62069 info@cicerone.co.uk
www.cicerone.co.uk and **www.cicerone-extra.com**